W. SOMERSET MAUGHAM
Portrait by Edouard MacAvoy

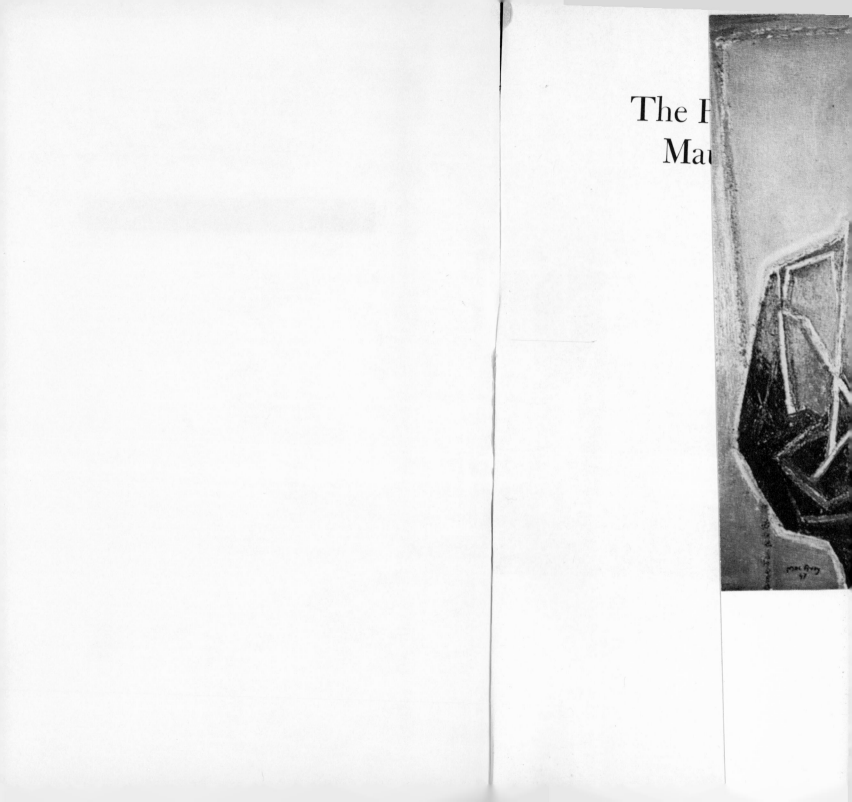

The P
Mau

The Pattern of Maugham

A CRITICAL PORTRAIT

'They say books about books are profitless, but they certainly make very pleasant reading . . .'

W. SOMERSET MAUGHAM, *The Book-Bag*

———

ANTHONY CURTIS

TAPLINGER PUBLISHING COMPANY
NEW YORK

First published in the United States in 1974 by
TAPLINGER PUBLISHING CO., INC.
New York, New York

Copyright © 1974 by Anthony Curtis
All rights reserved. Printed in the U.S.A.

Library of Congress Catalog Card Number: 74-3670

ISBN 0-8008-6240-6

Sarah's

Contents

Preface

I owe a debt to all previous writers about Somerset Maugham whom I have read and from whom I have profited even when I have disagreed with them. I have found especially useful the three bibliographies compiled by Raymond Toole Stott, the *Theatrical Companion* of Mander and Mitchenson, and the bibliography of criticism compiled and edited by Charles Sanders.

Mr Alan Searle has patiently answered a number of queries and encouraged me in my undertaking. Mr Spencer Curtis Brown, Mr Hamish Hamilton and Mr Roger Machell all read my manuscript and made valuable suggestions. Other people to whom I am indebted for various kindnesses in connection with this book are: Lord Boothby, Mr William Fox, Mr Roland Gant, Mr Patrick Gibbs, Sir Julian Hall, Mr G. Hattee, librarian of The King's School, Canterbury, Mr Richard Hough, Mr Roger Morgan, Mr P. Pollak, archivist of The King's School, Canterbury, Mr George Rylands, Mr Rivers Scott, Mr Denys Sutton, Mr John Symonds. None of the above are however responsible for any errors of fact or judgment which may be discovered and for which I alone am responsible.

In using the Maugham and related resources of the British Museum Reading Room, the London Library, the Library of The King's School, Canterbury, and the Garrick Club Library I have met with nothing but helpfulness and my thanks go to their officials and staffs.

For permission to quote copyright material by Maugham I am grateful to the Literary Executor of W. Somerset Maugham, for permission to quote from Max Beerbohm to Mrs Eva Reichmann.

A.C.

CHAPTER ONE

Œuvre and Environs

THE FIRST POINT to make about Maugham is that he trusted literature. It was the one activity in which he had complete and lasting faith. He made a wholehearted surrender to it from boyhood to old age. Medicine in which he qualified but never in fact practised was a kind of insurance cover. As soon as he had published his first novel at the age of twenty-three he determined to live if he possibly could by and for literature. He had inherited some money from his father, enough to give him a modest livelihood, and he gambled this on his future as a writer.

After about ten lean years the gamble paid handsome rewards; from then on his income from his writing was never in doubt. He made a huge fortune and lived the life of a rich man. Maugham's affluence, his love of money and his ability to make a great deal of it, has undoubtedly stood in the way of a just appreciation of his work in his native country and in other places where a puritan conscience encourages the view that a serious writer has no business making a lot of money out of his work until he is safely in his grave, or at least too old to enjoy it fully, and that he can only perform this singular feat of lucrativeness by forfeiting his seriousness. Edmund Wilson, to name the most influential of Maugham's detractors, clearly felt that Maugham had no right to be seriously considered and took the opportunity of knocking him off the perch of eminence onto which he had landed safely at the end of his life in a damaging review of one of his least characteristic books.[1]

From his middle thirties onwards Maugham suffered loud and long from a sense that 'the intelligentsia'—a word into which he always put a drop of venom—had written him off. It is true that he was given a great many damning reviews, even more perhaps than other popular authors, but the animus behind them bred by his phenomenal success, was often so blatant as to be no more than momentarily disturbing. And there were, as we shall see, notable exceptions. Desmond MacCarthy[2]—and if he did not belong to the literary intelligentsia, who did?—was among the earliest critics to see Maugham's work as part of literature and to make out a graceful case for it. Even the mistress of Bloomsbury, Virginia Woolf when she read *The Summing Up* asked Harold Nicolson to tell Maugham how much she admired the honesty with which he had laid bare the nature of a writer's life[3]; we do not know unfortunately whether this piece of intelligence was in fact transmitted from Rodmell to Cap Ferrat and if so what effect it had. My own position is that Maugham's seriousness is beyond doubt, as should be plain from my attempting to write this book and spending as much time with his work as this undertaking involves; but to determine where and how we place him among the writers of this century is, it seems to me, a task of stimulating difficulty and fascination.

Even Maugham's most severe detractors will usually grant that he was a great professional. By this one means in external terms that he kept regular writing hours and as soon as he had finished one work he began another. The only interruption to the routine of writing was when he went on his travels, as he did annually for many years, but these travels were all part of the writing programme. He went with both an open mind and a sense of purpose, and his wanderings rarely failed to provide him with the raw material for a book. New books by Maugham never needed to be heralded by his publishers as 'long-awaited' or 'breaking a long silence'; they appeared with unvarying punctuality from his twenties to his eighties.

One associates this kind of indomitable productiveness with a certain type of popular writer, a P. G. Wodehouse or a Simenon who is meeting a demand by writing the same book, or at least the same kind of book, over and over again. Maugham was both wonderfully prolific and wonderfully varied. In all the main genres of prose-writing, including the theatre, there was nothing he touched that he did not adorn. To be sure one can

cite previous instances of English writers who have made a
contribution to, say, both fiction and drama, Fielding in the
eighteenth century, Charles Reade in the nineteenth, but almost
no one who has had such sustained mastery of whatever genre
in which he happened at the time to be working. If Maugham's
senior contemporaries Arnold Bennett and H. G. Wells can
boast an even more extensive wordage on the clock they cannot
compete with his formal perfectionism or his literary ubiquity.
It is true that Arnold Bennett wrote plays but there are only
two that have survived, one of those being composed in collaboration with someone else, and as a novelist he is tiresomely
prodigal of detail at the expense of that much more difficult
economy at which Maugham excelled. Wells was a fine short-
story writer and novelist but much of his output consisted of
journalism by its nature ephemeral: how much of what remains
will survive as literature is today a very open question.

But then Wells was a curious instance of an artist who became
impatient of his own art. He aimed by the quickest means
possible to change society, and to change social attitudes, and
he often succeeded. Maugham had no such aim, or if he did it
was finely concealed. He was a conservative in both literature
about which he said a great many wise things and politics on
which he almost never pronounced publicly. He has the cool,
the poise, the irony of the eighteenth-century English essayists
and like them his concern is to uncover attitudes and to penetrate the dishonesties on which social life depends. He was in
this sense a realist as much as in the narrower meaning of pro-
ducing fiction in a manner derived from certain nineteenth-
century French novelists. Maugham's conservatism was seen at
its staunchest in his lifelong faith in the sovereign power of
narrative; all his books are constructed on the principle of a
sequence of events that first of all arouses, and then prolongs
and ultimately satisfies the reader's curiosity. Maugham clung
tenaciously to the linear logic of narrative at a time when his
colleagues appeared to be abandoning its consecutiveness in
favour of much greater psychological immediacy and were
experimenting with ways of expressing inward irrational confusion in works that deliberately left curiosity unsatisfied whatever else they did. Maugham's faith in the enduring power of

traditional narrative did not let him down throughout this revolution. But if he had the faith in his own art that moved mountains he was not complacent about it. He was never content to rest assured; his conservatism, his sense of literary tradition and social tradition, was combined with tireless intellectual curiosity. He was continually extending his scope even though he sometimes re-worked a plot he had used before: he never wholly profited by the acquired élan. In his own story-telling way he had the equipment of a good journalist: the 'nose' for copy, the rapid power of assimilation and quick seizing of the salient features of a situation, the ability to present complex matters in simple arresting paragraphs, above all the capacity to provoke a reaction rather than to follow a trend.

Maugham's whole career was a masterpiece of literary strategy, planned and executed with ruthless precision. He had an unerring way of finding subjects that although not tied to topical events were of the moment and of great popular interest. He sensed the zeitgeist and contributed to it from his own standpoint as a story-teller. His offensives were brilliantly timed and so were his withdrawals. Unlike his mentors in the theatre, Henry Arthur Jones and Pinero, he bowed out at a time when his public would probably have welcomed more even though they misunderstood some of his last plays.

As he grew in stature as an author he adopted the habit favoured by Monty and other successful generals of chatting to the troops: the mature Maugham cultivated a friendly working relation with his readers that became the constant feature of his vast many-sided œuvre. You can always tell one of his books in outward appearance by the spiky wigwam, the emblem against the evil eye found by his father in Morocco, that sits on the binding,[4] and in inward appearance by the presence in the narrative of Maugham's professional self, a creature who is witty, courteous, gentlemanly, commonsensical, sceptical, agnostic, hedonistic, totally absorbed in the technique of his craft. Let us imagine that we are in the library of some great Maugham collector such as Jerome Zipkin or Bertram Alanson,[5] one-time head of the San Francisco Stock Exchange, who possess every one of Maugham's books in its first edition and that they are ranged side by side across the shelves. What an impressive sight it is! Such industry, such dedication, such singleness of purpose! Lucky indeed the fellow-writer who can gaze thereon without a creeping paralysis of guilt at the pitiful smallness of his own output!

Here is *Liza of Lambeth* in her original green cloth as she appeared in Fisher Unwin's pseudonym library in 1897 and ranged beside her are those early offspring whom the Master later disowned *The Making of a Saint* (1898), *Orientations* (1899), *The Hero* (1901). 'I have never met with a fine copy,' said Maugham's bibliographer Raymond Toole Stott in his *Maughamiana*. *Mrs. Craddock* (1902) next: eventually she was awarded her place in the Collected Works. Then three more outcasts *The Merry-Go-Round* (1904), *The Land of the Blessed Virgin* (1905) earliest of his travel books and first fruit of his lifelong infatuation with Spain, and *The Bishop's Apron* published by Chapman and Hall in 1906, and then again in Newnes Sixpenny Novel Series in 1908, looking for all the world like a genuine housemaid's novelette with an artist's impression of the aforesaid bishop among the illustrations. *The Explorer* (1907) and *The Magician* (1908), emphasize the young writers regularity and persistence, also how long it is taking us to reach familiar ground. At last with *Of Human Bondage* (1915) we have arrived and here beside the British Heinemann edition stands the American published by George H. Doran one day earlier in the same year, thus establishing a transatlantic link that was to endure for the next forty years. Next to them is the German edition of *Bondage Dasselbe* (Berlin 1930), the French edition *Servitude Humaine* (Paris 1937), the Swiss edition *Der Menschen Horigkeit* (Zürich 1939) and the Spanish edition *Servidumbre Humana* (Barcelona 1945) plotting a representative pattern of territorial expansion. Now the eye begins to skim rapidly over titles that are household words *The Moon and Sixpence* (1919), *The Painted Veil* (1925), *Cakes and Ale* (1930), *The Razor's Edge* (1944) up to *Then and Now* (1946) and *Catalina* (1948) with which the novels ended. In a separate section are the short stories that began with *Orientations*. Next to it is a curiosity, a thin volume called *Flirtation* (1904). Inside appears to be an almost illegible galley proof in diamond print chopped up into a handful of pages. It is of a story that appeared in the *Daily Mail* and was registered in the British Museum to establish copyright. It is not until 1921 that the next volume of stories appeared, it was *The Trembling of a Leaf*, after which came *The Casuarina Tree* (1926), *Ashenden or the British Agent* (1928), *Six Stories Written in the First Person Singular* (1931), *Ah King* (1933), *Cosmopolitans* (1936), *The Mixture as Before* (1940), *Creatures of Circumstance* (1947). The ideal way to read Maugham's stories is in this chronological sequence of book publication rather than in the re-shuffled order of *Altogether*, or the three hardback Collected volumes or the four paperback ones in which they were re-issued. Apart from the print being bigger there is geographical unity in the original volumes and such luxuries as the author's prologues justifying his titles.

The plays were first collected in six volumes in a shiny brown cloth in 1931 onwards spanning the Master's retirement from the theatre, volumes for which he wrote prefaces of scintillating brilliance. They were doubled up later into the three volumes of Collected Plays we now can buy. But looking along the shelf we see a number of plays published after their production that never made the collected edition: the first play of all for example *A Man of Honour* (1903) which exists in more than one edition because it was issued as a supplement to *The Fortnightly Review* edited by W. L. Courtney. Then there are such rarities as *The Explorer*, *The Tenth Man*, *Loaves and Fishes*, *Landed Gentry* in smart red boards with lists of the original casts, but afterwards repudiated.

In another section are works of travel and autobiography— the former *On a Chinese Screen* (1922), *The Gentlemen in the Parlour* (1930), *Don Fernando* (1935) have all been combined in one volume in the Collected edition and ought surely to be better known than they are. Then there are those crucial books *The Summing Up* (1935) and *A Writer's Notebook*, and books of literary *causerie*, *Books and You* (1939), *Great Novelists and Their Novels* (1948), *The Vagrant Mood* (1952), *Points of View* (1958). For someone who often referred to himself as 'but a story-teller' he would seem to have published a sizeable amount of non-fiction.

A complete Maugham collection will include not only his own books but those by other people for which when he was eminent he wrote prefaces. They tell us much about his interests and his circle. Here is the American Bridge expert Charles H. Goren on *The Art of Bidding* and here are the memoirs of the Aga Khan. Here are theatrical memoirs by the matinée idols who contributed to his own success as a playwright, Gladys Cooper and Charles Hawtrey, in which Maugham confessed that there was no greater illusion than the naturalism of the theatre. Here is Doris Arthur Jones, daughter of the dramatist, in whose *What A Life!* Maugham recalled the first hostess to take him up, a Mrs. George Stevens. Here are people whom later on he took up, people like Louis Marlow, Noël Coward, Dorothy Parker, Edward Marsh, Peter Arno.

After scanning this prefatory *galère* we must quickly flick our eyes along the shelf that holds those imaginative works, mainly stage plays, made by other hands from novels and stories by Maugham. Here is *Rain*, perhaps the most famous single work of Maugham's, which in its dramatic form turns out to be by two American writers, John Colton and Clemence Randolph. Then Edith Ellis's play of *The Moon and Sixpence* in 1925, Bartlett Cormack's of *The Painted Veil* in 1931, Guy Bolton's of the novel *Theatre* in 1937 and S. N. Behrman's of the short story *Jane* (1931) and Rodney Ackland's of the story *Before The Party* (1949). From these we pass to the film scenarios that were published after the Second World War when selected groups of three or four stories were presented in dramatic form in the cinema: *Quartet* (1948), *Trio* (1950), *Encore* (1952), with work on them by R. C. Sherriff, Noel Langley, T. E. B. Clarke, Arthur Macrae and Eric Ambler. The television scripts that followed these when many of the stories were dramatised again in that medium by writers like Hugo Charteris in the BBC series produced by Verity Lambert have not been published but had they been we should have to add them. It is difficult to think of another writer whose creative bounty has spilled so richly into other men's laps.

It amused Maugham to pretend that he was more or less ignored by serious critics during his lifetime. In fact he received an inordinate amount of critical attention. If you were to put all the reviews and articles devoted to his work in English alone end to end they would stretch from Cap Ferrat to Los Angeles.

A whole book has been published by the Northern Illinois Press, in a series with the resounding title of Annotated Secondary Bibliography Series on English Literature in Transition, 1880–1920, on Maugham, compiled and edited by Charles Sanders, which lists critical references to Maugham from 1897 to 1968. It contains nearly two and a half thousand entries and is still incomplete though it remains an invaluable work of reference to any student of Maugham, and one to which the present book is much indebted. So far there has been no Critical Heritage volume on Maugham from Routledge but what amounts among other useful things to an anthology of reviews of his plays may be found in the superbly researched *Theatrical Companion to Maugham* by Raymond Mander and Joe Mitchenson (1955). These two works together with the fine scholarly bibliographies of Raymond Toole Stott—the latest and most complete revision arrived just as this book was going to press—are the essential tools in any serious appraisal.

Books *about* Maugham range from the academic to the scurrilous and by now occupy several sizeable shelves of their own. With his global audience and his portraits of English people all over the world Maugham was a natural subject for university study abroad. Paul Dottin's *W. Somerset Maugham et Ses Romans* appeared as long ago as 1928. But North America has led the field in professorial industry with Richard Cordell and Klaus Jonas outstanding for their devotion to the subject over many years; since Maugham's death in 1965 they have been joined by M. K. Naik and by a Canadian scholar Robert Lorin Calder whose *Somerset Maugham and the Quest for Freedom* (1972) pursued the theme of its title with great erudition and posited real-life originals for several of Maugham's most famous characters.

In his native Britain critical studies of Maugham's work are harder to find though we may boast a succinct and pertinent Reader's Guide by Laurence Brander (1963); here it is the man of letters and literary journalists who have contributed major reviews and essays starting with Desmond MacCarthy followed among others by Cyril Connolly, V. S. Pritchett, David Paul, and two men of the theatre, St John Ervine and

Ivor Brown. Fellow novelists who have written with critical insight about Maugham include Frank Swinnerton, Richard Aldington, H. E. Bates, Cecil Roberts, Graham Greene and John Brophy.

This brings me to the last shelf of all labelled rather ominously Family and Friends. Here is Robin—the present Lord—Maugham's *Somerset and All the Maughams* (1965) which contains in addition to the author's recollections of his uncle a historical account of the rise and rise of the Maugham family from modest beginnings, and here is Lord Maugham's later autobiography *Escape from the Shadows* (1972), one of these being his uncle Willie. Next to this we see *A Case of Human Bondage* (1966) by Beverley Nichols with some rare glimpses in print of Syrie Maugham, and containing a violent personal attack on Nichols's former mentor. Much more cheerfully there is Garson Kanin's *Remembering Mr. Maugham* (1966). Mr. Kanin did a very valuable thing. He Boswellized Maugham. Whenever he met him he went away and wrote down exactly what Maugham had said. The result is one book where we do hear the real voice of Maugham speaking about everything from form in writing to royalty on the Riviera. Another American Wilmon Menard tried to perform the same task in his *The Two Worlds of Somerset Maugham* (1965) but here it is not at all clear when he is quoting from Maugham's published writing and when he is claiming to report Maugham's conversation. Still, Mr. Menard is informative about Maugham in the South Pacific.

The only volume that appears to be missing from these bulging shelves is an official biography, the equivalent of Ray on Thackeray, Johnson on Dickens, Baines on Conrad. Whether there will ever be such a biography of Maugham I would not care to predict but it is quite clear that he did not wish that there should ever be one.

No one in the history of literature was ever so determined to cover his tracks. Maugham forbade any posthumous publication of his letters. The copyright of an author's letters is vested in his estate: this prohibition can be (and is being) enforced. In his lifetime he destroyed much of the documentation on which a biography might be based. *A Writer's Notebook* (1949) contains only about a quarter of the material he amassed as jottings during his working life; the remainder was destroyed. Towards the end of his life he went in for what he called 'bonfire nights' in which vast quantities of mss. material and letters were committed to the flames. Fourteen unpublished Ashenden stories went this way, so did a number of unperformed plays.

Maugham's secretary and devoted friend, Alan Searle recalls how the morning after one of these conflagrations Maugham said to him: 'That was a good evening's work. Now we'll burn everything you've hidden under the cushions on the ss-ofa.' One can only speculate about the motivation behind all this. If he feared posthumous revelations about his marriage by the end of his life these had been made by himself in a way that was far more damaging than if they had been seen in the full context of his life's achievement by some sympathetic biographer. As an omnivorous reader of literary biographies himself Maugham must have realized what a superb full-scale Life he would have made; it would have spanned so much of late nineteenth- and twentieth-century history, beginning with the last years of Queen Victoria, including the Boer War, the Edwardian age, the First World War, the early rumblings of the Russian Revolution, the uneasy peace, the British colonial administration in the Far East, and switching in the later chapters to the world of the French Riviera before and after the Second World War, to China, to Indo-China, to India, to New York, to South Carolina, to Hollywood, to Japan . . . For steady involvement with the deepest concerns of the time and some of its most powerful personalities, such as Churchill and Beaverbrook, one cannot think of any other literary biography of the modern period to rival it. But Maugham wished to be judged only in his own terms as a professional author not as a private individual. He wished for no more to be revealed about himself posthumously than he had revealed already in his lifetime. He had a great reluctance for the image of Maugham so carefully planted and cultivated by him over more than fifty years of writing to be altered or corrected or modified in any way however deftly it was done. One of the difficulties—and hence one of the fascinations—of writing about Maugham is to get past Maugham's apparent self-detachment. Everything there is to say about

Maugham has (so it seems) already been said by Maugham himself. He appears so open with the reader about the nature of the problem before us and his own equipment for dealing with it that further comment seems superfluous. If we wish to assess his place in literature or point to the shortcomings of his style we find that he has been there already and come up with an answer as judicious as it is modest. He told us as much about his own life as would enable us to follow his career as an author, and to understand the events that had influenced that career. In *The Summing Up* he combined one part autobiography with about six parts general reflection rather like those marvellous martinis that Gerald Haxton used to mix for him. The pithy and illuminating prefaces he wrote in his later years for the Collected Edition of his works are rich in personal anecdote. What he showed us on these occasions was a mask by no means unrelated to his 'real' or private self but used to establish the character of a professional author who was as much a creation of Maugham's as any of his other characters. This professional self was a creature of infinite good sense; he was a living example of the Golden Mean of Aristotle in action: we know from books that have been published by his intimates since his death that in fact the 'real' Maugham was by contrast a creature of fluctuating extremes and like the rest of us capable of behaving at times in a completely irrational and totally indefensible way. Moreover, in his last five years though the body was kept alive his mind had clearly gone, and that once superb flow of clarity and precision had deteriorated into a dreadful doddering senility.

Machiavelli [Maugham writes] has told us that when he retired to his study to write he discarded his country clothes and donned the damask robe in which as Secretary of the Republic he was wont to appear before the Signoria. So, in spirit, did Burke. In his study he was no longer the reckless punter, the shameless sponge, the unscrupulous place-hunter (not for himself, but for others), the dishonest advocate who attacked measures introduced to correct scandalous abuses because his pocket would be affected by their passage. In his study he was the high-minded man whom his friends loved and honoured for his nobility of spirit, his greatness and his magnanimity. In his study he was the honest man he was assured he was. Then, but only then, can you say of Burke: *Le style c'est l'homme meme*.[6]

In his study Maugham never became the malicious, gratuitously offensive man whom those he snubbed recall, nor was he the twisted self-conscious stuttering individual, warped by the consciousness that he was three-quarters queer and a quarter normal, as he confessed to his nephew. In his study he was the humane and courteous, the generous and fluent, the amusing and stimulating companion whom those few fortunate people who had his confidence recall. In his study he was a story-teller of genius, inheritor of the major literatures of the world and mediator of their riches to the common reader. Then and only then can you say of Maugham: *Le style c'est l'homme même*.

In reality the two selves cannot always be so conveniently separated. Maugham could be utterly charming to total strangers and sometimes we detect a rent of anger in the damask robe. In his writing he often showed us how someone who has lived hitherto by the light of reason fails to overcome a self-destroying passion: self-mastery and the roads by which it may be attained or lost is a theme that gives a kind of unity to everything Maugham ever wrote. In his own case it was not so much a road as a flight of stairs that led him to his rooftop writing-room at nine o'clock punctually every morning, the start of the sacred hours before lunch spent religiously at his desk mastering all the main literary forms—novel, drama, short story, travelogue, essay; a lifetime of dedicated effort in which he managed to excel in all that he attempted. There has never been a more perfect 'case' than Maugham's of success in the profession of literature.

The nature and the pattern of that success is my concern in this book. Because of the ubiquitous presence of the Maugham figure in the work I cannot wholly ignore biography. On the other hand it is not my intention to try to out-wit Maugham by writing his life in spite of him. He has dealt me my cards which are his published works; it is up to me to play them as best I can. In short what follows is an appraisal in the form of a critical portrait. Its main lines are chronological with a bit of dodging about in order to group together works of a similar kind whose composition was separated in time.

[2.]

Many of the most important English writers at the turn of
the century have a sense of exclusion from the full process of
formal education culminating in a period at a university. The
classic statement in fictional terms of this feeling of being a cultural pariah is the unsuccessful efforts of Hardy's Jude—the
novel was published in 1895—to get into Christminster. Admission to Christminster would seem to be a prerogative of the
gentleman by birth rather than of any natural endowments to
benefit by exposure to its civilized richness. Jude turned to the
Church, but the choice of literature as a career became another
way of continuing the educative process indefinitely, of making
the reading public subsidize the writer's own self-education
through his books, and enabling the reader who is in the same
plight to enjoy the cultural process at one remove. Writers like
Gissing, Bennett, Wells—to name but three of the most obvious
—all manifest this strategy in various ways. They are part of a
great heroic wave of self-education that had its origin in the
lower-middle and working-class, and that preceded the belated
acceptance of universal university education as a basic right in
England after the Second World War.

Maugham was part of this 'movement', if you can call it that,
for a strangely capricious reason. His brother who later became
Lord Chancellor went to Cambridge and Maugham should have
followed him there after he had left The King's School,
Canterbury. But by the time Maugham was at his public school
both his parents were dead and he was in the care of his Uncle
the Vicar of Whitstable. As many precociously clever boys do,
Maugham went through a phase of disillusionment with school
after a break through illness and, being a headstrong and determined youth, he persuaded his guardian to allow him to give up
the idea of going to Cambridge and to let him go instead for a
period to the University of Heidelberg. His aunt was of German
origin and her support for the plan was a deciding factor. Now
at this time the University of Heidelberg was just about the
most culturally exciting place anyone could find in the whole
world. Kuno Fischer was electrifying the minds of the students

with his lectures on Schopenhauer; Ibsen's plays were being translated into German and performed at the theatre; Wagner was in the air and his theory of music drama was being avidly discussed; students from all over Europe congregated there to take courses and to enjoy a precious sense of freedom.

It would, then, seem to be slightly absurd that someone who had at his own volition gone there and been intensely stimulated by his exposure to all these influences should later in life have any regret that he lacked a proper university education. But Maugham did suffer from remorse on this score. Heidelberg was splendid but it was not Christminster. He wished that he had been to Cambridge where he would have had someone to guide his reading and to correct his English. If he had it might have had the effect of curtailing his gifts to the impoverishment of our literature. Maugham might easily have stayed there as a scholar and a don and written stories merely for fun in his spare time. But this is idle speculation. What actually happened was that as Maugham's days as a student of the humanities were cut short in the formal sense, they continued actively to the end of his life. The literature and the art of the world were his university; he was never happier as a story-teller than when he is breaking off the narrative to expound about literature. Readers of *The Book Bag* will recall that Maugham used to travel across Malaya with a portable mini-library, and that when he came to unfold his hair-raising tale of brother-sister incest in that story he uses carefully planted analogues from Racine and Byron; indeed Maugham is so discreet that it's only through the Byron reference that you realize exactly what went on.

Maugham used sometimes to go to Cambridge to visit his friend George Rylands at King's and as he listened to Mr. Rylands taking up a point about Shakespeare or Donne with his pupils he saw what he had missed. But Maugham believed that it was never too late to do what you wanted to do and he asked Mr. Rylands to give him a supervision. 'It amused him,' Mr. Rylands writes, 'to sit at my feet for academic instruction—sometimes of course scoring off me in the event! . . . He loved to "draw" me because I *taught* English Literature and he was a great admirer of Shakespeare on whom he pretended I was an authority and scholar (which I am not) and got me to compose an anthology for his bedside book. We talked also of course about the theatre as I was a keen amateur actor and director. But much time was spent happily dissecting our friends and foes. He thought human beings very peculiar and contradictory and absurd and lovable and ghastly; the fascination was perpetual. And although he belonged to the *fin de siècle* pessimist group in a way—Housman, Hardy, James Thomson, Gissing— his cynicism was the relish or sharp sauce to his meat—to flesh and blood; not the dish itself; more romantic than cynical indeed with a temptation to the mystical. However you will have realized all this long long ago. His books tell the whole story for the man who can read. He was always very good and encouraging to me and I was deeply devoted to him—marvellously entertaining—he loved to make one laugh *aloud*—he loved to tease.'[7]

This *fin de siècle* pessimist group—one hadn't quite thought of them as a group before—did have a common concern in their various writings which was the evil environment of the great city in which the vast mass of humanity was at the end of the nineteenth century condemned to live and to find some means of subsistence. The glow of silent purity which had enveloped the London skyline for Wordsworth in his Sonnet Composed Upon Westminster Bridge in 1802 and that 'soul of Beauty and enduring Life . . . Composure and ennobling Harmony' which he had discerned beneath the myriad activities of the capital in 'The Prelude' had by 1874 (the year of Maugham's birth) been overshadowed by the Dantesque vision of Thomson's City of Dreadful Night, and Darwin had published his *Origin of Species* in 1859. There was a copy in the Vicarage at Whitstable and in *Of Human Bondage* Maugham refers to it simply as 'that great book'. The view of human life as one vast battle for survival,

> The sense that every struggle brings defeat
> Because Fate holds no prize to crown success

and of the city-dwellers looking at the statue of Melancolia dominating them,

> The strong to drink new strength of iron endurance
> The weak new terrors; all, renewed assurance
> And confirmation of the old despair . . .[8]

was one that was common both to Thomson and to Gissing. It was to this city instead of Cambridge that Maugham went to live at the impressionable age of 18 after he had finally left the King's School and his uncle's vicarage for good. As a medical student attached to one of the great teaching hospitals on the edge of one of its poorest areas he would have the opportunity to discover how much of fact and how much of fantasy there was in the writings of the pessimists.

CHAPTER TWO

Orientations

[1.]

THE MANUSCRIPT OF *Liza of Lambeth*, Maugham's first
published novel, belongs now to The King's School, Canterbury.[1]
The story was written on three *cahiers* apparently purchased by
Maugham in Paris from the Papeterie F. Brocchi at 30 Faubourg
St. Honoré. On the inside cover of the first volume is a map
showing the eighty-eight departments of France. The hand-
writing is bold and confident, the text has some corrections but
is fairly clean. The last four pages disappeared; and when he
made his gift to his old school Maugham wrote them out again,
adding a P.S.: 'This novel, my first, was written in 1895 at 11
Vincent Square Westminster'—that is to say, two years before
publication in 1897.

The most interesting features of the manuscript are the
original title 'A Lambeth Idyll' which is shown crossed out, and
the author's name which is given as 'William Somerset'. This
has puzzled people and some splendid theories have been
advanced such as that the *nom de plume* is evidence of Maugham's
impersonal detachment from his own work showing at an early
age. Raymond Toole Stott who includes a fascinating description of the publishers folder relating to *Liza* in his latest
bibliography says: 'whether because he was training as a doctor
and did not want his identity revealed, or he wished to remain
anonymous in case his book was not a success, are matters for
conjecture.'

I don't think that there is really much room for conjecture.
The story was originally intended to appear in a series called
The Pseudonym Library, published by T. Fisher Unwin, devised
by his reader Edward Garnett. *Pseudonyms* attracted a glittering

array of new writers including Ouida, Olive Schreiner and W. B. Yeats. As the title implied each of the books in the series appeared under an assumed name.[2]

> They were slim volumes [said Maugham in the preface he wrote to the 1930 Travellers Library edition of *Liza of Lambeth*] bound in yellow paper and they had a dashing look. I wrote two longish stories and sent them to Mr Unwin with a suggestion that he might think them suitable for this series. After some time he returned them to me with a letter that filled me with exultation. He said that they interested him, but that they were not long enough for the Pseudonym Library; if, however, I had a novel he would be glad to read it.

Ten minutes later Maugham was at work on his Lambeth Idyll, having pushed aside his medical studies. When it was completed, far from wishing to remain anonymous, the pseudonym he chose was as close to his real name as possible. The shocking and offensive nature of Maugham's material to the drawing-room taste of the 1890s produced qualms in at least one of the readers to whom the publisher sent the manuscript, but it was Garnett's view that, 'if Mr. Unwin does not publish A Lambeth Idyll somebody else will ... We should say *Publish*.' This view prevailed but it was decided to publish the story *hors de série*, and under the author's own name so that he could take full responsibility for it. Meanwhile the two short stories, *A Bad Example* and *Daisy*, the first Maugham ever wrote, had to wait awhile for publication.

There was nothing particularly original in Maugham's writing a tale about the inhabitants of the London slums at the tail-end of the Victorian period. Ever since George Gissing had brought out *Workers in the Dawn* in 1880 more and more writers had been attracted to describing the dark regions of the capital. 'As for that great and daily increasing school of novelists,' wrote Oscar Wilde in *The Decay of Lying*, 'for whom the sun always rises in the East End, the only thing that can be said about them is that they find life crude and leave it raw.' Nor was it merely in fiction that the life of the poor was recorded: Henry Mayhew had started the record in the 1850s with his factual surveys, and in 1886 the shipping magnate Charles Booth and his assistant Beatrice Webb (as she later became) began what was to be for Booth a seventeen-year stint of noting and codifying the way the other half—more than half in fact—lived or failed to in his monumental *Life and Labour of the People in London*.[3] It would be over-simplifying a confusing climate of attitudes to say that the cult of the Poor had taken over from the cult of Beauty but certainly the pendulum of taste among the young littérateurs in the late 1880s was swinging between the aesthetic affirmation on one hand and commitment to social realism on the other. One has a sense of this swing in motion in the recollections of Arthur Quiller-Couch looking back on his undergraduate days:

> In this autumn of 1882 the 'aesthetic movement' had—in Oxford at any rate—almost run itself out of breath; while Pre-Raphaelite enthusiasm was fading almost with famous Union frescoes, and in Oxford the neo-Gothic craze in architecture had lost its edge . . . poetry and the arts for a while gave place in discussion to philosophy (notably that of T. H. Green) and social philanthropy—*The Bitter Cry of Outcast London*, Toynbee Hall, the crusades of W. T. Stead, etc.—a backwash from the prophetic preachings of Carlyle and Ruskin.[4]

In fact aestheticism still had quite an impetus behind it in the persons of Oscar Wilde and Walter Pater both of whom were still active in the early 1890s, Wilde avowing that it was the business of life to imitate art. But at the same time the backwash of literature about the Nether World—to use the title of Gissing's greatest working-class novel, appearing in 1889— was also continuing to gather strength. As a young man of letters, Maugham inherited both these traditions for the moment, though, it was in the direction of slum realism that he looked for a model. In 1895 Arthur Morrison, who was himself of working-class origins although he liked to conceal the fact in later life, published *Tales of Mean Streets*, sketches and stories that had originally appeared in the Strand Magazine about life in the East End where the author had worked in the newly-built People's Palace.[5] It was in the tales of Morrison that Maugham, as he afterwards acknowledged, found his immediate model.

But what is remarkable about *Liza* is not that it had models but how much more readable and alive it is today than any of them. It may well be true, as P. J. Keating says in his valuable pioneer study *Victorian Working Class Fiction* that, 'the three principal qualities that Morrison believed dominated working-class life (monotony, a yearning for respectability and violence) all feature in Maugham's novel',[6] but *Liza* is an unflawed work: it is totally free from the ineptitudes of construction, the biblical afflatus, the 'whereuntos' and 'heretofores' and the sentimentality ('the trotting of sorrow-laden little feet . . .') which spoil Morrison's worthy stories and have prevented him from finding many readers today. Maugham is not only more detached, he manages somehow to cover a much greater amount of the actual life of the poor in its different phases throughout the day and throughout the year. To begin with Liza is not just the typical work-girl who, arrayed in her Bank Holiday finery, meets a bloke, yields to him, and after a brief idyll, becomes exhausted by child-bearing and the brutality inflicted on her by her husband when drunk: that role in Maugham—the role of Morrison's Lizerunt—is filled by Liza's friend Sal who marries her chap Harry, after which she undergoes the familiar metamorphosis. Liza is something much more original in terms of working-class fiction. She is a real heroine; someone above the common ruck, a Carmen or Lola of Vere Street. Maugham has the Italian organ-grinder churning out the Intermezzo from Cavalleria as she dances beneath the Lambeth sky:

> Liza outdid them all; if the others were as stately as queens, she was as stately as an empress; the gravity and dignity with which she waltzed were something appalling, you felt that the minuet was a frolic in comparison; it would have been a fitting measure to tread round the grave of a *première danseuse*, or at the funeral of a professional humorist. And the graces she put on, the languor of the eyes, the contemptuous curl of the lips, the exquisite turn of the hand, the dainty arching of the foot! You felt there could be no questioning her right to the tyranny of Vere Street.[7]

The street dance was a conventional episode in a story of this kind and so was the Bank Holiday outing which follows; the trip to Chingford sets the seal on Liza's love-affair with Jim Blakeston, a married man with wife and kids, which is the heart of Maugham's tale. This was, as Dr. Keating points out, the first time that a love-affair, and an adulterous one to boot, had

been made the theme of a slum novel: previous writers had
regarded the love-life of the poor as being either comic or
merely bestial or both. Maugham's approach was considered
greatly daring. At one point the word 'belly' had to be changed
to something less offensive. The staider members of Fisher
Unwin's staff wondered whether the book should be published
at all and there was much apprehension in the office when the
book at last came out after the excitements of the Queen's
Diamond Jubilee had died down. To the modern reader the
passage of time has dulled the shocks and given a pastoral tone
to the work. Maugham started his history of Jim and Liza's
passion in the high summer August days when life was more
than bearable, being lived largely out of doors, and showed it
coming to grief in the chilling isolating fogs of November. He
succeeds in dramatizing Liza's fluctuating feelings about
brawny Jim and her ever-loyal admirer Tom: she won't at first
go on the Bank Holiday jaunt because it would compromise her
position and then her sense of fun becomes too much for her self-
respect and she joins the throng only to become singled out
from them again by her involvement with Jim. Her crude
innate moral sense, if you can call it that, is no match for her
bouyant animal appetite and eventually she becomes an object
of scorn and hatred among the community of Vere Street. Thus
the slanging and scratching match between Liza and Jim
Blakeston's wife to be followed by the beating up of Mrs.
Blakeston by Jim are pieces of violence that have been most
skilfully prepared as parts of a whole process of degradation. By
contrast the bashing given to Morrison's Lizerunt by her husband seems merely gratuitous. Liza's death which soon follows
is another triumph, this time of bitter farce in the Gamp-like
reactions of Mrs. Kemp and her crony from upstairs who is
getting her cut on the funeral:

' "Hoak *versus* helm, thet's the question." "Well, Mr Footley," says
I, "for my own private opinion, when you've got a nice brass
plite in the middle, an nice brass 'andles each end, there's nothing like hoak." "Quite right," says 'e "thet's wot I think; for
coffins give me hoak any day, an I 'ope," says 'e, "when the Lord
sees fit ter call me to 'Imself, I shall be put in a hoak coffin myself."
"Amen," says I.'[8]

Maugham's ear for the speech of the people whether in a comic set-piece like the above or in Liza's more passionate exchanges with Jim is finely attuned. The passage I have just quoted might rival in its vernacular Kipling whose story *The Record of Badalia Herodsfoot*[9] was, Dr. Keating suggests, a landmark in the treatment of the working-class in English fiction. One contemporary reviewer of Maugham's book was not afraid to put Liza in the same class of achievement as Badalia, even to give the palm to Maugham. 'We are not indeed sure,' said the *Standard* critic 'that this new story does not beat that one in vividness and knowledge of the class it depicts . . . he has an almost extraordinary gift of directness and concentration, and his characters have an astounding amount of vitality.' Both Liza and Badalia happen to be masterly creations; if anything, I would rate Kipling's (like Maugham he made but the one direct excursion into slum life) the more extraordinary in that apart from all the vividness and wealth of authentic detail it takes no less a theme than a Christian martyrdom (that is what Badalia becomes when she is kicked to death by the Herod's foot of her husband) and transposes it to the life of those mean streets.

Maugham had other models beside Morrison and Kipling. If he had learned from those two how to handle the Cockney vernacular, and the rough violent life suffered by its speakers, he went across the English Channel for the things that gave his book its greatly superior form and proportioning. Maugham's parents were living in Paris when he was born. His father was a partner in a firm of solicitors acting for the British Embassy in whose august portals William Somerset Maugham was born in January 1874, technically speaking on British soil. Until the age of seven when he was left an orphan through the deaths of both parents in fairly rapid succession he had been brought up in the Embassy circle, and he never lost his love of Paris nor his ease with the French language even after he had moved to his uncle's Whitstable vicarage and gone to The King's School, Canterbury.[10] Maugham was a natural linguist among his other gifts and he tells us in *The Summing Up* how as a youth he would slip over to Paris and browse in the bookshops in search of work by Maupassant, buying the cheap reprints and reading the others piecemeal on the spot:

The attendants in their pale grey smocks took no notice of me and it was often possible when none of them was looking to cut a page or two and continue the narrative without interruption. Thus I managed to read most of Maupassant before I was twenty. Though he does not enjoy now the reputation he did then, it must be admitted he had great merits. He was lucid and direct, and he knew how to get the utmost dramatic value out of the story he had to tell. I cannot but think that he was a better master to follow than the English novelists who at that time influenced the young.[11]

Several English writers of Maugham's, and the preceding generations, drew strength from French naturalism, but with Maugham the transfusion 'took' at once without endangering the life of the patient. The rigorous discipline of the French masters suited Maugham's literary temperament. He enjoyed taking pains. He revelled in the difficulty of relaying his story pictorially, through external events and minutely observed detail. During his work as an obstetric clerk he spent long hours in the dwellings of the Lambeth poor and his novelist's eye would take in the ornaments and furnishings for use later on. Thus, after Liza has become Jim Blakeston's mistress for the first time she sleeps late through Sunday morning and on waking contentedly stares at her room:

The decorations of the room had been centred on the mantelpiece; the chief ornament consisted of a pear and an apple, a pineapple, a bunch of grapes, and several fat plums, all very beautifully done in wax, as was the fashion about the middle of this most glorious reign. They were appropriately coloured—the apple blushing red, the grapes an inky black, emerald green leaves were scattered here and there to lend finish, and the whole was mounted on an ebonised stand covered with black velvet, and protected from dust and dirt by a beautiful glass cover bordered with red plush. Liza's eyes rested on this with approbation, and the pineapple quite made her mouth water. At either end of the mantelpiece were pink jars with blue flowers on the front; round the top in Gothic letters of gold was inscribed: 'A Present from a Friend'—these were products of a later but not less artistic age. The intervening spaces were taken up with little jars and cups and saucers—gold inside, with a view of a town outside, and surrounding them, 'A Present from Clacton-on-Sea', or, alliteratively, 'A Memento of Margate'. Of these many were broken, but they had been mended with glue, and it is well known that pottery in the eyes of the connoisseur loses none of its value by a crack or two.[12]

This would have won Flaubert's approval for being not just *any* working-class room but one we might recognize if we saw it, and just as Flaubert follows Emma's surrender to Rodolphe with a description of the sunset on the road to Yonville so Liza's reactions to her surrender to Jim are felt through these clearly visualized objects. But unlike a practised realist Maugham finds it difficult to keep the mask of the detached observer strictly in position; every so often he lowers it and permits us to see (as in the Coridon and Phyllis episode) his contempt for the hideous taste of all that he beholds. The response on the part of the novelist to the tragedy he is about to unfold is not so much compassion or Olympian aloofness as a well-bred horror. As he grew older and more accomplished this was something Maugham learned to conceal and even here it is not allowed to spoil the strict proportions of the whole performance: the theme of the extra-marital affair is perfectly measured against the norms of life in Vere Street. There is nothing in the whole book that is not relevant to its heroine.

T. Fisher Unwin knew how to push his wares and *Liza* was widely reviewed, remarkably so for a first book. There were the expected complaints about the coarseness of it from the primmer critics but some of them were favourable and welcoming of a new talent. 'He has performed his task with singular ability,' said the *Literary World*, while 'Liza is a living creature from the beginning to the end' said the *Queen*. Meanwhile of the more intellectually grand journals *The Academy* spotted the Morrison influence calling it 'deliberate and unashamed mimicry' and the *Athenaeum* praised the 'fidelity and care' of the treatment even if the result was 'unpleasing'. And the appearance of the book set in motion wider ripples than just reviews: Augustus Hare's friend Basil Wilberforce used the story as a text for one of his sermons in the Abbey—to the delight of Maugham's landlady—and the French critic Augustin Filon writing in *Le Journal des Débats* on *Le peuple de Londres et le roman naturaliste* made the book the centre-piece in a discussion between the English and the French attitudes to naturalism.

It was Maugham's first taste of success and of fame, and though the young author took it in his stride, it was all very gratifying. News of the novel even reached St. Thomas's where the Senior Obstetric Physician offered Maugham a job as his assistant. This he turned down. Maugham had made one of those crucial decisions that sprang from his unshakable belief in himself from the very beginning. From now on though hardly begun his days in medicine were already over; he would live by his pen.

[2.]

There is never a time in England when it is a good moment for a young man in his early twenties to set up shop as a writer, but if one was inflexibly minded to do just that, with unlimited energy, huge resources of talent and an iron will, then 1897, the year of Queen Victoria's Diamond Jubilee, was a slightly less bad moment than most moments. Literateness was spreading rapidly. The 1890s saw the founding of several lively general publishing houses, Heinemann, Hutchinson, The Bodley Head, J. M. Dent, Sidgwick and Jackson, Methuen, Duckworth, whose names are still household words in the London book-trade. The art of fiction had three years earlier in 1894 been liberated from the albatross of the obligatory three-volumes for a novel thanks to a joint decision of Mudie's and W. H. Smith's circulating libraries henceforth to stock novels in one volume only.[13] Earlier the Copyright Act of 1886 had meant that British authors were now able to reap the financial benefits of American publication denied to their great Victorian forebears, and in the 1890s they began to employ agents to protect them from the astuteness of their own English publishers.

The first literary agent historically speaking was William Maurice Colles of the Authors' Society who acted for Gissing for many years. He also handled Maugham's earliest novels until after *The Merry-Go-Round* Maugham broke with him and joined the redoubtable J. B. Pinker, just as Gissing had done at the end of his life. Pinker also numbered Bennett, Wells, Stephen Crane and Conrad among his clients.

Among the novelists of an earlier generation the most tireless campaigner for the respectability of literature as a profession, and for improving the working conditions of those who practised it, was Walter Besant who had also taken a look at poorest London in *All Sorts and Conditions of Men* (1882) and *Children of Gibeon* (1886). He had produced a paper in 1892 on 'Literature as a Career'[14] which the young Maugham might have read with with some flexing of the creative muscles, for it went into the whole question of the rewards, monetary and otherwise, to be gained from creative writing. The general picture was not encouraging.

There were perhaps fifty novelists in Britain, Besant reckoned, making a thousand a year. The greatest prizes were to be had from the theatre: 'but' he said ruefully, 'the stage is a fortress very hard to take: many there are who sit down before it and presently retire vanquished.' Besant's more famous lecture on 'The Art of fiction' had been given at the Royal Institution in 1884. In it he urged that there should be knighthoods for authors—in the end he received one himself—and that the novel should be taken seriously as an art-form. He formulated some rules to be observed by the novice writer of fiction, one of them being never publish at your own expense; another, never go beyond your own experience; and yet another, keep copious notes. Whether he read Besant's talks or not, Maugham obeyed these precepts throughout his career and would certainly have been more impressed by them than the beautiful plea by Henry James[15] in a rejoinder to Besant for a much wider notion of the idea of reality in fiction. At any rate, as artists these two men represented the polar extremes of the profession he had just elected to enter.

Maugham reviewed the position that had been won by his *succès d'estime*. *Liza* had been, if not exactly dashed off, written rapidly in response to Fisher Unwin's invitation to produce something of suitable length for his Pseudonym Library. But Maugham had no intention now of becoming a specialist in the working-class novel as his publisher urged. Fisher Unwin wanted him to follow his *novella* with a long book set in a similar milieu. It was sound business advice and it would have been followed by ninety-nine ambitious young men out of a hundred. Maugham was the hundredth. He looked a long way beyond Lambeth to his future. In his final year at St. Thomas's he went through a period of intense soul-searching, of reading widely in European literature, history and philosophy. From this haphazard study he struggled to find some sort of order. 'I have,' he confided to the notebook that he now began to keep, 'collected a mass of facts, ideas, experience, but I cannot yet arrange them into any system or order them into any definite pattern.'[16] His need to reshape experience, whether from books or from the encounters of life, into a pattern remained with Maugham for the rest of his life. It was his greatest drive. He caught it from the aestheticism that was in the air when he came to manhood; the urge was strengthened by the fractured history of his youth, the broken flow of his own speech, and by his rejection of the narrow snobbish provincial form of Christianity that he had been exposed to in his uncle's vicarage:

> I do not believe in God. I see no need of such an idea. It is incredible to me that there should be an after-life. I find the notion of future punishment outrageous and of future reward extravagant. I am convinced that when I die, I shall cease entirely to live; I shall return to the earth I came from. Yet I can imagine that at some future date I may believe in God; but it will be as now, when I don't believe in him, not a matter of reasoning or observation, but only of feeling.[17]

The drift of these reflections is towards the sceptical and agnostic position, the faith in will-power and self-discipline to control instinct and passion, and the admiration for isolated acts of courage, familiar to readers of the mature Maugham. It is remarkable how early he made up his mind on all the important questions and how rarely he altered a notion once it had been formed. He considers his friend B. who believes in God, and the object of life is self-fulfilment. He concludes that he 'has no will, no self-restraint, no courage against any of the accidents of fortune . . . He is a selfish creature, indifferent to other people's feelings and the only thing that makes him behave with any semblance of decency is his conventional view of the conduct proper to an English gentleman.'[18]

During most of his literary career Maugham would be observing this code of conduct and this motivation, and subjecting it to many different kinds of tests; for the moment though he was more concerned with the conduct proper to an Italian nobleman of the fifteenth century. He had taken to heart some bad advice of Andrew Lang's who urged that the historical novel was the only one that a young writer could hope to write with success because he lacked sufficient experience of life to write about his own time. To a romantic escapist like Lang who adored Stevenson's novels there may have been something in this but it seems strange that a budding realist like Maugham should have fallen for it. Perhaps he felt then that he would be able to discern a pattern more clearly in the past than in the present.

In his last long vacation at St. Thomas's he spent six weeks in Italy visiting Genoa, Pisa and Florence, immersing himself in Italian art and history. He found his story for *The Making of a Saint* in Machiavelli's *History of Florence*: the insurrection at Forli in 1487.[19] The material was, as they say, action-packed; first the chain of events leading to the conspiracy, then the murder of the tyrant, and then the way everything falls apart for the conspirators after his death, with his widow shutting herself up in the fortress while her little sons are used as hostages. Maugham blushed for it in after-years and would hear no good of the book. Its main fascination now is to observe him finding in the aggressive life, rich in culture and personality of the Renaissance, a mirror of his own world and of his own attitudes. He explains in a preface that he is 'painfully aware that the persons of this drama were not actuated by the moral sentiments which they might have acquired by education at a good public school . . .' and he identifies with his narrator, a young man who is one of the conspirators and present at every important event that led to the overthrow of the tyrant. He is ambitious, vulnerable and sharp-eyed, very like the young Maugham, except that his current concern is murder rather than literature, Plato and Socrates rather than Wilde and Pater. Before the conspirators move in for the kill he is sent on a mission to Florence to canvass the opinion of Lorenzo di Medici from whom he receives the following message to report back to his boss:

'The wise man knows,' he said earnestly, 'for he has made up his mind what will happen, and goes about to cause it to happen. It is only the fool who trusts to chance and waits for circumstances to develop themselves . . .'[20]

Lorenzo is referring to the seizure of power through assassination, Maugham is thinking the same thoughts about getting his plays produced in the West End. But he has certainly done his Italian homework: he moves around with ease conjuring up the whole cultural and moral ethos, the courts, the condottieri, the favourites, the humanists and the women with two of whom in particular, one worldly-ambitious and one carnally-lustful, the young hero becomes ensnared. It was easier in those Mrs. Grundyish days to discuss sex in fancy dress. In later years the narrator of the book became a saintly Franciscan friar while Maugham became a saint (mornings only) of literary production but the life of holiness does not form part of this novel, only the worldly preparation for it.

There was general bafflement at the title, a sense of disappointment after Liza, and the inevitable attempt to compare Maugham's Renaissance ladies with his Cockney ones. The luke-warmth of the reception did not sow any doubts in Maugham's mind about the wisdom of abandoning medicine. He had gone to Spain for the first of many visits and had spent many enchanted hours in wanderings around Andalusia. In 1897 and 1898 he worked on a long autobiographical novel called *The Artistic Temperament of Stephen Carey*. On his return to England this was turned down by Fisher Unwin, and the book was never published. Maugham came to regard this set-back as a stroke of good fortune: years later he was free to return to the project of an autobiographical novel and write his masterpiece, *Of Human Bondage*. On his return home he rented a flat in Victoria with a friend Walter Payne who was a chartered accountant; while he was at his chambers Maugham had the place to himself. He worked assiduously: he wrote plays; he wrote fiction, long and short. In the 1890s there was a considerable market for short stories in England from the rare orchids of *The Yellow Book* to the earthier nosegays of the new gutter press. Besant had touched on the possibility of a writer supporting himself by some form of creative journalism in his lecture:

. . . all these papers vie with each other in getting the best fiction, the most striking articles possible; they offer a means of subsistence —not a mere pittance, but a handsome income—to hundreds of writers. Out of one office alone there is poured every week a mass of fiction representing as much bulk as an ordinary three-volume novel.[21]

Maugham addressed himself to the superior end of this demand represented by such publications as *Punch*, the *Strand Magazine*, *The Bystander*, *Casell's Magazine*, the *Illustrated London News*.[22] He had more than a dozen stories published between 1898 and 1908, that miraculous year when he was to have four plays on in the West End, and no doubt there were other tales that never saw the light of day. Seven short stories made up Maugham's next book, *Orientations* published by Fisher Unwin in 1899. When he came to compile his volumes of Collected Stories Maugham said of these early efforts: 'They are not worth bothering about.' Yet they anticipate in so many different ways what was to come that they are of some considerable interest if one is trying to trace the pattern of his development. Several of them do indeed crop up vestigially in the mature work.

Social realism, picaresque adventure, fairy-tale, melodrama, satire, these are some of the possible directions in which the author of *Orientations* might have seemed to be orienting himself. If there was a dominant mood it lay in a sense of enchantment and a faith in the spirit of adventure; and if there is a single influence it is one of the books Maugham found on the Vicar's shelves in Whitstable, *The Thousand and One Nights* in E. W. Lane's translation. Total immersion in this work was Maugham's early baptism as a story-teller. In later life he lamented that he would never be able to read it in the original Arabic. He had to make do with Mardrus's French translation in sixteen volumes. The underlying Islamic sense of the futility of the individual's attempt to defeat the operation of fate, with all the marvellous unexpected incidents that happen to him in the process, appealed strongly to Maugham's outlook on life. He recalled the story of the merchant who tries vainly to evade his appointment with death by leaving Baghdad for Samarra in his farewell to the theatre. In the figure of the Departer who tries to change the pattern of fate by leaving one city for another we have the most persistent theme in the whole of Maugham.

There are several such Departers in *Orientations* both to places abroad and in England, and the stories may be divided neatly between the exotic and the homebred, another foretaste of things to come. So far as one can see *The Punctiliousness of Don Sebastian* was Maugham's earliest published story appearing first in a trilingual magazine *Cosmopolis* in 1898.[23] Here the Departer is really a tourist who arrives one day at the Castillian city of Xioromonez. He has an ominous feeling of being at the world's end but all that happens to him is a conducted tour of the cathedral from the local Duke who tells him how his ancestor had poisoned his brother, the archbishop, on discovering his wife's infidelity with him through a scribble in a breviary. It is Maugham's earliest attempt to fathom a code of honour more ruthless than the English gentleman's. By contrast O'Donnell in *An Irish Gentleman*, first published in *The Strand* in 1904, is a much more typical Maugham figure, an exponent of burning your boats. He arrives in the principality of Wartburg Hochstein where he flings away his last fifty pounds in a gesture of pure chivalry. He keeps a volume of Virgil in one pocket and Childe Harold in the other, thus combining Maugham's two great passions for serious reading and travel. But the most typical Departer to exotic climes is the hero of *The Choice of Amyntas*. Despite his name Amyntas is the first-born of an English country schoolmaster; he goes out into the world with ten guineas from the parson to make good:

> So may Dick Whittington have meditated as he trudged the London road, but Amyntas had no talismanic cat and no church bells rang him inspiring messages. Besides Dick Whittington had in him from his birth the makings of a Lord Mayor—he had the golden mediocrity which is the surest harbinger of success.

He turns his back on his rustic English origins and goes to Cadiz where an enchanting young woman relieves him simultaneously of his virginity and his purse; now destitute, he wanders through the country in search of food and work and his own identity. He comes to a parting of the ways and a peasant in terror bids him avoid the path of evil fortune. This naturally he is drawn towards irresistibly until he finds himself afloat on a lake whose current bears him over-poweringly forward into an Aladdin's grotto of plenty where he has to make a choice between three young women who represent respectively beauty, wisdom and love. To his everlasting credit he chooses the Lady of Love and he does not return home to England. Amyntas is the forebear of Strickland in *The Moon and Sixpence* and Charles Battle in *The Breadwinner* and a number of other Maugham heroes of a later vintage for Maugham never ceased to be attracted by characters who abandoned their families in pursuit of a quixotic ideal.

He used the Spanish setting in another story in *Orientations* called *Faith* and here we have the first sounding out of another favourite theme—the unbeliever who had to suffer a profound disruption on account of his unbelief. In this instance he is a monk in the closed society of the monastery of San Lucindo. Brother Jasper confesses his unbelief to his superiors and is made to suffer the torments of the damned; the description of the flagellation ordered by the fanatical prior is a unique rendering of physical violence in Maugham's writing. Maugham the sceptic shows how the intense physical agony produces in the man's mind the hysterical illusion of a vision of the Redeemer. There is great jubilation. But as his wounds heal he returns to his former condition of chronic doubt. Maugham sees the whole thing as an illusion of his imagination. 'The wretched monk,' Maugham writes, 'who had not the faith to cure the diseases of his own mind, cured the diseases of those who had faith in him.' Maugham was to wait half a century before he again took up the question of miraculous healing in his last novel *Catalina* also set in Spain; this notion of the illusion that inspires faith he explored again in the various studies throughout his work of different kinds of artist.

His first long trip to Spain provided him, therefore, with much fruitful material; he acquired a whole lot more by simply breathing the air of London and his home county of Kent. In 1903 Maugham had indigenous stories printed in the *Pall Mall Magazine*, *Punch* and *The Strand*. If they contained such stock characters as compromised parliamentary candidates, hypocritical fortune-hunters, old family solicitors and exploited spinsters, everywhere the dialogue has freshness and sparkle:

'My dear Edith,' rejoined Lady Proudfoot. 'I think it would be disagreeable for all of us. You know she's inclined to be frightfully religious already.'

'Oh six months of marriage with the Vicar would quite cure her of that.'

A perceptive literary tipster chancing upon this kind of thing might have suggested that the young man should try his hand at writing for the stage. The young man had as it happened been filling notebooks with dialogue for plays he intended to write for years and had already had one play produced by the Stage Society. His comic touch with dialogue was seen again in the trifling *Flirtation*, published in the *Daily Mail* in 1906 but written two years earlier, in which a middle-aged bachelor proposes to an elegant, much sought-after widow in terms which announced another theme to be more fully fleshed out later on: 'After all,' he says, 'with the sort of people we know marriage is still the only respectable means of livelihood for a nice girl.' Maugham forgot that he had written this piece and when it was pointed out to him late in life he said it reminded him of the Dolly Dialogues by Anthony Hope.

The two most interesting stories in *Orientations* are in fact the earliest, *A Bad Example* and *Daisy* originally submitted by Maugham for the Pseudonym series. Set in Camberwell and Whitstable they show Maugham not merely finding a target in the social attitudes of the respectable folk among whom he moved, but ripping the middle of it to pieces. In the former a Cockney clerk is summoned to jury service at the coroner's court where he has to sit through three pathetic cases of suicide, three victims of social exploitation; the grisly spectacle of the bodies in the mortuary shatters his complacency. 'Bring me a Bible Amy,' he tells his wife afterwards, and after reading it proceeds to donate all his money to the poor out of a burning desire to do 'something for my feller creatures'. In the end his family and society regard him as certifiably mad. It is the theme of Maugham's last play *Sheppey* and it suits the social ambience of the nineteen hundreds just as well as that of the 1930s, if not better.

Daisy has an honoured place in Maugham's œuvre for it reveals him using his boyhood country in a literary work for the first time. It is based on the real life episode of a Whitstable girl who eloped with an army officer in Canterbury causing a tremendous flutter in the seaside dovecote. Her father has a respected position as the local undertaker. Her mother ascribes her daughter's lapse to the evils of education: 'I didn't want her brought up above her station, I can assure you.' Here is *le vrai Maugham* in full satirical control of his material, making a complete exposure of the cruelty inherent in the moral society while at the same time his romantic heart goes out to the courage and magnanimity of the Departer who returns as the wife of a baronet to reveal a streak of humanity lacking in her detractors. Before making such a brilliant marriage she appears as the Principal Boy in a tour of Dick Whittington:

> As Daisy waved her hand and gave a kick the audience broke out into prolonged applause; Tercanbury people have no moral sense although Tercanbury is a cathedral city.

Daisy was to be seen in Blackstable a second time reincarnated as Rosie in *Cakes and Ale*.

[3.]

The appearance of *Orientations* did nothing to raise the critical temperature. 'An average book, fairly readable, but with no serious interest or promise about it' commented the Bookman damningly and typically. It was not going to make his fortune. Maugham often said that he hated poverty, referring to his way of life at this time. Poverty is a relative term and I do not think that Maugham was ever poor in any absolute sense. He was never as poor as Philip Carey was in *Of Human Bondage*. He came into a sum of money from his father when he was twenty-one that gave him £100 a year; his literary earnings were not negligible, and life in those days was cheap. The Mrs. Barton Traffords of London literary society welcomed him to their salons little knowing what they were letting themselves in for. Edmund Gosse patronized him. Max Beerbohm was a friend, and many Fridays to Monday would be taken care of by invitations to houses in the country like Holmhurst owned by

Augustus Hare where 'sharp at eight in the morning a maid in a rustling print dress and a cap with streamers came into your room with a cup of tea and two slices of thin bread and butter, which she placed on the night table . . .'[24] By poverty Maugham meant begrudging the half-a-sovereign given to the butler on departure and enduring a stony glance or two from that worthy official. Still, he was in constant danger of living beyond his means and to meet the threat of bankruptcy he turned his mind to writing novels about the kind of English society he knew best, doctors, the clergy, the military, the lawyers, and the formidable womenfolk who ruled their servants and their husbands with rods of iron: the good people who were the traditional fodder of the English novelist. Their fathers and grandfathers had furnished many a three-decker. They had been immortalized in Jane Austen, in George Eliot, in Trollope. More recently they had found a champion for their chauvinism and a strident new voice for their patriotism in Kipling who at this time was touring the battle-fronts of South Africa. The Boer War was the first indication that some of their most firmly held beliefs were to be put to the test; and that with the passing of the Queen they would have to endure an era of radical change.

In 1901 Maugham published *The Hero* in which the chief character is conscious of a new mood of public breast-beating and of failure of nerve when he returns to his home land from the war:

> James had been away from England for five years; and in that time a curious change, long silently proceeding, had made itself openly felt—becoming manifest, like an insidious disease, only when every limb and organ were infected. A new spirit had been in action, eating into the foundations of the national character; it worked through the masses of the great cities, unnerved by the three poisons of drink, the Salvation Army, and popular journalism. A mighty force of hysteria and sensationalism was created, seething, ready to burst its bonds . . .[25]

The main novels in which we find Maugham's anatomy of Edwardian England and its values are *The Hero* (1901), *Mrs. Craddock* (1902), *The Merry-Go-Round* (1904) and *The Explorer* (1909). All of them have at their centres situations in which the

English gentleman finds his code of conduct woefully inadequate in dealing with the realities of life and in which he arrives through crisis at a painful maturity.

Maugham belonged to the last generation of English writers to inherit this code which has such a remarkably long life. Nevill Coghill in his English Association Lecture 'Chaucer's Idea of What is Noble' (1971) points to the origin of the term in *gentil* and *gentillesse* and associates it through medieval tradition with behaviour in imitation of the Founder of Christianity. Because of the ultimate Latin source of the term *gens* (family) there was 'a popular fallacy that there was something *hereditary* in being *gentil* and that there was such a thing as gentle blood, a mystical thing, that showed through all efforts to disguise it . . . Also popularly connected with the idea of heredity is the idea of wealth . . . *Generosus*, which in classical Latin meant *eminent* or *distinguished*, is the normal word in medieval chronicle Latin for a gentleman, as we would have to translate it; it implied wealth and hereditary station.' A history of English Gentlemen would trace the fortunes of this conception through Chaucer, Shakespeare, Congreve, Richardson, Thackeray, showing all manner of interesting fluctuations. What is remarkable is how much of the original conception remained intact at the end of the nineteenth century waiting to be inherited and re-examined by Maugham.

The novelist who precedes him as an ironic chronicler of English life, George Gissing, was also obsessed by the gentlemanly ideal, especially in his novels of the 1890s when he had ceased to write about the working-class. Like Maugham, Gissing felt socially disoriented: like him he lost his father when he was a boy; like him he suffered from a break in his education; like him he found social life an intense strain and always longed to get back from people to the peace of the library; like him he was a man of culture whose public persona was that of a story-teller. Gissing called one of his most deeply felt novels *Born in Exile* (1892) by which he meant that the intellectually brilliant hero was not born a gentleman. This young man explained his predicament to a friend thus: 'Put it in correct terms: I am a plebeian, and I aim at marrying a lady.' The friend then cross-examined him:

'One question. You seriously believe that you could find satisfaction in the life to which such a marriage would condemn you?'

'What life?' asked Peak impatiently.

'That of an average gentleman, let us say, with a house in town and country, with friends whose ruling motive was social propriety.'

'I could enjoy the good and throw away the distasteful.'

'What about the distastefulness of your wife's crass conventionalism, especially in religion?'

'It would not be *crass*, to begin with. If her religion were genuine, I could tolerate it well enough; if it were merely a form, I could train her to my own opinions. Society is growing liberal—the best of it. Please remember that I have in mind a woman of the highest type our civilization can produce.'

'Then you mustn't look for her in society!'[26]

Maugham did not quite have Gissing's paranoiac sense of social exile in spite of his stammer and he writes out of a privileged position within the social system but he is equally critical of it. In *The Hero* he presents us with a young Englishman all set to make just the kind of marriage for which Gissing's outcast longs when through his experience of life in the Boer War he gains a totally new perspective on the society in which he has been brought up. He is Captain James Parsons V.C., a Departer who comes back covered in a glory that is all the more gratifying because it atones for a costly military error of judgment on the part of his father; when in India the old boy had 'acted like a gentleman and a Christian; but the enemy was neither.' Parsons goes through the triumphal arch erected in his honour and the lines of cheering choir-boys but he is a changed man from the one who left home four years earlier. He sees his heroism as a futile gesture that may have cost the life of the brother-officer he was trying to save; the Kiplingesque patriotism of his father's friends in the village of Little Primpton he has come to regard as a sham and his own motivation as actual enjoyment of killing his fellow-men rather than any altruistic sense of duty. On top of all this, he has had a romantic experience with the wife of a man in a native regiment that has completely altered his attitude to the sacred institution of marriage as understood by the country gentry of latterday Victorian England.

Mary Clibborn is a complete gentlewoman who has waited

patiently and chastely for his return. She is a girl 'with a fine digestion and an excellent conscience; if not very pretty, obviously good . . . she enjoyed a long walk in a gale, with the rain beating against her cheeks.' Mary is motivated by a puritanical sense of duty and an unshakably loyal devotion to James. She occupies her days usefully as a district visitor to the sick and needy and she has a class of village girls 'to whom she taught sewing, respect for their betters, and other useful things.' Maugham is alert to the unconscious cruelty in Mary's strong-minded pursuit of duty. She forces an ailing labourer to lie in a painful position against the man's own better judgment; she provides an ill woman with the comfort of a bottle of port against the wishes of the doctor and tries unavailingly to rub into her girls a sense of their wretchedness. Mary is in a sense the first of Maugham's missionaries.

> 'I'm seriously distressed about my girls. They live in nasty little cottages, and eat filthy things; they pass their whole lives under the most disgusting conditions and yet they're happy. I can't get them to see that they ought to be utterly miserable.'
> 'Oh, I know,' sighed the curate, 'it makes me sad to think of it.'
> 'Surely, if they're happy you can want nothing better,' said James, rather impatiently.
>
> .   .   .
>
> 'Happiness is not the chief thing in this world, James,' said Mary gravely.
> 'Isn't it? I thought it was.'
> 'Captain Parsons is a cynic,' said Mr Dryland, with a slightly supercilious smile.[27]

The fatal word, the fatal reproach, comes out there for the first time as Maugham subjects his handful of characters, the two sets of parents and the vicar and his wife, to a scrutiny that beautifully places them in their period. They have a passion for Marie Corelli, Mendelssohn, backgammon, bagatelle, blanc-mange on the one hand, and temperance on the other; above all they are bounded by a parochial exclusiveness and snobbery that the returning hero finds stiflingly imprisoning. Primpton in all its awfulness comes alive for us through a series of neat strokes.

For James the moment eventually arrives when he has to tell
Mary that he no longer loves her and wishes to be released from
the engagement. The scene between them in which the news is
broken to her is strongly wrought and perfectly positioned at
the heart of the book. In working out the aftermath Maugham
was luckier than when years later he came to use the basic plot
again for his play *The Unknown* which hinges on the returning
hero's atheism and the girl's bigotry. Here in the novel
Maugham is concerned with the local repercussions of James's
jilting of Mary. It is the most deliciously heady storm in the
Primpton teacup. James's quondam bravery in winning the V.C.
does nothing to expiate the crime he has committed in their
eyes against the narrow ideal of gentlemanly conduct on which
the morality of Primpton is founded.

The Hero (1901) is an early landmark in Maugham. It is his
first sustained attack on contemporary middle-class values from
within the framework of English society and it shows his
remarkable ability among his countrymen to mount the attack
in a spirit of truly Gallic concentration.

[4.]

The family who bore the brunt of this attack were gentry,
but they were not very grand. To penetrate more deeply into
the English society to which they belonged Maugham had to
see it from the vantage-point of the Great House as so many of
his fellow English novelists had done. Like the courts of the
medieval kings and the palaces of the Renaissance princes, the
English country house was a world of autonomous rule in which
a novelist such as Trollope could find an inexhaustible concentration of the social, political and moral life of his period. To
the American expatriate Henry James, the House was the
Garden of Eden in which beneath the silken rustle of the ladies'
gowns, the intensely private conversations and the nightly click
of the billiard balls, the Fall of Man was re-enacted. Maugham
was never enamoured of the House like James and he never discovered there the richness of a Trollope. He had from the first
an artistic wanderlust that made him impatient with its

insularity. By the time he began to write he saw it as already in decline. His most damning picture of it is in the play *Our Betters* where it has come under the opulent, energetic, adulterous sway of Lady Pearl Grayston and her American compatriots who have bought themselves into London society and taken it over. The House upon which Maugham focused in his fiction at the turn of the century was a stately Kentish pile called Court Leys. It lay somewhere in between Whitstable and Canterbury. The mellow elderly Maugham who chanced to re-read his own novels of this time was harsh about the young man who held the Georgian architecture of Court Leys in such contempt. It may be that, as Maugham says, he was not a very nice young man, but his description of the House has a well judged accuracy as an image of social decline, mirroring the lost ascendancy of its inhabitants:

> The avenue of elm trees reaching from the façade of Court Leys in a straight line to the gates had once been rather an imposing sight, but now announced clearly the ruin of an ancient house. Here and there a tree had died and fallen, leaving an unsightly gap, and one huge trunk still lay upon the ground after a terrific storm of the preceding year, left there to rot in the indifference of bailiffs and tenants. On either side of the elm trees was a broad strip of meadow that once had been a well-kept lawn, but now was foul with docks and rank weeds; a few ship nibbled the grass where upon a time fine ladies in hoops and gentlemen with tie-wigs had sauntered, discussing the wars and the latest volumes of Mr Richardson . . . The house stood out in its squareness without relation to its environment. Built in the reign of George II, it seemed to have acquired no hold upon the land that bore it; with its plain front and many windows, the Doric portico exactly in the middle, it looked as if it were merely placed upon the ground as a house of cards is built upon the floor with no foundations.[28]

The owner of Court Leys in this state of decrepitude is a lively girl called Bertha Ley. She has a similar dissatisfaction with the gentlemanly assumptions and values of English county society to that of Captain Parsons; her intellectual awakening has come about through her education and extensive travel on the Continent like the heroine of Gissing's *The Emancipated* and like Maugham himself. She shares her cultivated cosmopolitanism with her formidably outspoken maiden aunt, Miss Ley, whom Maugham uses in this novel and in *The Merry-Go-Round* as the reasoner and confidante of the other characters, the role filled so urbanely in his later work by Maugham himself. She quotes Montaigne and La Rochefoucauld; 'the passion to analyse the casual fellow creature was the most absorbing vice she possessed'. Maugham tells us that he conceived her when he saw the portrait-statue of the ruthless Empress Agrippina in the Naples Museum. At any rate, she and Bertha show up the insularity of the worthies of the county who from time to time receive invitations to Court Leys, and who have splendid Thackerayan names: Mrs. Mayston Ryle, Lady Waggett, General Hancock and Mr. Atthill Bacot. Maugham later felt he had been rather hard on these people as well as on the architecture of Court Leys and he tried to make amends:

> They were devoid of envy. They had good manners and were kindly and hospitable. But they had outworn their use and perhaps it was inevitable that the course of events should sweep them away.[29]

The usurper who puts the House in order, Edward Craddock, is a gentleman farmer, that is neither a gentleman nor a farmer, as one character puts it, though in fact he proves himself to be both. Maugham's placement of him at a point in the social scale where he is initially unacceptable but afterwards capable of scaling all the heights of local eminence is very exact and very clever. Much thoughtful and damaging detail has gone into the portrait of this handsome specimen of good yeoman stock. His peculiar combination of philistinism, insensitivity and innocence emerges on his honeymoon with Bertha in London where he cries at a crude melodrama and loves a vulgar musical comedy, but is bored to death by the pictures in the British Museum; his politics are a Joseph Chamberlain-like imperialism, and protectionism derived from his farming experience, and he turns out to be deeply intolerant as a husband. His attitude to women he has learnt from many years spent rearing chickens: 'give 'em a good run, properly closed in with stout wire-netting so that they can't get into mischief, and when they cluck and cackle just sit tight and take no notice.'

Maugham shows how easily Craddock can combine an essential inhumanity manifested in various ways in his behaviour towards Bertha, and a hard blinding egoism, with his assumption of the gentlemanly role in which he is so triumphantly successful. To the world at large he is the perfect husband and an admirable master of Court Leys: they take back all their reservations about him and elect him to the town council. His respectability is complete. Only Miss Ley penetrates his outward front; she is stricken with horror at his vulgar improvements (gold-paint and lopped elms) to the old house. Several critics have pointed to the shadow of *Madame Bovary* looming over this novel and to be sure it has the same painful progression, beginning with the steady corrosion of the marriage through the husband's unawareness of the wife's inner nature, and moving with Maugham to the wife narrowly escaping death as she gives birth to a still-born child, this last episode being most authentically depicted by the former obstetric clerk of St. Thomas's. We may also wish to see *Mrs. Craddock* as a horrible realistic refutation, a decade in advance as it were, of the novels of D. H. Lawrence. Certainly Bertha obeyed the 'wisdom of the blood' when she married beneath her in defiance of society but where did it get her? It seems right that Craddock in a fit of arrogance should die in a riding accident at the end of the book while Bertha recovers, goes abroad, takes a lover and ends emotionally numbed and moribund with only her friendship with Miss Ley to support her.

At this stage in his career Maugham did not have the self-confidence to appear in his own books in person; when he needed a reasoner to enunciate the truths of which the antagonists seemed unaware he used Miss Ley. She became the axle of his next book *The Merry-Go-Round* (1904) in which he tried the experiment of linking together dramas involving separate sets of people. He hoped, as he explained later, to give 'a truer picture of life' like this than the 'partial' one of most novels. 'I was myself,' he said, 'living in several sets that had no connection with each other . . .'[30] As later novelists like Gide and Huxley demonstrated you need to counterpoint the material somehow if this aim is going to be realized, otherwise the novel will tend to read rather like a collection of short stories in spite of the presence of one ubiquitous figure like Miss Ley with whom all the others claim acquaintance. However, Maugham's book does have an organic unity of a kind through his continued examination of the gentlemanly code as a guide to right action in the relations between men and women belonging to the ruling social class. He presents his examination dramatically, perhaps one should say melodramatically, through a number of stock situations, such as the respectable married woman who has to confess to her husband that she has a lover, the gentlewoman who falls in love with a young poet of the humblest origins and therefore socially unacceptable who is dying of TB. This situation also occurs the other way round, with the gentleman who has an affair with a barmaid who becomes pregnant by him; and then there is another unwanted pregnancy, that of the gamekeeper's daughter who thereby threatens the security of her entire family because her father's livelihood depends on the head of the estate whose gentlemanly sense of propriety she has mortally offended. With a deterministic pessimism Maugham shows us how the code, which long ago had its origin in a great counsel of forgiving, exacts the maximum cruelty on those who become unwittingly caught up in its mechanical operation: each of the three main liaisons comes to grief in either betrayal, early death or suicide; two young women take their own lives, victims of masculine idealism; the only marriage that shows any sign of being happy is between an upper-class blackguard and a blowsy, level-headed, ungentlewomanly actress.

Maugham confessed to being much under the influence of aestheticism when he wrote the novel. He claimed he had made everyone much too beautiful. Certainly he was given to patches of descriptive over-writing which he later disciplined himself to avoid: 'the fields were gay with flowers, a vernal carpet whereon with delicate feet might walk the angels of Messer Perugino . . .' Aestheticism was at this time more than just a style: it was Maugham's answer to the code. He makes Miss Ley eloquently voice his credo to a young doctor Frank Hurrell, an agnostic who refuses to jump on the sexual merry-go-round at the first opportunity; he represents what Maugham felt he might have turned into had he stayed on in medicine. Hurrell elicits this confession from Miss Ley:

> I aimed at happiness, and I think, on the whole, I've found it. I lived according to my instincts, and sought every emotion that

my senses offered; I turned deliberately away from what was ugly
and tedious, fixing my eyes with all my soul on Beauty—seen, I
hope, with a discreet appreciation of the Ridiculous. I never
troubled myself much with current notions of good and evil, for
I knew they were merely relative, but strove always to order my
life so that to my eyes at least it should form a graceful pattern
on the dark inane.[31]

She sustains this Wildean pose while grisly things are happening to all the people in the circles around her—to Herbert, the
young working-class poet denied a sight of Greece (pure
Gissing, this) before death cuts short a life watched over by the
Dean of Tercanbury's daughter Bella, to pathetic Mrs.
Castillyon who is powerless to help the girl on her estate being
disgraced for the same 'crime' of which she herself is guilty, to
poor Basil Kent the barrister-author in love with Mrs. Murray
but married to Jenny Bush, the barmaid whose vulgar sponging
brother has the whip-hand over him. 'Oh, I think I've had
enough of duty and honour,' Basil says despairingly. In com-
menting upon the fate of this couple Miss Ley and Frank
Hurrell might be pronouncing judgment on all the chief
antagonists. Frank says:

> The only excuse I can see for them is that they're blind instruments
> of fate: Nature was working through them, obscurely, working to
> join them together for her own purposes, and because Jenny came
> between them she crushed her ruthlessly.[32]

To which Miss Ley replies:

> I can find a better excuse for them than that. I forgive them
> because they are human and weak. The longer I live, the more I
> am overwhelmed by the utter, utter weakness of men; they do try
> to do their duty, they do their best honestly, they seek straight ways,
> but they're dreadfully weak. And so I think one ought to be sorry
> for them and make all possible allowances. I'm afraid it sounds
> rather idiotic, but I find the words now most frequently on my lips
> are: 'Forgive them, for they know not what they do.'[33]

Miss Ley and Frank visit the grave of Jenny Bush who drowned
herself in the Thames. Her husband and Mrs. Murray have
placed roses there. On her way back from the cemetery Miss

Ley sees the hedges ablaze with wild roses. Frank gathers a
huge bunch to give her. As she takes it she says:

'. . . there is one thing that compensates for all the rest, that
takes away the merry-go-round from a sordid show, and gives it a
meaning, a solemnity, and a magnificence, which makes it worth
while to live. And for that one thing all we suffer is richly over-paid.'
    'And what the dickens is that?' asked Frank, smiling.
    Miss Ley looked at him with laughing eyes, holding out the
roses, her cheeks flushed.
    'Why beauty, you, dolt!' she cried gaily, 'Beauty.'[34]

End of novel. Maugham blushed as scarlet as the reddest rose
for that affirmation in after-years. He poured scorn on those
who burned with a hard gemlike flame and he described Pater
as a feeble creature whom 'it was unnecessary to condemn with
intensity.' He hated the cultural exclusiveness of aestheticism
and felt that appreciation of beauty should lead on to behaving
well. So much for Miss Ley. She had served her turn and does
not reappear. It seems unjust that so coolly rational a lady
should have been made in the end to represent so decadent an
attitude. Maugham was quick to see through the cult of beauty.
He would spend the rest of his life looking for something else
by which to live. But did he ever really find it?

[5.]

Maugham at thirty: he had now published four works of fiction in book form and was earning a modest competence from
his writing. His play *The Man of Honour* had been produced by
the Stage Society and published by *The Fortnightly* in a special
literary supplement. He was distinctly a man of promise.
Pinker was getting him fresh contracts to write more novels.
The anti-evil eye symbol had started to appear (upside down on
The Hero) on the bindings of his work. Was it inspired by
Kipling's swastika, plus the desire of the dedicated professional
to have his own personal trademark? William Heinemann had
taken him on and it was with his firm that henceforth Maugham's
fortunes would be linked in England. He had gained that

respected, not very lucrative reputation as a serious novelist he later felt he had forfeited through his success as a fashionable dramatist. The influential journal of opinion *The Speaker* had for instance reviewed *The Merry-Go-Round* to the tune of half-a-column in a joint article with Hall Caine. It showed that the reviewer was aware of Maugham's previous work. Mr. Maugham had

> 'written a very readable novel, but one that has perhaps more interest as a social document than as a work of art. *Liza of Lambeth*, the author's first book, was also a social document, clever but smacking somewhat too much of the novelist's notebook; then came *A Making of a Saint*, [sic] a study of Italian Renaissance life, which came a great deal nearer to penetrating psychologically into the subject than does the work of most of our solemn English historians; and afterwards came *Mrs Craddock*, a study of "the misunderstood women." The reviewers gave a great deal of praise to this last mentioned book, saying the author had torn the veil from a woman's heart, in the burgeoning of her love, in the full glory of its blossom, in its fading, decay, and death, etc. as the publisher's advertisements prefixed to *The Merry-Go-Round* remind us. But *Mrs Craddock* was, in effect, done with a masculine heaviness and solemn thoroughness that would not impose on any witty woman of insight. Everything was there but the one important thing—the essential subtlety of a woman's feeling. In *The-Merry-Go-Round* Mr Maugham has succeeded somewhat better . . .'[35]

and so on. Not a word about the formal experiment or about Miss Ley.

In 1905 Maugham somewhat preciously recorded his impressions of Andulasia in his first book of travel, *The Land of the Blessed Virgin*. This was another work that he did not see fit to have reprinted in his lifetime. Another was a 'novelization' the following year of a play called *Loaves and Fishes*, itself made out of an abortive early novel that held the cloth to ridicule in the person of a fashionable London cleric. *The Bishop's Apron*, as the novel was called, and *The Explorer* (1907), which had a similar genesis, for long lay upon Maugham's conscience like 'discreditable actions' since they were run up rapidly to raise money. The money thus raised was intended to be spent on 'a young person of extravagant tastes' but by the time it actually

arrived his passion for this individual was extinct and Maugham
spent it on a trip to Egypt thereby gaining material for a play
to be written some years later called *Caesar's Wife*. In *The
Explorer* we return for the last time to Court Leys. But by now
Bertha Craddock—did Miss Ley ever succeed in marrying her
off to Frank Hurrell?—has let the place to a lady she met in
Rome, an American widow, Julia Crowley, who gives the old
house a new lease of life by breathing into it the air of the
twentieth century, cigarettes, cocktails and games of bridge plus
volumes by Nietzsche and William James. One of her guests
is the superman himself in the person of Alec Mackenzie—said
to be based on H. M. Stanley—and embodying the patrician,
courageous, adventurous, expansionist aspect of Edwardian
England. Alec is an English gentleman in the heroic mould, 'an
ancient Roman who buys his clothes in Savile Row' who loves
to read Greek literature but only when he is not penetrating the
African jungle with a band of trusty comrades. At the heart of
the story he finds himself trapped like Basil Kent and James
Parsons in the toils of the gentlemanly code of honour. The code
suffers first when the heroine's father is convicted of financial
malpractice, that quintessential Edwardian crime, and dies on
his release from gaol. He leaves behind a son and a daughter,
and never were the characters of two siblings more in contrast.
The son is a blackguard of a more violent truculent kind than
his dad; the daughter is the sum of all that is purest and fairest
in English womanhood. Maugham developed a trick at this
time under the influence of Pater, about which I shall have more
to say later on, of finding analogies for his main characters
among well-known works of art; in this way he was able to stay
outside the character while assigning to him the moral qualities
he found in the painting. For Lucy Allerton it is a picture by
Furse, Diana of the Uplands, as the memory of it occurs in the
mind of the lively American:

> This portrait of a young woman holding two hounds in leash, the
> wind of the northern moor, on which she stands, blowing her skirts
> and outlining her lithe figure, seemed to Mrs Crowley admirably to
> follow in the tradition of the eighteenth century. And as Reynolds
> and Gainsborough . . . had given a picture of England in the age of
> Reason, well-bred and beautiful, artificial and a little airless, so had

Furse in this represented the England of today. It was an England that valued cleanliness above all things, of the body and the spirit, and England that loved the open air and feared not the wildness of nature nor the violence of the elements. She noted that Lucy had just that frank look . . . etc. etc.[36]

Allerton *père* has sullied that clean spirit; Alec gives his son the chance to redeem the family honour by accompanying him on a dangerous mission designed to quell the East African slave trade. In the course of it he meets his death while the rest of the party including Alec escape. His sister's Volumnia-like reaction 'it gives me back my self-respect' proves to be premature because what really happened was that her brother drunkenly raped one of the native women after which he was sent off by Alec to almost certain death. Unfortunately the news of this last fact leaks in England without the explanation for it. Alec appears to have violated the gentlemanly code by sacrificing the boy. Maugham skilfully shows how an evil reputation may spread through this society like wildfire. Alec has the choice of either standing idly by while his character is assassinated or breaking the heart of the woman he loves by posthumously assassinating that of her brother. *The Explorer* contains patches of crude prentice work but it does show Maugham getting to grips for the first time with an individual of mythical potency, his relation to society and to the current morality. Alec is the first portrait in Maugham's gallery of exceptional individuals that will include such different kinds of people as Oliver Haddo, Charles Strickland and Larry Darrell.

For the moment however Maugham's creative thought was aimed in a wholly different direction. The clue to his immediate future lay in the Mirabel and Millamant-like conversations between Julia Crowley and her lover Dick Lomax, all flowering out of the story *Flirtation*. Cosily ensconced in the refurbished drawing-room of Court Leys, Mrs. Crowley brought to the business of courtship a refreshing wit and freedom from cant. This was the tone that Maugham aimed to sustain throughout full-length stage comedies. The new orientation would be London, Monte Carlo, places where the fashionable world assembled.

CHAPTER THREE

Going Lightly

[1.]

MAUGHAM'S DETERMINATION TO storm the fortress of the theatre was unwavering throughout his twenties. Behind his persistence at writing fiction lay the hope that a reputation as a novelist would ease the way for acceptance of his plays. His earnings from fiction added to his private income were still not enough to meet his fashionable needs, and as the level of his balance at the bank ebbed the awful vision of capitulation to a job as a ship's doctor hove threateningly into view. A golden carrot dangled in front of his nose, as has happened to many an unperformed young playwright, only with him it was no plodding donkey but a mettlesome prancing talent that he spurred on mercilessly.

The first encouraging breach in the outer fortifications came not in London but in Berlin. Although Maugham had been to the theatre in Paris as a very young boy his formative playgoing had been while he was a student at Heidelberg and when he went on his vacation trip to Italy it was a German version of *Ghosts* that he took with him to translate into English to learn the technique of construction.

One of the few ways in which an unknown playwright might hope in those days to see his work performed was by writing the one-act curtain-raisers that were still much in demand by the actor-managers. Maugham had turned out several of them and so good was his German that he translated one of them, *Marriages are Made in Heaven*—written around the time *Liza* was being published—into a German version as *Schiffbrüchig* (*Shipwrecked*) and sent it to the Café Theatre Society, one of whose principals was Max Reinhardt.[1] It was accepted and produced, probably by Reinhardt, in 1902 at their premises in Unter den Linden, Schall und Rauch (Rumour and Smoke). The entertainment, consisting of cabaret, satire and drama, all under the sway of a master of ceremonies, was clearly *avant-garde*. It seems unlikely that Maugham was able to get to Berlin to see his work but the following year he printed the English text of the play in a handsome literary annual he edited with another young man who was later to have a success as a playwright, Laurence Housman; it was called *The Venture* and the contributors included E. F. Benson and Maugham's childhood friend from the British Embassy in Paris days, Violet Hunt (also a one-act play); and some of the illustrations were by Lucien Pissarro. This was the kind of thing Maugham meant when he said that he too had lived in Arcadia.

It is tempting to peer into a famous playwright's first performed play and to say which grains will grow and which will not. How many dozen Anouilh innocents were subsequently pressed from the matrix of *Humulus le Muet*? Likewise this trifling piece of Maugham's contains the seeds of ideas that were to flower theatrically from his pen over the next decade. It is about two not so young people who decide to fly in the face of the current notion of propriety and go their own way; or again, it is about the need for innocence to be disillusioned if life is to continue. There is much talk of honour and dishonour and social ruin but it is happiness that wins in the end, as it does in many of the later full-length comedies. The innocent party is Jack Rayner's best friend Herbert who tries to persuade Lottie Vivyan voluntarily to give Jack up. She refuses, after which he reveals to Jack that her income derives from her former lover. This is no revelation to Jack. He knew that already and he does not care. Urbane conversation floating along above a ground-swell of sex and money, culminating in doing your own thing, putting pleasure and inclination before honour and duty, these are the ingredients with which Maugham would flavour some of his most famous dishes.

They were not entirely new ingredients, but what was new in 1897 was the note of acceptance of Lottie's past on which the play ended. A fashionable London audience would have found this shocking. In looking back at the difficulty he had as an

unknown in getting his plays performed, Maugham complained
that the West End theatre managers at the turn of the century
were most reluctant to experiment with new writing talent;
when they needed a new play, he said, they either put on one in
translation, or one by Pinero, Henry Arthur Jones or R. C.
Carton. While it is true that these men represented the theatrical establishment around 1900 it was not so long ago since they
had been in the vanguard of a dramatic renaissance. It was
during the 1890s that playwrights who had something challenging to say about contemporary life emerged in the fashionable
London theatre; Pinero and Henry Arthur Jones were among
the vanguard. Far from being reluctant to experiment with new
writers, George Alexander had, when he took over the St.
James's Theatre in 1890, perceived the need to attract distinguished authors into the theatre, and had encouraged Oscar
Wilde to write plays. After the disgrace of Wilde he turned his
attention to the work of Pinero, while his rival actor manager
Charles Wyndham formed an association with Henry Arthur
Jones.[2] Maugham knew Jones's daughters and when their father
read Maugham's first novel he remarked with great discern-
ment that the author of it would be one of the most successful
playwrights of the day. Between 1897 and 1907 Maugham was
writing plays in the theatrical climate largely created by Jones
and Pinero.

They judged to a nicety just how far they could go in the
examination of sexual morals. Their work, owing much to
French masters, echoed the drawing-room conversation of the
English upper-class. They pleased and shocked by exposing the
values with their curious inconsistencies, and different codes of
conduct for men and women in sexual matters, underlying that
conversation. The playwright's ultimate reluctance to follow
their plots through to the subversive conclusions to which the
action logically might tend is seen in Pinero's *The Notorious
Mrs. Ebbsmith* (1895) when the free-thinking heroine throws
the Bible she has just been given into the fire but then with a
pang of remorse pulls it out again singeing herself. Mrs.
Ebbsmith is a most singular creation. She only becomes sexually
attractive when she ceases to be intellectually committed, and
the actress playing the role has a costume change to mark this

transition. She is notorious because of her views and her rabble-rousing public speeches and because she believes in 'free union'. Most of the heroines who gave their names to these authors' plays, women such as Mrs. Dane and Mrs. Tanqueray, were notorious because of some former liaison involving some tacit transaction between sex and money. The French had a whole gradation of terms for such women, maîtresses, courtesans, demi-mondaines, cocottes, grisettes, and so on, precisely delineating their social status. In England they were merely 'notorious', or vaguely 'kept', the most notorious of all being Paula Tanqueray who first wrung the hearts of audiences at the St. James's Theatre; at that time Maugham was translating Ibsen in Italy.

Ibsen had first been performed in English in 1891 at the Independent Theatre started by the Dutchman J. T. Grein and had provoked the celebrated 'muck-ferretting dog' reaction to *Ghosts* from the *Daily Telegraph* critic, Clement Scott. Bernard Shaw's first play *Widower's Houses* had been performed there in 1892, the same year that saw the theatrical debut of another Celt who was to succeed in storming the fortress, J. M. Barrie with *Walker London*. A slightly later platform for Shaw and other unconventional young playwrights, such as Granville Barker and St. John Hankin, which had been founded in 1899 with the aim of securing 'the production of plays of obvious power and merit which lacked, under the conditions then prevalent on the stage, any opportunity for their presentation' was the Stage Society.[3] The Society took over a West End theatre for a Sunday evening and a Monday matinée and invited all the leading critics to the performance. Its criteria of taste veered between Ibsen and Maeterlinck, both of whose plays it presented. Shaw was on the selection committee at one time, and so was another keen Ibsenite, W. L. Courtney, the editor of *The Fortnightly* and former Oxford don. It was to the members of this committee that Maugham submitted his play *A Man of Honour*, who soon recommended it to the Society for production. Not only that, Courtney was so impressed by the play that he printed it in full as a special literary supplement to his magazine in 1902. It was produced with Granville Barker in the lead at the Imperial Theatre in February 1903.

A Man of Honour, which might be sub-titled 'The Barrister and the Barmaid', is one radial of *The Merry-Go-Round* adapted for the stage. The audience watches Basil Kent do the right thing, to the dismay of his friends, by Jenny Bush and the wrong thing by himself: in other words Basil's honourable marriage is an utter disaster. I do not know whether Maugham was aware of the marriages that Gissing, who had about eight months to live, had made with two women of the working-class but some of the dreadful scenes in real life between Gissing and Edith or Nell must have borne a remarkable similarity to those between Basil and Jenny. Like Gissing Basil is torn between his sexual involvement with a work-girl and his longing to marry a cultivated woman who can comprehend the books he plans to write. Listen to him as he explains his plight to a friend:

> Basil: I gave the world fine gold, and their currency is only cowrie-shells. I held up an ideal and they sneered at me. In this world you must wallow in the trough with the rest of them . . . The only moral I can see is that if I'd acted like a blackguard—as ninety-nine men out of a hundred would have done—and let Jenny go to the dogs, I should have remained happy and contented and prosperous. And she, I dare say wouldn't have died . . . It's because I tried to do my duty and act like a gentleman and a man of honour, that all this misery has come about.
>
> John (looking at him quietly): I think I should put it another way. One has to be very strong and very sure of oneself to go against the ordinary view of things. And if one isn't, perhaps it's better not to run any risks, but just to walk along the same secure old road as the common herd. It's not exhilarating, it's not brave, and it's rather dull but it's eminently safe.[4]

That might easily be a transcript of a real-life conversation between Gissing and Morley Roberts.

The theme of the mis-mating was a commonplace of the Victorian and Edwardian theatre but no one before Maugham had viewed it quite so unglamorously. In plays like Robertson's *Caste* (1867) often quoted as the onlie-begetter of realism in the English theatre, and Pinero's *Trelawny of the Wells* (1898), the girl is an actress with all the Bohemian allure of her profession;

she is capable of melting parental opposition and nimbly over-leaping the class barrier, as so many of them did in real life. In Shaw's early plays *Widower's Houses* (1892) and *Mrs. Warren's Profession* (1893) the misalliance of the plot is a mere stepping-stone, lifted to reveal the crawling iniquities of the socio-economic system; later in *Pygmalion* (1912) Shaw takes the highly original view that the division between the classes is largely one of speech habits and that it can be eliminated by a quick ear and an expert in phonetics. Maugham's remains the classic straight treatment of the mis-mating in its most extreme form for Edwardian England.

The critics' reactions were mixed but whether favourable or unfavourable they all bore the marks of the considerable impact that the play had had on them. It went straight to the heart of the Ibsenite and Shavian, J. T. Grein who, in a review of wild enthusiasm, declared the piece to be 'the (prose) play of the first triennium of the twentieth century'[5] and bracketed it in importance with *The Second Mrs. Tanqueray*. At the other extreme was the witty and anonymous A. B. Walkley in *The Times* who felt that the play was 'so ugly in subject and so dismal in tone that it ought to give deep and abiding satisfaction to all playgoers who take their pleasures sadly . . . The moral seems to be—don't make an honest woman of your humble victim, or, if you do, make haste to drive her to suicide, and, almost before she is buried, remarry in your own station in life.'[6] Walkley's most perceptive point came when he said that Maugham's work 'had some claim to belong to that category of plays which at M. Antoine's playhouse used to be called *le théâtre rosse*.' He concluded, prophetically as it turned out, that 'a man of his manifest ability is bound to become more cheerful by and by.' Max Beerbohm, who was now 31 and for the past four years had been writing a weekly theatre article in *The Saturday Review*, especially enjoyed the handling of the crumbling affection between Basil and Jenny—'the second act in which the husband and wife are bickering is admirably conceived . . .' but what, like Walkley, he most objected to was the finale with Basil and his true love Hilda practically in each other's arms almost before the dead wife's body had been fished out of the muddy slime of the Thames. At this stage in his

career Maugham was more than ready to listen to serious con-
structive criticism and he set about revising the play and
changing the ending, substituting a scene in which the *raisonneur*
friend of Basil's bribes the wife's vulgar brother not to make a
fuss. In this form it was revived a year later at the Avenue
Theatre with Ben Webster and Muriel Wylford, preceded by
one of Maugham's own curtain-raisers *Mademoiselle Zampa*, a
piece with a music hall setting that has not survived. Grein liked
the new ending; but Max didn't nor did he admire the acting:

> Mr Maugham's play is performed by clever people but it is not well
> performed by them. They are on the wrong tack. This is not surpris-
> ing. It would be surprising to find a poetic romance acted in the
> right manner: for poetic romance though we still have examples of
> it, is a bygone dramatic form; and when it dies, the right way to
> act it dies also. Prosaic realism is the form towards which we are
> tending; but we have not reached it yet: such plays as *A Man of
> Honour* are only as it were the outposts of the form; and con-
> sequently our mimes have not yet acquired the right method of
> interpreting it.[6]

In other words Maugham was not only probing an outmoded
conception of honour, he was forging a new instrument with
which to conduct the examination. But it was not one that
appealed to the general public and after a run of about a month
the play was withdrawn. What now for its author?

There were two views about what Maugham's next move
should be, and it was in the delightful setting of Merton Abbey,
the house that Nelson had lived in with Lady Hamilton before
Trafalgar, that they emerged. The house was occupied at the
beginning of our century by a Mrs. George Steevens, who was a
real-life example of a woman-with-a-past, having suffered social
ostracism through her involvement in Sir Charles Dilke's
divorce; later she married the *Daily Mail* correspondent George
Steevens who was killed at Ladysmith. As an old woman—one
of the models for Miss Ley?—she used to entertain a great
many writers and painters and actors at Merton Abbey at week-
ends. Maugham was part of her circle and so was Max, who
after luncheon one fine day talked to his friend like a Dutch
uncle about his future. Let Max recall the conversation in his
own words:

One sunny afternoon, when the twentieth century was younger than it is now, a novelist and a dramatic critic might have been observed pacing up and down a lawn, in deep conversation. The novelist had not long ago written a play, which had been produced by some society and so much admired that some manager had presently put it into the evening bill. There the critics admired it as much as ever, repeating their praises of its truthfulness, its humanity, and all that. The public, however, had not taken the advice to go and see it. It was, indeed, a play foredoomed by the melancholy grimness of its subject. The author had extenuated nothing. There was no gilding of the pill; and the pill, accordingly, was not swallowed. Disappointed, but unbowed, the author was now declaring to the critic his resolution to write more plays. The critic, who had always admired greatly the author's novels, urged him to leave the theatre alone. He pointed out that, good as the play had been it had not been so good as the novels. Drama, he insisted, was a damnable business, at best. The outlines had to be so arbitrary, the colours so thickly laid on. The most subtle of characters on the stage was far more obvious than the simplest and most straightforward of one's fellow creatures. In writing a novel one did not have to make these wholesale surrenders. One could be as subtle as life itself, said the critic. And, since the talent of the novelist to whom he was talking 'like a father' was essentially a subtle talent, the less traffic it had with the theatre the better it would thrive. The theatre could gain little by it, whereas, insidiously, the theatre would mar it for its proper use. Commercially, of course, the theatre was a tempting thing. There were pots of money to be made out of the theatre, by some people. 'But,' said the critic, pausing in his walk and tapping the novelist on the breast, rather impressively, 'you, my boy, are not one of those people.' The novelist seemed to acquiesce, not without a certain gloom. And the critic, sorry for him, yet conscious of having done a good afternoon's work, briskly changed the subject.[8]

He may have *seemed* to acquiesce but inwardly he remained utterly resolute. If he could not take the fortress by storm then he would take it by siege. It was simply a question of tactics. Max's point about the unsubtlety of the theatre was a sound one but he was reckoning without Maugham's power to communicate his peculiar subtlety in combination with the broadest of effects. From the commercial point of view *A Man of Honour* may have been a flop but Maugham had learned an enormous

amount about stagecraft from the rehearsals and the re-writing.
A scene between two newly-weds in the first act had in particular a light humour that promised well. Lines planted for laughs,
in a sub-Wilde manner, like, 'If you wanted to make love to me
you ought to have married somebody else,' actually succeeded
in getting laughs. Maugham took great heart from this, and
decided from now on to aim mainly for laughs. In those wise
and witty prefaces to the Collected Edition of his plays written
wearing his ironic disillusioned author's mask he protested that:

> ... it was not without misgiving that I turned to comedy. I knew
> the drama could only regain its proper place in the literary life of
> the time and be of serious import to intelligent men if it dealt in a
> sincere spirit with life. In my day we meant by this prostitution.
> We were willing, it is true, to consider adultery if the consequences
> were harrowing; but we had no patience with the quality and were
> interested in the proletariat only if it was vicious or starving: it was
> the middle class with its smug respectability and shameful secrets
> that offered us our best chance to be grim, ironical, sordid and
> tragic. We were not gay, life was too grave for that; we were not
> light, our admiration for Ibsen had taught us to leave that to the
> French.[9]

In fact Maugham turned to comedy not with misgiving but
with relish. As for the social evils of prostitution he was more
than willing to leave them to Shaw or to Brieux whose play
about V.D. *Les Avariés* (*Damaged Goods*) was a current sensation on the Continent, or to anyone else who thought them
suitable matter for drama. And Maugham had plenty of patience
with the quality when it came to writing plays. He realized
the truth exhibited in the work of Wilde and Pinero that everybody loved a lord, or rather loved to see a lord in a tight spot:
The Gay *Mr.* Quex would not have done nearly so well. He
knew that if he was ever going, as a later age would put it, to
break the big-time, he would have to turn his sights from the
experimental theatre and focus them upon Society and the West
End. In his two next plays, *The Explorer* and *Loaves and Fishes*,
we can observe him beginning in a somewhat blurry and uncertain fashion to bring his target into focus. In *The Explorer*
everything, as we saw, turned on that great preoccupation of
Society, reputation; and in the other play Maugham takes Canon

Spratte, the brother of a peer, and revolves the whole play around this worldly old rascal in his fashionable parish of South Kensington. But the main mood is still much more Shavian than Wildean. It is about a twentieth-century Tartuffe and though in places very funny it is a distinctly unpleasant play. It shows the Canon intriguing for his own preferment on the one hand and trying on the other to break the engagement of his daughter to a young man of the humblest origins who has written a book on *The Future of Socialism*. Like Candida two years earlier she has to make up her mind between two contrasting males, but unlike Candida she makes a thoroughly despicable choice, ditching the young author after a hilarious scene (the best in the play) where the Canon invites his old Mum to tea and she asks for a drop of 'white satin'; at this first breath of plebeian reality, the daughter lowers the flag and later confesses: 'I hate grime and dirt. I think the slums are horrible.' So much for social realism! It was something which Maugham would be very pleased to hand over to his contemporary John Galsworthy. Meanwhile he pursued the Canon with savage gusto; like the Vicar of Swale, in an early story published in *Punch* (February 1900) this worthy cleric discovers that the income of the widow he has been wooing ceases on her re-marriage and he makes haste to back-double ungallantly out of the engagement. Maugham was fond enough of the monster to reward him with his bishopric and most improbably to give him for his second wife a girl originally destined for his son. The play had to wait until 1911 for its production when it only achieved a brief run, and until 1951 for its revival (by Peter Cotes at the Boltons) when it seemed to the present writer still to have a great deal of fun left in it.

Loaves and Fishes was but one of at least five plays that Maugham wrote after *A Man of Honour* in 1902, until his next production in 1908. The more they were rejected by the managements, the harder he worked: but in spite of this whole-sale rejection the picture was not unrelieved gloom. During the period of rejection the novice is tantalized by mirages; a nibble here, an option there, a suggestion that if certain scenes were to be re-written and others substituted a production *might* be possible. Maugham had plenty of that. The American managers who crossed the Atlantic in search of new young playwrights were aware of his name. This was largely thanks to the efforts of R. Golding Bright who was destined to become the leading play-agent of his day and who at this time believed in Maugham's future as a playwright strongly enough to take him on to his books and to organize the arduous task of submission. His brother Addison Bright who, after a financial scandal committed suicide in 1906, had had good contacts as an agent among the moguls of Broadway; 'Goldie' inherited these, and he pulled off a coup for the young author when he negotiated a contract with the American impresario George C. Tyler to cover the rights of a comedy Maugham had written called *Lady Frederick*, for both London and New York with an advance of a thousand dollars. On the strength of this sum Maugham gave up his London abode and went to live in Paris. He met Mr. Tyler while he was there who was deeply impressed by Maugham's determination. He told him that one day he would be a distinguished dramatist and he gave him his first cocktail, thus starting a habit that was to last a lifetime and to which another American, Gerald Haxton, would expertly minister.[10]

Tyler was not the only person to be struck by Maugham's self-possession at this period of comparative obscurity. Louis Marlow, who met him at Cambridge when *A Man of Honour* was produced there after the London production, registered an impression of 'an unobtrusive, rather wary, unusually good-looking man',[11] and while in Paris, Maugham went to see Arnold Bennett (who had given up his job as editor of *Woman* in 1900 at the age of 33 and had been writing industriously ever since).

> He [Maugham] has a very calm almost lethargic demeanour. He took two cups of tea with pleasure and absolutely refused a third; one knew instantly from his tone that nothing would induce him to take a third. He ate biscuits and gaufrettes very quickly, almost greedily, one after the other without a pause, and then suddenly stopped. He smoked two cigarettes furiously, in less time than I smoked one, and solidly declined a third. I liked him . . .[12]

At this period Maugham found a more intimate friend in a young old-Etonian painter called Gerald Kelly who had a studio in the rue Campagne Première. 'He was highly talented, abundantly loquacious and immensely enthusiastic. It was he who first made me acquainted with the Impressionists . . .'[13] Through Kelly, Maugham began to frequent a restaurant known as Le Chat Blanc in the rue d'Odessa, the regular haunt of a number of artists and writers and the scene of discussion about the principles of post-Impressionism in painting and realism in fiction. Bennett was often to be found there and so were people like Auguste Rodin and Marcel Schowb (who had a great admiration for Stevenson and a passion for the South Seas). Clive Bell was there too, and W. E. Henley and all manner of curious flora and fauna from both sides of the Channel. Perhaps the most curious was Aleister Crowley, 'the Great Beast', founder of an order of Magick and self-styled Magus, who married the sister of Kelly:

> I took an immediate dislike to him [Maugham later wrote of Crowley] but he interested and amused me. He was a great talker and he talked uncommonly well. In early youth, I was told, he was extremely handsome, but when I knew him he had put on weight and his hair was thinning. He had fine eyes and a way, whether natural or acquired I do not know, of so focusing them that, when he looked at you, he seemed to look behind you. He was a fake but not entirely a fake . . . He was a liar and unbecomingly boastful, but the odd thing was that he had actually done some of the things he boasted of.[14]

When Maugham came by and by to put Crowley into a novel called *The Magician* (published in November 1908) he searched for a painterly analogue for him and found one in 'the arrogant attitude of Velasquez's portrait of Del Borro in the Museum of Berlin; . . . his countenance bore of set purpose the same contemptuous smile.' We need not linger over this novel with its homunculi and its account of the Magus's abominable experiments; it must be the most implausible story Maugham ever wrote. Maugham did allow it to be re-printed in his lifetime and wrote a preface from which I have just quoted, but he hated the book so much that when a friend of mine, B. A. Young, asked him to autograph his copy he refused. Did Charles Williams read it at some stage and think how much better he could do? Williams's magicians, like Oliver Haddo, the name Maugham

gives to the Crowley character, turn innocent young women
into slaves of their evil wills but they do so through some
strange heretical perversion of Christian doctrine; Maugham
has done his homework on the occult in his usual thorough way
but the real source of Haddo's power is in his pseudo-scientific
dabblings and in a spell derived from—wait for it!—'the
honeyed words in which Walter Pater expressed his admiration
for that consummate picture [La Gioconda]'. Maugham clearly
half-admired Crowley's demonic will-power and he also had a
score or two to settle with both him and Pater. Crowley had
been somewhat patronizing to 'that nice young doctor' he met
in Paris.

By the time the book was published Maugham had already
lost interest in it. It was, however, sent to Crowley who
reviewed it in *Vanity Fair* and who commented when he caught
sight of the volume:

> So he had really written a book—who would have believed it! . . .
> the Magician, Oliver Haddo, was Aleister Crowley; his house
> 'Skene' was Boleskine. The hero's witty remarks were many of
> them, my own . . . But I had jumped too hastily to conclusions when
> I said 'Maugham has written a book.' I found phrase after phrase,
> paragraph after paragraph, page after page, bewilderingly familiar;
> and then I remembered that in my early days of the Golden Dawn
> I had introduced Gerald Kelly to the Order, and recommended
> him a selection of books on Magick. I reflected that Maugham
> had become a great friend of Kelly, and stayed with him at Camber-
> well Vicarage. Maugham had taken some of the most private and
> personal incidents of my life, my marriage, my explorations, my
> adventures with big game, my magical opinions, ambitions, exploits
> and so on . . . I was not in the least offended by the attempts of the
> book to represent me as, in many ways, the most atrocious
> scoundrel, for he had done more than justice to the qualities of
> which I was proud . . . *The Magician* was, in fact, an appreciation
> of my genius such as I had never dreamed of inspiring.[15]

[2.]

Tyler showed *Lady Frederick* to a number of leading ladies
but none of them would contemplate the scene in the last act

where the heroine appears in deshabillé in broad daylight and eventually his option lapsed. The tide turned at last when Otho Stuart, who was running a season at the Royal Court, had need of a play to put on as a stop-gap between two productions and decided to run Maugham's comedy for six weeks. It lasted a year. Ethel Irving had an immense success in the title role which she repeated when the play was revived in 1913. And sadly enough for Tyler it was Charles Frohman who produced the play on Broadway with Ethel Barrymore as the Irish widow.

In after years Maugham liked to give the impression that after so much rejection he had turned himself into a sort of play-making computer, feeding into the programme all the elements required for a fashionable success: epigrams, an adventuress with a heart of gold, blackmail, and a touch of brogue. There is slightly more to the piece, and those that followed it, than that. Maugham has found his own way of dis-distilling the essence of that over-fed, exclusive, insolvent, elegantly covertly libidinous Edwardian society, that had repudiated its greatest wit and sent him to Reading gaol and was now ready to acclaim a new Jester.

Society was still exclusive but because of its insolvency it was beginning to have to relax some of the qualifications required for membership and it is this process, threatening a widening of the ranks, which is what Maugham's early Society comedies are about. For Maugham it is still true, as it was for Wilde, that 'To be in it Society is merely a bore. But to be out of it simply a tragedy.' Yet exclusion is no longer the ultimate sanction that it was; for a woman with a past there is less sense of transgression and expiation below the comic or farcical surface and more of a feeling of a poker game in which you both have to hold the right cards and have sufficient nerve to raise the stakes and bluff your way to triumph through superiority of will-power or magnanimity of character. The scene has shifted significantly from Mayfair to Monte Carlo.

Maugham gave his Irish heroine an intriguing (in both senses) hand to play. She is up to her ears in debt and so is her brother. She has young Lord Mereston in her toils; his fortune could easily obliterate her creditors: his family are doing their damnedest to undermine her influence. Against this, she holds a bundle of letters from the young man's father that will destroy his posthumous reputation of having led a life of blameless piety (Cf Pinero's *His House in Order*). They can cap this with a letter that compromises her. She had an explanation that nullifies the force of that . . . and so on, and so forth. Maugham keeps the see-saw swinging cleverly until the last act. In the end she does something quite incredible but utterly in keeping with the character of a magnanimous Maugham adventurer. She throws away her advantage, and she weans the young man of his love for her. She shows him herself stripped of her social mask; he sees her at her toilette in her boudoir by the pitiless light of day. Here is a perfect theatrical image for one of Maugham's most cherished themes, the process of youthful disillusionment, and liberation.

The piece pleased both critics and public. 'A very charming and persuasive piece of work it is,' said *The Times* voicing the general sentiment. Success snow-balled rapidly. At the end of April 1908 the *Pall Mall Gazette* reported that: 'Mr. Somerset Maugham's sound and clever comedy of *Lady Frederick*, which moved first of all from the Court to the Garrick, and again last night from the Garrick to the Criterion, resembles another traveller in that it "drags at each remove a lengthening chain" of popularity. Its merits are of a kind that grow upon intelligent audiences for while it was launched originally without any splutter of fireworks, it has steadily enlarged its circle of admirers, and no piece of the present season has gained a more substantial or legitimate success.' One success led to an immediate demand from the managements for further work of the same kind. The author beheld the gratifying spectacle of competition for scripts that previously had been rejected.

In this same year *Lady F.* was followed on the stage by *Jack Straw* with Charles Hawtrey in the eponymous role and *Mrs. Dot* with Marie Tempest, thus reversing the order in which these two comedies had actually been written. Already there were those who were sounding a note of caution amidst all the jubilation. The following appeared in *The Referee* in May:

> Now success has come with a rush to Mr W. Somerset Maugham. Certainly he is a writer with a sense of the theatre and with talents that should be welcome there; but with three of his plays running

concurrently in London and a fourth already waiting for production at another theatre, it looks very like overdoing it: either he is writing too much or he is giving us, one after the other the plays he may have written before 'Lady Frederick' established his reputation. Whichever way it may be, it is a mistake . . .

It was certainly not a mistake from the point of view of the box office. *Mrs. Dot* ran for 272 performances, *Jack Straw* for 321. These two comedies show Maugham enlarging his satirical portrait of Edwardian society by caricaturing the different elements of which that society was composed—minor foreign royalty, impoverished peers, affluent mercantile vulgarians, dangerous well-endowed widows, languid men-about-town, dogmatic husband-vetting mamas, suppressed daughters, indefatigible duns pursuing dandified younger sons, exploited and insolent servants. They were all like so many coloured balls juggled about by Maugham with dazzling aplomb around the career of the adventurer hero/heroine who is the rude shock that brings them all momentarily to their senses. The plays have as much permanence as the clouds of cigar smoke floating off a hearty group of male supers as they discuss some demmed good-looking filly at the start of an act above the ephemeral melodies of a distant orchestra, but while the airy pattern lasts it is worth trying to trace it. Opulence does battle with effrontery and effrontery always wins in the end. Here is a world obsessed by money and by manners; a snub or a slight has as much weight as an inheritance or a bankruptcy and sudden reversals of fortune must be met with outward nonchalance and inward fortitude. The one thing common to everyone, except the servants, is abundant leisure. To the grape-shot of aphorisms the heavy veil of hypocrisy surrounding the Edwardian marriage market is rent apart:

Gerald: You married for love, Lady Sellenger.
Lady Sellenger: I'm anxious that my daughter shouldn't make the same mistake.

.   .   .

Gerald: What is your ultimatum?
Lady Sellenger: Well, Gerald, I'm not in the least mercenary. I know that money can't give happiness. But I do

feel that unless you have two thousand a year you
can't even make my daughter comfortable.
Gerald: I'm sure that's very modest.
Lady Sellenger: It's not even love in a cottage. It's not love in a
palace. It's just matrimony in Onslow Gardens.[16]

In *Mrs. Dot* (her name is a pun on the French *dot*—dowry)
from which this exchange comes the adventuress is herself
immensely rich. She is the widow of a brewer (the play was
originally called *Worthley's Entire* after his ale) and a bankrupt
younger son comes into his inheritance in the first few minutes.
It seems as if Maugham is throwing away his aces far too soon
but these stock motifs are but a preliminary to Mrs. Dot's
scheme to disengage the above-mentioned young lady from the
newly ennobled and enriched Gerald and to marry him herself.
She is a Maugham manipulator in the guise of a fairy godmother
who casts her spell by making two of her young guests feign the
opposite emotions from the ones they feel. There is a scene
between them in her garden both wearing white to receive
the other's declaration of love that is like something out of
Marivaux, and shows Maugham's lightest touch. In the last act
when they are trying to summon up enough courage to bolt
together, they are already anticipating his mature comic
masterpiece, *The Circle*.

In *Jack Straw* this purity of tone is marred by a streak of
malice though Jack Straw himself is an innocuous enough
invention. He is 'a man with an uncontrollable love of adventure' and he has here a multiple role to play: waiter, impostor
and archduke. He exhibits the insatiable Edwardian appetite for
practical jokes and disguises. Straw is used by an outraged pair
of English aristocrats ostensibly to punish an odious family of
upstarts for a snub delivered to the inoffensive little wife of a
country vicar, in reality for their penetration of the charmed
circle of county society. The punishers propose to pass off Straw
as the Archduke of Pomerania (Maugham's only excursion into
this kind of operetta country) to enjoy the discomfiture of the
upstarts when they reveal he is a waiter at the Grand Babylon
Hotel where the play opens in fine style. The thing redounds on
them because Jack Straw is in reality the missing archduke, a
fact plain to us from the beginning of the play. The blatancy of

the parvenus—'all the very best people in Cheshire, no out-
siders today what ho!'—is as Beerbohm pointed out in his notice
completely incredible:

> A humble family resident in Brixton, suddenly inheriting two
> millions of money, and thereby launched into the great world
> would become more humble in its new environment. It would
> certainly not assume blatant airs. It would provide a case for
> sympathy, not for ridicule. By immemorial tradition of the stage,
> however, *nouveaux riches* are always blatant, always ridiculous;
> and Mr Somerset Maugham lays the colours on with a trowel.[17]

To be sure Maugham was never afraid of the obvious, but he still
had one trick left when he makes the odious snobs become
accomplices to the deception to save their own faces with the
county. As that tireless Maugham champion Grein put it in the
Sunday Times: 'We are always ready to say: "Ah! but see how
French playwrights manage it." Well here is an English—real
English—play which is every whit as good as the Palais Royal
and Nouveauté's plays, and a great deal better . . .'

These three comedies were, as *The Referee* had predicted,
followed by *The Explorer*, and in 1908 Maugham had achieved the
miraculous feat of having four plays on in the West End at the
same time. *Punch* printed a drawing by Bernard Partridge
showing Shakespeare outside the theatres enviously looking at
the billboards advertising Maugham. 'Why shouldn't all the
theatres in London be Maughamized?', asked Max in a sparkling
review of *The Explorer* in which the main part was played by a
great matinée idol of the period, Lewis Waller, who had his own
fan club, the K.O.Ws or Keen On Wallerites; clearly Max was
a member:

> See him standing in the centre of the drawing-room, his heels
> joined, his shoulders squared, his fists clenched, his lips com-
> pressed as if by a vice of steel, his eyes flashing luminous shafts
> as he turns his profile this way or that, with the abruptness of the
> ventriloquist's puppet! See him as he paces the drawing-room carpet,
> and admit how inadequate is the simile of the caged lion![18]

One interesting point to emerge from the play was that young
George Allerton for all his blackguardism remains the one
person in it who is not subject to the idolatry, the silent authority

of the Explorer: otherwise when the plot is detached from the civilizing aura of Court Leys it is the twin themes of financial disaster and the lost column that hold the stage to provide some harrowing moments.

The popular acclamation that Maugham had striven so hard for over a decade had come at last in a manner beyond even his most ambitious dreams. He was not however going to let himself be bowled over by it. As he put it in his Notebook:

> Success. I don't believe it has had any effect on me. For one thing I always expected it, and when it came I accepted it as so natural that I didn't see anything to make a fuss about. It's only net value to me is that it has freed me from financial uncertainties that were never quite absent from my thoughts.[19]

He remained aloof, then as always, but this does not mean that he failed to enjoy the suits and trappings of success. He and Walter Payne moved to 23 Mount Street, Berkeley Square. He began to look for a house to buy in Mayfair. He was put up for membership of the Garrick Club—'Maugham, William Somerset. Profession: Dramatist'—by the actor Arthur Bourchier and elected in January 1909. A varied cluster of theatrical and literary lights supported his candidature including A. B. Walkley, Nigel Playfair, Alfred Sutro, Edward Terry, W. Pett Ridge, George P. Bancroft, J. Forbes-Robertson, W. W. Jacobs, Sidney Low, John Hare and F. C. Burnand.[20] He continued to see something of Max, and such friends of his as Rothenstein and Conder, and in the spring of 1909 he went to stay with Oscar Wilde's charming friend Reggie Turner who declared Maugham to be: 'very good, I know. And good to be with. But not as good as Oscar. Not like Oscar. Oh, no, he'd never be like Oscar! . . . Yes, we are leaving tomorrow. The distinguished playwright and the unsuccessful novelist will depart by the evening train for Paris.'[21] Apart from considerably enlarging his circle of acquaintances Maugham was beset by journalists who wanted his views on the drama. In its review of the past year's achievements in the theatre *The Referee* noted in January 1909 that,

> Among the new authors who have sprung up Mr W. Somerset Maugham has been easily the first . . . [He] quickly cut himself

away from melancholy and morbidity . . . It is rather refreshing to listen to Mr Maugham talking about himself. As a man in the street might say, there is no dashed nonsense about him. Mark, learn, and inwardly digest this, ye superior people:

> With those who maunder about plays dominated by a great central idea I have no sympathy. I am sure that the theatre is not the place in which to air third-rate notions or to give morbid currency to a hash of Neitszche or a rechauffée of Schopenhauer.

> Mr Maugham goes on to declare that it is most unwise for dramatists to take themselves so seriously; that people go to the theatre to be entertained, and that to entertain should be the chief aim—perhaps the only aim—of the playwright . . . it may be hoped that the day of the morbid is ended.

The Jester had spoken. He had jumped down off the theatrical fence and said his farewell to the alternative theatre. One of the people who maundered about plays dominated by a great central idea was Granville Barker whose season at the Court had preceded *Lady Frederick* there and who was in 1910 to bring his wares to the West End. Among the playwrights he invited to join him and write a new play for the season was Maugham; but he had never taken to Granville Barker ('a young man brimming over with other people's ideas', he called him) and the proposal fell through. Meanwhile the currency given to Maugham's off-the-cuff attack on the play of ideas (to be elaborated later in his prefaces and also partly repudiated by his own practice) ranged several of the leading critics against him, led by none other than his old friend Max in *The Saturday Review* before he finally bowed out of drama criticism.

> They told me [Maugham said] I had sold my soul to Mammon; and the intelligentsia, of which I had been a modest, but respected member, not only turned a cold shoulder on me, that would have been bad enough, but flung me, like Lucifer, headlong into the bottomless pit.[22]

There is an element of exaggeration in this as if Maugham rather revelled in his rôle as a fallen archangel. What had happened was simply that he had discovered his audience. He had acquired a hold that he was never to relinquish for long, retaining it in the end through other forms than the drama. His nonsense, if you like, suited their nonsense, except I do not believe

that it was nonsense. I do not believe that you can acquire that
kind of hold upon the fashionable West End audience for that
long without an understanding of the secrets that it wishes to
conceal from the world and from itself; and by exposing them,
enabling it to change its pattern of life.

> If [Maugham continued in self-justification] I had continued to
> write plays as bitter as *A Man of Honour* or as sardonic as *Loaves
> and Fishes* I should never have been given the opportunity of pro-
> ducing certain pieces to which not even the most severe have
> refused praise. The critics accused me of writing down to the
> public; I did not exactly do that; I had then very high spirits, a
> facility for amusing dialogue, an eye for a comic situation, and
> a flippant gaiety; there was more in me than that, but this I put
> away for the time, and wrote my comedies with those sides of
> myself only that were useful to my purpose. They were designed
> to please and they achieved their aim.
>
> I had no intention of fizzling out with a passing success, and I
> wrote my next two plays to consolidate my hold on the public. They
> were a little bolder and, mild and unsophisticated as they must
> seem now, they were attacked by the more straight-laced for their
> indecency.[23]

Nowadays the two plays mentioned here, *Penelope* and *Smith*,
do not strike one especially by either their mildness or their
unsophistication but in comparison with what has gone before
by a significant shifting of the sights on to the world of the
affluent middle class and by the use of a dialogue that is even
more colloquially closer to actual speech. The whole Edwardian
boiling, lords and ladies, parvenus and charmers, epigrams and
bundles of compromising letters, has been swept away; in its
place are doctors, lawyers, bridge-players, and mansion-flats
containing 'the kind of drawing-room which every woman of
the upper-middle class has in London. It is agreeable to the
eye, unoriginal, artistic and inexpensive.'[24] We are now unmis-
takably into the twentieth century even if human beings are still
subject to the same laws of pique and pride, avarice and snobbery, that they were in the latter days of the nineteenth; if anything they have got meaner and more petty and lost much of
the preposterous grandeur of the Edwardian fantasticks. What
has not changed at all is the playwright's skill in moulding his

work around a single starring role without sacrificing opportunities for the other characters to make their marks. Indeed with each fresh play Maugham's stagecraft grows more assured, his construction neater and happier.

Penelope, which was written in 1908 for Marie Tempest and produced a year later, is the first of Maugham's many portraits of the modern wife. Penelope is cool, calm and collected; she is childless, idle and married to a successful London doctor. She has just discovered his infidelity with her best friend, Ada Fergusson, and she has called a family council to announce her intention to start proceedings for a divorce. It is her father who causes her to stay her hand. Maugham plants the clue as to how he thinks she should deal with the matter in his surname, Golightly; he is a professor of mathematics who while the women chatter and wax indignant scribbles the sum $2+2$ on a piece of paper. Golightly is our mentor, our reasoner, our Maugham mask who knows how to cope with everything under the sun including his own wife:

> Mrs Golightly: Dickie's behaviour is abominable, and there are no excuses for him. It's a mere matter of common morality.
> Golightly: My dear, I have no objection to you talking common morality if you'll let me talk common sense.[25]

Common sense recommends going lightly, in other words postponing the crunch indefinitely in the hope that it may never come. Now we all know what that unfortunate movement led to politically, but as a working philosophy of how to stay married it has its points, even today. When in the brilliant third act Penelope drops her mask she admits to her husband that she has known about his liaison with Ada Fergusson all the time; she tells him to his astonishment that she regarded it as 'a matter of no importance', a phrase which he repeats in a painful colloquy with his mistress. As Vyvyan Holland pointed out, the word 'importance' was one of Oscar Wilde's favourite words;[26] in his work it always bore a heavy burden of irony: the woman of no importance was of the greatest importance to the man who made the remark because she was his erstwhile mistress and the mother of his son; similarly it *was* important *not* to be earnest in the sense in which the Victorians used the word. Maugham gives this irony to Penelope who adopts a pose of aesthetic insouciance involving her in almost insupportable self-control and, like her Homeric forebear, is rewarded by the return of her husband. In her outward unpossessiveness lies her constancy, a female virtue that Maugham was to define more than once in his comedies.

In *The Times* of April 28, 1908, Walkley began by adducing other contemporary instances of the theory that 'the best way to kill a flirtation is to let the flirtation have free play' such as Sardou's *Divorçons* and 'a play now running at another theatre, *What Every Woman Knows . . .*' and then went on to give an interesting account of the impact of the play upon its first night public. 'The audience, which was manifestly becoming tired—or beginning to be afraid that it was about to become tired—by the elaboration of a too familiar stage idea, was swept away in the sudden delight of this right-about-face [the husband's shock at his wife's complaisance] burst into a great roar of inextinguishable laughter, and the play, you felt, was safe. [Marie Tempest] absolutely revelled in the opportunity and made of it what she alone could make.'

The tone of this, which was typical of the reaction to the play of the more serious critics, can hardly be described as casting Maugham into outer darkness.

Penelope was presented by the American impresario Charles Frohman, who operated from both New York and London and who later shipped Miss Tempest over to Broadway to act it there. Like Barrie and other fashionable playwrights Maugham grew very fond of this dark vital little man in his huge fur coat with his unerring flair for discovering new talent in the theatre. Frohman more than anyone was the financial brain behind Maugham's first wave of success and helped him to lay the foundation of his fortune. When Maugham bought a house in Mayfair at 36 Chesterfield Street he was the first person to be invited there to dinner; the invitation read: 'Will you come and see the house Frohman built?'[27] Frohman was the most outstanding of the new race of impresarios—to use that rather unsatisfactory term—who were to replace the actor-managers. Not that the actor-manager tradition ever completely died out during Maugham's playwriting career. Beerbohm Tree was, for instance, still very much in evidence at His Majesty's. Moreover any leading player might at any time decide to go it alone, to run a season of plays in which he or she was the star, and would approach someone like Maugham for a piece. In 1909, for instance, Charles Hawtrey (to whom the success of *Jack Straw* had owed so much) took over the little Royalty Theatre in Dean Street and he had asked Maugham to make an English version of Grenet-Dancourt's *The Noble Spaniard* for him to perform there. Its simple fun and wealth of good parts has down the years proved a boon to repertory companies and amateurs. An even slighter job of the same kind was a comedietta in one act called *A Trip to Brighton*[28] which Maugham adapted from the French of Abel Tarride for a Charity Matinée arranged by Sir Charles Wyndham at the New Theatre in May 1911 in aid of the City of London Hospital for Diseases of the Chest. Mary Moore played the role of a peer's wife who decides to give her husband tit for tat when she discovers that he has been carrying on a flirtation with a friend. When Mander and Mitchenson drew Maugham's attention to the existence of this work in 1957 he denied all recollection of it. It was obviously one of those chores that a successful playwright finds himself undertaking against his will. Another more difficult task was an adaptation that Maugham did of Molière's *Le Bourgeois Gentilhomme* at the request of Beerbohm Tree. But it was Frohman in 1909 who put on the second of the two original plays Maugham had written, called *Smith*.

It came six years after Barrie's *The Admirable Crichton* and takes an equally searching look at a set of people whose self-satisfaction is jolted by a servant. Maugham does not need a desert island to make his point about the superior moral worth of the servant; he does it right in the heart of the Kensington drawing-room. In recent years Miss Margaret Powell and others have recalled what it was like to be a parlourmaid at this time, a being who could hardly be said to have full human status. As Smith's mistress puts it tartly: 'A parlourmaid isn't a handsome woman, Tom; she has a good appearance.' The only escape route from such servitude was, as Miss Powell says, marriage with the footman, the postman or the milkman. To this classic prospect Maugham offered an intriguing alternative in the person of the mistress's brother. He is significantly called Mr. Freeman;[29] returning home from a spell of farming in Rhodesia he views his sister and her odious bridge-playing friends with a devastatingly fresh eye. Maugham was already confident enough in his hold to let his customers have it on the chin: the sensation of the play was the scene in which they refuse to interrupt their game at the news that one woman's baby is dying. By contrast its most charming moment is a cork-pulling in which the Freeman proves the superiority of his muscle-power over that of his rival, the porter in the block of flats. The whole thing was all much more closely related to actual life than anything Maugham had done before in the theatre, while the courtship across the class barriers (beautifully played by Robert Lorraine and Marie Lohr, and later by Irene Vanbrugh) offended some critics but delighted the audience.

Walkley called the play 'a curious blend of the fresh and the stale' and contested the proposition that an addiction to the card-table stultified the maternal instinct. 'Some of us', he declared, 'at any rate are acquainted with London matrons who are equal at once to a good deal of nursery-filling and a good deal of bridge-playing.' Even so, the success of the comedy 'was beyond all doubt'.[30] But it was Archer who most warmly welcomed the new pugnacious note of social satire that the piece combined with its romantic interest and he gave Maugham the accolade in the colums of *The Nation*:

> 'I will not go so far as another critic and say that *Smith* is worth fifty *Lady Fredericks* but I will say that it is far the best thing Mr Maugham has done since *Lady Frederick* and is a work that deserves to count more seriously even than that charming comedy.'

In *Penelope* and *Smith* Maugham had at last found his own tone, his place in the tradition of artificial comedy in the English theatre reaching back through the Restoration playwrights to Beatrice and Benedick, Katherine and Petruchio. The main concern was to expose the nature of marriage to its audience, marriage à la mode; and latterly it was always trying and nearly always failing to do this with the style and elegance and symmetry of the French. Maugham, who was aware of both the French and the English tradition, succeeded where so many had failed and he added an attack on a certain type of contemporary English woman for good measure. At Frohman's behest he was soon to produce his own modern version of *The Taming of the Shrew* set in the wilds of Manitoba. This work was his next great leap forward in 1913, but before that he made two steps backward with *The Tenth Man* and *Landed Gentry*, both of which were a reversion to Pinero-type drama touching such sensitive Edwardian nerves as high finance, gamekeepers' daughters and illegitimate babies. As Maugham said about these plays later: 'They were neither frankly realistic nor frankly theatrical. My indecision was fatal. The audiences found them disagreeable and not quite real.'[31] He also had an unhappy time over the Molière adaptation which was cut down from a full-length play by Beerbohm Tree to one act to serve in a double bill with the first London performance of Strauss's *Ariadne* and was savagely attacked for the ineptitude of the translation. But with so much success and so much money pouring in from both London and Broadway this could be shrugged off as all part of the night's work. In the Fall of 1911 Frohman wrote to Maugham to say that he was 'still down with rheumatism—partly on account of the weather but more especially because you are not doing any work.'[32] It was not true. It was never true of Maugham at any time in his whole life. What was true was that for the moment he had decided not to write any more plays.

CHAPTER FOUR

Limping Earnestly

[1.]

IN HER NOVEL *The Limit* (1911) Oscar Wilde's friend Ada Leverson 'the Sphinx' has left us an amusing caricature of Maugham riding his first great wave of theatrical glory:

> To have eleven plays, all written 'out of one's own head' and all being performed simultaneously in American, in Eskimo, and even in Turkish, besides in every known European language; to have money rolling in, and the strange world of agents and managers pursuing you by every post and imploring for more contracts by every Marconigram; and these triumphs to have come quite suddenly was really enough to have turned the head of any young man; yet Hereford Vaughan's (known by his very few intimate friends as Gillie) had remained remarkably calm. He was not even embittered by success.[1]

The calm was, as always, a mask; if he was not embittered he was not ensweetened either. He had wanted the release of fame and had achieved the imprisonment of notoriety. Vaughan, or rather Maugham may, to all outward appearance, have seemed 'quiet, reserved, and as apparently modest as ever' but within he had begun to suffer the anguish of that peculiarly twentieth-century malady in which the pressure of the past renders the present insupportable.

His condition could not be cured, or even stated, in the Jester's mask before a West End audience; it could be nowadays perhaps in the theatre of Strindberg, of O'Neill, of John Osborne, but not then. Maugham put away his cap and bells for the moment, and resumed his more private *persona* as a novelist. Fifteen years of writing professionally had taught him that the most satisfying reward of the literary life is to be found

not in either fame or fortune but in catharsis, in the purging of
the writer's past. As it turned out, Maugham's withdrawal from
the limelight for a couple of years in order to write a very long
novel about himself in his youth was not only a rather risky
thing to do but also a very clever one. It was one of those far-
seeing moves on the chessboard which in the games of the
grandmasters get an exclamation mark for brilliance. He was to
become one of the small band of writers in English who have
contributed significantly to both the novel and the drama.

What Maugham had for the present given up was not just
the theatre but the going lightly that had brought him success
there. The matter of importance throughout a long, reverberat-
ing work of fiction was to be the growing consciousness, the
process of disillusioned self-discovery of the author. Life hacks
away at him; its blows give his personality its unique form: *la
vie me sculpte*, as Cocteau once put it. A novel in which the hero
is really a portrait of the author may be read in different ways
at different times. The first readers read it for the story, later
ones for the autobiography. Maugham succeeded in *Of Human
Bondage* in integrating the two aspects to a point where they are
almost inseparable. He avoids mere self-indulgent reminiscence
by the rigour of his narrative method. He uses the straightforward 'biographical' approach of the great Victorian novelists
but with the advantage of shorter chapters and freedom from
the exigencies of serial or part publication. The movement of
the book is classically linear without flashbacks or short-cuts,
from the moment when Philip Carey is left an orphan after the
death of his beautiful mother, involving him in an abrupt change
of setting from his fashionable, cushioned and cosseted home in
Paris to the austerities of his uncle's seaside English vicarage,
to his emergence many years and much hardship later as a
qualified doctor; throughout, his life is viewed as a chronological sequence of actions each of which has its own dramatic
development. It is the *donnée* of orphanhood that gives a
peculiarly mid-Victorian air to the whole operation. Carey,
like Copperfield, discovers at a tender age that life is lived with
a much greater intensity of consciousness by the person who
does not in childhood possess that blanket guarantee of love
with which most of us are fortunately endowed. He has to seek

alternatives in the 'real' world; he gains a precocious understanding of the compensations of friendship, ambition, the aesthetic life, religious faith, and of their limitations. He learns more rapidly what we all learn in the end when the blanket guarantee must be put aside and the voluntary love of others must be won, the meaning of human bondage.

Philip Carey, whose date of birth is the same as Maugham's (he is nine when the novel opens in 1885), is not only vulnerable because he is an orphan but much more obviously and continually because he has a club-foot which sets him apart from the other boys and debars him from joining in their more extrovert activities. On one level this is clearly analogous to Maugham's stammer, on another to that sense of apartness whose complex roots it was the purpose of the novel to uncover. Philip's vulnerability is a much more inward trait than anything we have seen in a Maugham hero up to now. It does not make him very likeable, deeply as we may sympathize with him in the cold climate of the vicarage. Maugham was not prepared, any more than E. M. Forster was, to break all taboos. He did not depict his sexual ambivalence, but with this large exception he was ruthlessly honest, realizing that he would only exorcise the ghosts of the past by dragging the ugly contradictions of his own nature into the light of day.

Basic to it was that insatiable love of reading that was his lifelong consolation for the sense of alienation from other people. As a boy his book-knowledge fed him with a vanity that made him contemptuous of his contemporaries while his witty insights into their characters gained him many more enemies than friends. 'He was developing a sense of humour, and found that he had a knack of saying bitter things, which caught people on the raw; he said them because they amused him, hardly realizing how much they hurt, and was much offended when he found out that his victims regarded him with active dislike.'[2]

This role of the wounded wounder is one that we watch acted out by Philip in many different situations on his way through life. The syndrome is set early on at school in Tercanbury (The King's School, Canterbury, a tough snobo-sadistic place in those days that he finds dislikeable while acquiring a rudimentary education). He has his first crush there,

though he does not recognize it as such, on a boy called Rose
with whom Philip shares a study. For a while he forgets his disability in the warmth of Rose's companionship but as this ripens
to inseparability he becomes over-demanding. Then fate inter-
venes; he catches scarlet fever; when he returns to school Rose
has moved in with someone else and the fellow-feeling with
Philip has evaporated. His vanity cannot accept this over-throw
and in making a fuss he brings upon himself the inevitable
wounding appellation of 'cripple'. In the fury of enraged consciousness of self that this reversal brings about, his reaction is
the desperate one of cutting short his school career and abandoning his attempt at a university scholarship. It is a frightening
example of the wound mechanism at work; even then it would
not have come to anything after his anger had cooled were it
not that to uphold his decision becomes an irresistible challenge
to his will. His uncle the Vicar, one of the most richly depicted
comic characters in the whole of English fiction, a supreme
study of an egoist, opposes his nephew's wishes in a particularly
devious way. This so incenses him that he works upon his aunt
through whose intervention he manages to get both his uncle
and the headmaster to accept his plan to go to Heidelberg. This
first great triumph of will is poisoned by his knowledge that he
has made a disastrous mistake; yet his pride will not suffer him
to change his mind. In real life it was, as Maugham revealed in
Looking Back, part one, a bully of a form-master who showed
hideous insensitivity to his pupil's stammer, that proved this
psychological chain of cause and effect that robbed Maugham of
his Cambridge education.

    There was, when he was about the same age, a parallel
moment of dislocation in the life of Gissing when he was dismissed from Owens College, Manchester, for theft, and thereafter
thrown upon his own intellectual resources unaided by official
tutors and professorial guidance. At least for Maugham there
was no public disgrace, no prison sentence; instead his first
exposure to the real world was at Heidelberg where he was able
to continue that process of omnivorous reading that had begun
in his uncle's study with the Bible, The Lives of the Saints and
the secular works of adventure and romance that the vicar
collected. The life that greets him now is rich in intellectual

prospects and, to the student of human nature that he has become, equally rich in eccentric material among his fellow boarders chez Professor Erlin. It was the period in Germany of Goethe's greatest fame, the beginning of Maugham's lifelong fascination with his genius. Several critics have pointed to Werther as a distant forebear of Maugham's novel. At the same time Kuno Fischer introduces the hero to the pleasures of abstract thought: 'it was a little like watching a tightrope dancer doing perilous feats over an abyss; but it was very exciting.' Metaphysics is not the only revelation; another, even more intoxicating perhaps, is the new theatre. Philip finds himself in the midst of an Ibsen season. His host, the professor, has the greatest revulsion for *The Doll's House* along with Wagner whom he regards as a joke. In Heidelberg Maugham had the same arguments about the new drama that Joyce had in Dublin.[3]

His reading comes under the influence of two of his fellow boarders in the Issyvoo-like atmosphere of Frau Erlin's, the kind of people who to a gifted young man are stages on life's way. In later life Maugham realized that their originals' interest in him was probably much more sexual than intellectual but this is not even hinted at in the novel. One is Hayward (based on an Englishman called Brooks), a precious aesthete, a feckless cultivated failure who 'talks of *Richard Feverel* and *Madame Bovary*, of Verlaine, Dante and Matthew Arnold.' He knows Fitzgerald's Omar by heart and reads Newman's *Apologia* for its stylistic beauty. But it is the American Weeks who, in giving Philip Renan to read, works the great change in him. In a section which every reader of this novel will remember, Philip had lost his faith in a paternalistic miracle-working God when his childish prayer for the removal of his disability had not been granted; now the whole concept of God leaves him like a cast-off garment. He observes the golden Rhine in the distance and he is filled with a Wagnerian sense of exaltation and all-conquering freedom.

All kinds of new intellectual and literary influences now begin to crowd in upon Philip. Maugham is skillful in making the individuals he encounters naturally respresentative of all the myriad swirling thought-currents at a time of turbulent change.

He meets on his return to Blackstable a Miss Wilkinson, a rector's daughter who has been to Paris as a governess. She boasts of an acquaintance with Daudet and Maupassant, plays him airs from Massenet and lends him Murger. He becomes enamoured, not so much of Miss Wilkinson, whose lover he in fact becomes, as of the whole romantic idea of *la vie de bohème*, starving in a garret in Paris.

At this point I find it helpful to think of Maugham's novel as a tale of two cities, the city of grim necessity, of wearisome toil and incarceration within one of the most class-conscious societies the world has ever known, which is London; and the city of art, of the aesthetic life, of self-fulfilment and freedom which is Paris. That at least was how Philip saw it at this time and naturally he longed to enter the latter while his uncle was determined that he should pursue some regular, secure occupation in the former. Thus before the Parisian section of the book begins Philip is packed off to London as an accountant's articled clerk and we hear a little menacing tune, a hint of things to come, that tells of frustration, melancholia, genteel Gissingesque poverty and sense of social ambivalence: Philip is too much of a gent for his fellow clerks and not enough of one for his employer. He compensates in the classic manner by seeping himself in Ruskin and Vasari, mooning about the National Gallery. Maugham deliberately emphasized the hopelessness of his own early London life to create that sense of environmental imprisonment he had inherited from the masters of the naturalistic novel. It takes another great battle of wills with the vicar before he can give up accountancy and depart for Paris. He carries in his pocket a paper sack bulging with sovereigns given him in a touching scene by his aunt. Once again he leaves the vicarage ready for any adventure that may befall him, rather like the hero of his own early story, Amyntas.

The Parisian scenes of *Of Human Bondage* are a corrective to those of Murger and du Maurier. Maugham shows us what bliss it was to be alive in that dawn when everything was new under the sun but he tells us too the price in terms of blood, sweat and tears which has to be paid for the artistic life both by those who possess original talent, painters like Clutton, who owed a lot to Maugham's friend the Irish artist Roderick

O'Conor, and by those who do not, such as the pathetic trier
Fanny Price with whose suicide by hanging this part of the
novel melodramatically ends. In many of the great personal port-
manteau novels of the nineteenth century the intensity slackens
after the early childhood section, with its atrocities and con-
solations; the pressure here is kept up with wonderfully
consistent energy.

What is just slightly puzzling is the time historically when it
is all supposed to be happening. If as we may suppose Philip
was eighteen or nineteen, that puts it at some time in the early
1890s, yet Maugham appears to be writing of a period in
which Impressionism was the latest thing in painting and in
which the frank sexuality of Manet's Olympia was a revelation.
Yet this splendid painting was completed in 1863, creating a
rumpus when it was exhibited two years later. It had in fact
been shown in the Salon in a retrospective exhibition of Manet's
work in 1899, the year of his death. Manet would have been by
then as much and as little *avant-garde* as, say, Jackson Pollock
is now. In order to give us a sense of the modern movement
happening Maugham seems at times to project Philip back into
the Paris of George Moore. He *had* been there in the 1870s
while both Impressionism in painting and realism in fiction
were still exploding like fireworks along the banks of the
Seine. He had visited the Nouvelles Athènes during what R. H.
Wilenski called the Prologue[4] and—so he claimed—heard
'Manet, Degas, Pissarro, Débutin, Forain, Catulle Mendès and
Paul Alexis . . . the beloved café in which I learned French and
all I know of literature and art . . .'[5] and he had been out to
Medan to visit Zola. Maugham has somehow telescoped about
twenty years of development from the Impressionists to the
Fauves into a year or two with the aim of revealing to us the
radical change of taste and outlook suffered by Philip when he
crosses the Channel.

Thus before he arrived in Paris he 'had worshipped Watts
and Burne-Jones' and he had derived his view of the function of
art 'from his diligent perusal of Ruskin' but after a week or two
in Paris he is talking 'as emphatically as the rest on the merits
of Manet, Monet, and Degas. He bought a photograph of a
drawing by Ingres of the Odalisque and a photograph of the

Olympia. They were pinned side by side over his washing-stand so that he could contemplate their beauty while he shaved.'[6]

But he soon finds himself making friends through Lawson (based on Gerald Kelly) who have long since absorbed the influence of these masters of actuality in painting and are wondering whether something both more mystical and more structured should be introduced into a painting, who are in fact witnessing the end of Act I. It is Clutton who first brings the name of El Greco into Philip's ken, sounding a theme that will be developed fully in the last section of the novel with the appearance of Thorpe Athelney. It is Clutton who first tells Philip of a Parisian stockbroker who had just gone to Tahiti, leaving his wife and family behind in France to fare as best they could, adding 'if you want to be a gentleman you must give up being an artist. They've got nothing to do with one another . . .' sounding a theme that will not be developed fully until Maugham's next novel, *The Moon and Sixpence*. Clutton's real life original O'Conor had known Gauguin at Pont-Aven in the late 1880s and the expatriate Irish artist became very fond of Maugham whom he called 'that gentle Samson' and who bought some of his paintings.

Clutton, his fictional counterpart, was the one significant artist in the group and its arbiter on matters of artistic judgment. The layer-down of the law on everything under the sun and generator of cultural hot air was the writer Cronshaw, a kind of Enoch Soames (said to be based partly on the Canadian painter James Morrice). He epitomizes the 1890s, being a contributor to the *Yellow Book*, frequenter of Mallarmé's soirée's, drinker of whisky from a private bottle and lover of cricket. It is Cronshaw who has the crucial conversation with Philip about the meaning of life and the nature of art that occupies the same commanding place in the structure of the novel as does the conversation between Stephen Dedalus and Lynch about Aquinas's view of beauty in *Portrait of the Artist as a Young Man*. In his affected way Cronshaw probes Philip's values to discover a residual belief in the Christian ethic against which he puts his own hedonism: ' "Men seek but one thing in life—their pleasure." "No, no, no!" cried Philip.' It is Cronshaw who, in answer to Philip's agonized query, 'If you take away duty and

goodness and beauty, why are we brought into the world?'
leaves him with the suggestion that he should study the Persian
carpets in the Musée de Cluny.[7]

This was a dialogue that was to continue in Maugham's
mind, and in the minds of many of the writers of his generation,
for the rest of his life. One thinks again of Joyce in *Portrait*
hearing 'voices of his father urging him to be a gentleman' and
of his own urge 'to discover the mode of life of art whereby
your spirit could express itself in unfettered freedom.' In *Of
Human Bondage* we are not given one sovereign doctrine of
art, patiently worked out by a process of severe intellectual
effort but a multiplicity of impressions ar.d ideas, a *stimmung*
with which the mind of the hero is saturated. The Paris of the
period between the first Impressionist exhibition of 1874 and
the first Fauve exhibition in 1903 was in a ferment of artistic
revolution, distilled by Maugham into his novel. He did not,
like Joyce, have an original view of art that determined the
structure of the novel; he was a mediator who reflected the
current of ideas within the traditional form. Maugham beaut-
fully catches the mood of *avant-garde* Paris in the years before
the First World War and the post-war American influx. He
built a fitting memorial to a whole artistic era and proved his
power to depict not just a few individuals in rural England but
a whole new cosmopolitan society.

Philip leaves Paris abruptly, recalled to Blackstable because
of the death of his aunt. Maugham's genius for *comédie rosse* is
nowhere better seen than in his description of the self-regarding
way in which the vicar takes his bereavement; his dismissal of
his middle-aged female servant on grounds of propriety, his
continuing battle with the churchwarden flaring over the
inscription on the tombstone, and his handling of the impact of
the good lady's death on the town as a whole, even the dis-
senters paying respects. For Philip it is a moment of truth: the
decision to take up medicine as his career is born, for what may
to us seem the odd reason that, 'it was an occupation which
seemed to him to give a good deal of personal freedom.' He
buries himself in an extended course of philosophical and
scientific reading, Hobbes, Spinoza, Hume, *The Origin of
Species* ('Philip was born a generation after this great book')

confirming the scepticism on ultimate questions that had begun to dawn on him in Paris. This important bridge passage in the novel opens a window upon Maugham's state of mind when he entered St. Thomas's. Although he was about to start training to become a doctor he would seem already to have done much of the reading required of candidates for honours degrees in English, modern languages (French and German), and philosophy.

Philip's new self-knowledge does not unfortunately make it any easier for him to get on with other people. To be detached does not necessarily render one less vulnerable as he painfully discovers throughout the remainder of this very long book which offers us now vivid glimpses of a medical student's life in late nineteenth-century London. Many people must on first acquaintance have reacted to Maugham in the way that his fellow students reacted to Philip:

> A fear of rebuff prevented him from affability, and he concealed his shyness, which was still intense, under a frigid taciturnity. He was going through the same experience as he had done at school, but here the freedom of the medical student's life made it possible for him to live a good deal by himself.[8]

The stock reaction to such a degree of alienation was a déclassée affair with a young woman upon whom the isolated young gentleman could project his own vulnerability. Many late nineteenth-century English novelists play variations on this theme, especially George Moore in *A Modern Lover* and Gissing in most of his early books from *Workers in the Dawn* to *Eve's Ransom*. Maugham's contribution to this tradition is to strip the relationship of any romantic Victorian view of honour, such as he had examined in his play, and of all pity, compassion and social conscience. He shows its origin in psychological necessity, its development as a naked battle of wills. Mildred Rogers is a waitress at an ABC restaurant when Philip first sets eyes on her. She is rather odd-looking, slight of build with a boyish figure, anaemia giving her flesh a greenish tinge, a beautiful face, vulgar in her tastes, pathetically snobbish, an easy prey to the first blackguard she meets and, needless to say, possessing absolutely nothing in common with Philip. But once the deadly virus has taken its grip on Philip he becomes a notable sufferer from what Stendhal calls *l'amour pique* turning into *l'amour fou*. Philip is determined to make her his mistress simply to cure himself of his craving for her, but in her shrewd Cockney way she is superbly, aloofly unyielding. The progress of his passion at this point in the novel is a long *conte* about an irresistible male force and an immovable female object.

In spite of her boyish torso what a capriciously feminine creature Mildred is! Beverley Nichols in his vilification of his old friend in *A Case of Human Bondage* declared that, 'the Master's psychological make-up—unless his whole life was spent behind a mask—was not predominantly homosexual. He certainly had affairs with women, though these were neither as numerous nor as passionate as he would have liked the world to believe.'[9] Philip spends a lot of time as a medical student studying his own isolating disability and trying to discover if it can be cured; he even undergoes an operation on his foot from one of the surgeons at the hospital. The private meaning of this episode went much deeper into Maugham's complex nature than the conquest of his stammer.

After Mildred's departure from the scene, apparently to be married, Philip recovers his old bohemian self with immense relief:

> He was like a snake casting its skin and he looked upon the old covering with nausea. He exulted in the possession of himself once more; he realised how much of the delight of the world he had lost when he was absorbed in that madness which they call love; he had had enough of it; he did not want to be in love any more if love was that.[10]

But this is not the end of the affair. It is merely the respite from it. When Mildred seeks him out again, her baby has been born out of wedlock, V.D. has begun to poison her flesh, and if her spirit remains unbroken, her condition is desperate. Philip responds to her *cri de coeur* and takes her in. Now the delicate balance of the relationship has changed. He has become the dominant, she the dependant, a new form of bondage for him.

Before he is made to realize the full horror of it he has a period of renewal in which he resumes the aesthetic life, taking up again with such old friends as Lawson, just returned from

Spain, whose ruthlessly professional attitude to women he envies, and his old Heidelberg friend Hayward, who has turned up in London before departing for the Boer War, where he dies a hero's death. Philip himself day-dreams of escaping to the veldt; but without Mildred life in London has an enchanting freedom. Maugham finds a sentence worthy of the 1890s in which to express it:

> The delicate iridescence of the London air gave the softness of a pastel to the grey stone of the buildings; and in the wharves and storehouses there was the softness of a Japanese print.[11]

We are wafted back in such prose to the world of the Goncourts and of George Moore. These masters of expression and of taste shared one thing that Philip Carey now discovers to be a *sine qua non* of the aesthetic life: it is, simply and crudely, money. He meets a stockbroker with an unfortunate talent for speculation in both shares and metaphysics through whom he loses all his savings and he is so broke that he cannot even afford to go on studying medicine for the moment. Money, Maugham often told us, apologizing for his great commercial success as a writer, was a sixth-sense without which the other five did not function properly. Be that as it may, Philip's education is not complete until he lacks it. In poverty he discovers that condition of total dependence on life which the naturalistic novel so ruthlessly examined. He discovers Grub Street in the person of Norah Nesbitt, churner-out of penny novelettes and player of bit parts in the theatre. He learns about the purgatory of unemployment followed by the awful sycophantic servitude of a job as a floor-walker in a big department store in a sequence that out-Wells Wells as he drags his club-foot over the thick pile of the carpet bowing and scraping to the leisured customers of the carriage-trade. He learns the ignominy of being dependent for one's release on the death of another human being, the old Vicar from whom he will inherit a small amount of money, who in some masterly scenes back in Blackstable, shows an extreme reluctance to depart this life. Philip, as he re-reads *The Thousand and One Nights*, resists the temptation to speed him on his way by administering an overdose, not because he fears the crime but the remorse that would follow it.

Is it all too grim? Too loaded against the hero to prove on as grand a scale as he can Maugham's Darwinism? As in the rest of Maugham's work he does not wholly give up his belief in the power of the human spirit to rise above conditions of the bleakest hopelessness. Even in his present way of life Philip's ability tells. He gradually improves his status having a quiet success as a dress designer. At the same time we are shown other notable examples of that fortitude which Maugham prized above all else in human beings—in Norah Nesbitt, the novelette writer; in the gruff, tough Dr South in his scattered seafaring Dorset practice. But the most memorable specimen is Thorpe Athelney, whom Philip meets first when he comes for some treatment as an in-patient. With the appearance of Athelney, a mood of *con brio* begins to predominate in the last movement, as it were, of this ornately orchestrated novel. He shows more than mere fortitude at his plight: he adds a quixotic element that renders him indifferent to his surroundings and his fate in so far as this is humanly possible. He has some ill-defined job in what we should describe as public relations and lives in patriarchal glory with his wife and vast brood of children in an Inigo Jones slum near Chancery Lane. But his thoughts are as far away as a Huysmans hero. He gives Philip some translations he has done of St. John of the Cross, shows his photographs of Toledo:

> [Philip] could not take his eyes off it. He felt strongly that he was on the threshold of some new discovery in life. He was tremulous with a sense of adventure. He thought for an instant of the love that had consumed him: love seemed very trivial beside the excitement which now leapt in his heart.[12]

Athelney is the apotheosis of the Maugham adventurer who, though he may have his head in the clouds, is always ready to provide tangible help in the form of a square meal, or a bed for the night. He is a man who consistently lives his dream even to the names he gives his own daughters whom he introduces to Philip as:

> '. . . Maria de los Mercedes, Maria del Pilar, Maria de la Concepcion, Maria del Rosario.'
> 'I call them Sally, Molly, Connie, Rosie and Jane,' said Mrs Athelney.'

Whether or not Athelney really is a down-at-heel gentleman or just an impostor is irrelevant: he has escaped from the class-system and the cash nexus altogether by sheer indifference to it. *Of Human Bondage* opens with the sombre funeral chords of a death, the death of a mother that intensified the alienation from the world of her son, and it ends with a death, the death of the guardian that enables that son, now a young man, to regain his independence from the world at the same time as he re-discovers his mother in Maria del Sol, the full-breasted, broad-hipped goddess of the Kentish hop fields. In a final Elgarian fortissimo Maugham gives us the pastoral idyll of the hop-picking, the open fields and the contented workers who have momentarily escaped from the enclosed prison of the city.

We know this to be a fantasy and that at the historical moment when this novel ends the real Philip Carey, far from marrying an earth-mother and becoming a G.P. in a safe country practice, was embarking in unencumbered singleness of purpose upon one of the most hazardous things a man can do in this life, to live by literature alone. In the swelling pastoral chords we hear this theme, too, if we listen closely. Philip Carey's adult pattern was to be a conventional one circumscribed by marriage and a job; Maugham's was the eccentric one of the literary artist, the curious traveller and the connoisseur of humankind. In this ample novel both patterns are very fully sketched.

Had he only produced *Of Human Bondage* Maugham would be a much less important figure than he is, but it is nonetheless his most important book and one that will bear a great deal of re-reading; what it will not bear in my view is the kind of analysis that by intensive boring into its surface tries to make a 'strike' of the author's philosophy. If it has a philosophy it is one of events rather than ideas. I have used the image of a symphony to describe its shifting and blending moods of joy and sorrow but the sister-art from which this novel draws its strength is in fact painting. It is itself a most illuminating retrospective one-man show; as we patiently wander through its rooms absorbing one rich full canvas after another we take in an unforgettable series of impressions of what life was like at the end of the nineteenth and the beginning of the twentieth centuries. That kind of life continued into the period when the novel was being written, but now with the outbreak of the Great War it ended suddenly with a full stop.

[2.]

Of Human Bondage appeared both in England and in America in August 1915. It was a bulky work for the old kit-bag but at least one private soldier, J. Isaacs, later to become professor of literature at London University, remembers taking it to the front to read. For him at least its affirmative finale did nothing to dispel the gloom of the situation. The bulk also weighed heavily on those who remained at home to pursue the gentle art of reviewing. 'A very big book in every sense of the word,' said Gerald Gould in the *New Statesman* in September. It was a dense and difficult work for reviewers to assimilate at first blush, and one which completely shattered the brittle theatrical image they had of the author—'the merits,' Gould went on, 'are precisely not those one would expect from Mr. Maugham.' The reviewers were shaken by the immense scope and depth, the ambitiousness of the book, and they tried to cover their confusion in easy generalities, in attacks on the character of the hero, in complaints that it was not one novel but many, in scorn for the pattern-in-the-carpet approach to moral values, and in quick comparisons with other novelists such as Fielding, Arnold Bennett and Compton Mackenzie. Gould's review, which while inadequate is by no means ungenerous, reflects the general unease and puzzlement; although the book had been published for over a month by the time Gould pronounced at the end of September he seems to have neither had enough time to think about it nor enough space to deal with it. His piece is full of convoluted hedging sentences such as: 'I am not sure that he has not written a highly original book. I am not even sure he has not written almost a great one.' Gould's gloss on Maugham's depiction of the passions is just as ambivalent, and it is typical of many reviews:

Of this whole view of sex, the romantic (who is the best realist) will

say, as of the view of the [Bal] Bullier quoted above—It simply
isn't like that. And yet it is so far-fetched that from that very fact
it draws a certain convincingness. It *may* be true—*from the angle.*
But what an angle! And I am still misrepresenting Mr Maugham.
I have made his book sound revolting and it is not.

These are the words of a man who has not recovered yet from
the uncommon candour of the novel; his colleague on *The
Athenaeum* voiced a much less tolerant distaste for Maugham's
angle on life:

> The values accorded by the hero to love, realism and religion are so
> distorted as to have no interest beyond that which belongs to an
> essentially morbid personality. In such long novels reiteration is
> peculiarly tiresome and apt to reduce the gratitude which should be
> felt for the detailed portraiture and varied aspects of life the author
> presents to us.

It was among the American reviewers that the truth and
honesty of Maugham's outlook was immediately recognized,
particularly by his fellow novelist, Theodore Dreiser who, writing about the book in the *New Republic*, on Christmas Day 1915
under the heading 'As a Realist Sees It', acclaimed the novel's
frankness and genius in such a way as to leave no one in any
doubt about its importance. Maugham was enormously grateful
for this article. It represented the start of a steady growth of
critical interest in the book in the United States over the years,
and was the foundation of Maugham's future reputation as a
serious novelist.

CHAPTER FIVE

A Double Life

A scene in a little bedroom at Malo near Dunkirk comes back to me: a thick roll of proofs had arrived for him; he had corrected them and long strips were lying on the bed. Now although I was short of something to read, my interest in them was confined to noticing how very few corrections had to be made. When I remarked on it, he replied that he always went over his work carefully before he sent it to the printer.[1]

The writer is Desmond MacCarthy who at the beginning of the First World War belonged to the same ambulance section of the Red Cross as Maugham. The unit had been sent to France to help cope with the first wave of casualties after the battle of Ypres. Maugham told in *Looking Back* how at the outbreak of the war he had approached Churchill, then First Sea Lord, to try to get a job: the best he could do for the forty-year-old author was to send him with a letter to the Admiralty where he might have been taken on as a clerk:

Then [Maugham writes] I happened to hear that the Red Cross were sending to France a number of Ford ambulances and if I applied in the proper quarter I might be taken on as an interpreter. I took the necessary steps with the result that within a reasonable time I was wearing khaki and crossing the Channel with the ambulances.[2]

They soon found there was plenty of work for them. 'I have never seen such wounds,' Maugham wrote in his Notebook. 'There are great wounds of the shoulder, the bone all shattered, running with pus, stinking; there are gaping wounds in the back; there are wounds where a bullet has passed through the lungs; there are shattered feet so that you wonder if the limb can possibly be saved.'[3] The novelist who had dramatized death in action in *The Hero* and *The Explorer*, who had used war for its effect upon a man's character, was having a taste of the real thing. The few fragments of descriptive writing inspired by Maugham's stint at the front are graphic footnotes to the later first-hand accounts of Blunden and Graves, but the experience never emerged again in the form of fiction. There is nothing comparable in the Maugham canon to Kipling's story in *Limits and Renewals* of the doctor performing makeshift operations in the dug-out in inadequate light and without anaesthetic. All we have are these few unforgettable pages in *A Writer's Notebook* recalling the wounded being taken on stretchers to the railway station from the temporary hospital at Doullens, listening to a cracked bell heralding the funeral procession of one of their comrades. The trained observer missed none of the irony of a situation in which civilized elegance and barbarous horror combined: dressing and drugs on the grand piano in the eighteenth-century château, the patient waiting for his wounds to be stanched lying on a Buhl writing-table; and in the midst of such carnage, the irrepressible man of letters, the insatiable browser and burrower into old books, was from time to time delighted when he chanced upon such treasures as a gentleman's library in his billet at Montdidier: 'I found the picaresque novel *Don Guzman de Alfarache* and immediately below the *Memoires d'un Homme de Qualité*; then there are the complete works of Bossuet, the sermons of Massillon, and the works in a dozen volumes of a writer I have never heard of. I am curious to know how he deserved this splendid edition . . .'[4]

It was while he was serving in France that Maugham met Gerald Haxton, a handsome American who was a member of his Unit. Facts about him are sparse; the photograph about this time reveals a dapper, harsher Melvyn Douglas with an air of cruelty about the eyes but also huge reserves of gaiety and fun. The effect he had on you seems to have depended largely on how far gone he was in liquor at the time of the meeting. Robin Maugham as a youth in Vienna was 'impressed by his sophisticated man-of-the-world pose' and at times found him 'an excellent host . . . ebulliently, irrepressibly friendly.'[5] To

Beverley Nichols on the other hand in *A Case of Human Bondage*
'he stank. He had about him an aura of corruption. To say that
I did not know him well would be both true and untrue; for
though our meetings were few and far between they were so
intense, and sometimes so shocking, that I can recall many of
them with an almost painful clarity.' Maugham himself wrote:
'He had grave faults. He was a heavy drinker and a reckless
gambler. He had great merits. He had immense vitality. He was
fearless. He was always ready for an adventure and could turn
his hand to anything, whether it was to persuade a stubborn car
to behave reasonably or in the wilderness to cook a savoury
dinner.'⁶

[2.]

Apart from Gerald the years of the First World War were a
crucial time for Maugham in both his professional and his
private life. He had met Mrs. Syrie Wellcome in London in
1913, and had been in the midst of a love-affair with her when
the war had broken out. The daughter of Dr. Thomas Barnardo,
founder of the orphanages, she was the estranged wife of
Henry Wellcome, of the drugs firm Burroughs and Wellcome.
Her husband was some twenty years older than she though she
was already in her mid-thirties when she met Maugham.

In the spring of 1915 Maugham left the ambulance unit and
went with Syrie to Rome where they rented a flat. He had many
conversations with her about her early life; he played some
golf, and he began to write *Our Betters*, his first piece for the
theatre since his long lay-off from play-writing. It was through
Mrs. Wellcome that Maugham now met the British intelligence
chief he called R. who in real life was the lover of one of Syrie's
girl-friends. Maugham was anxious to find fresh work to help
the war effort and R, who was impressed by the playwright's
fluency in French and German, recruited him to replace an agent
of his in Switzerland who had cracked up. His first assignment
was to go to Lucerne to investigate an Englishman who was
living there with a German wife (which provided material for
the story *The Traitor*) and then on to a base in a hotel in Geneva.

Readers of *Ashenden* will remember the vividness with which Maugham evoked the sinister atmosphere of Swiss cities at this time, all teeming with agents of both sides engaged in a fantastic and dangerous game of deception and counter-deception. As he brooded upon the ever-present possibility of a spell in a Swiss prison Maugham noted the rewards of an agent's life as explained to him by his chief: 'If you do well you'll get no thanks and if you get into trouble you'll get no help.' The immediate reward for Ashenden—the persona under which Maugham himself appears in his spy stories—was time and opportunity to continue with his other career, both as a cover and in reality, as two Swiss policemen discovered one dark night:

'I am writing a play,' said Ashenden.

He waved his hand to the papers on his table. Four eyes followed his gesture. A casual glance told him that the detectives had taken note of his manuscripts.

'And why should you write a play here rather than in your own country?'

Ashenden smiled upon them with even more affability than before, since this was a question for which he had long been prepared, and it was a relief to give an answer. He was curious to see how it would go down.

'*Mais monsieur*, there is a war. My country is in turmoil, it would be impossible to sit there quietly and write a play.'

'Is it a comedy or a tragedy?'

'Oh a comedy, and a light one at that,' replied Ashenden.[7]

This play was real enough. It was called *Caroline* and was the second in a trio of comedies with rather similar plots about women whose eminently reasonable behaviour in Maugham's eyes turns the current conception of matrimony inside out. Maugham described how he finished it in Geneva and when he got to London to find it already in rehearsal he discovered he had made a miscalculation about the mood of the final act and had completely to re-write it eliminating a whole character for whom a well-known actor had been engaged. Fortunately Dion Boucicault the director (son of the author of *London Assurance*) bore with him and all was well.

[3.]

The severe Swiss winter had however taken its toll on Maugham's health. He had had a bout of bronchitis. He decided to make a trip that he had been planning for a long time to the South Seas both for his health and because he wanted to investigate the life of the stockbroker-turned-painter about whom he had quizzed O'Conor in Paris. It seems unlikely that he had any intelligence mission on this occasion although it was an area where the German colonial empire was considerable: two years earlier the battleship *Graf von Spee* had been chased from cover across the Pacific by the Royal Navy. Before he left England Maugham had been told that Wellcome had started divorce proceedings against his wife; he was cited; Gerald Haxton had meanwhile left the ambulance unit, been declared an undesirable alien in England, and was at a loose end in Chicago. He had a sort of literary link with the South Seas through Lloyd Osbourne, Stevenson's friend and collaborator, who was also a friend of Haxton's father. Maugham now approached Haxton to come with him on the trip as his secretary assistant-companion and together they left San Francisco in 1916.

On arriving at Honolulu the ticker-tape of Maugham's storyteller's brain worked overtime recording reams of raw copy for future refinement and use. Whether it was in the Union Saloon, the Chinese quarter, the stews of Iwelei or the volcano of Kilauea, Maugham filled pages and pages of his notebook with striking contrasts between the breath-taking natural beauty of the islands and the driftwood of humanity that had washed up on them. No one escaped the lazer-beam of his attention, from his Australian and Jewish fellow-passengers to the administrators, missionaries, medicos, traders, and the chiefs, half-castes and humbler members of the native population. From Hawaii they took to sea again, and entered Samoa at Pago-Pago. Here Maugham, the writer, made the most famous encounter of his life. It was with a young woman 'plump, pretty in a coarse fashion, perhaps not more than twenty-seven'—she was a prostitute on the run from Iwelei where the brothels had been raided. Maugham put her down in his notebook alongside a description of two American medical missionaries, Mr. and Mrs. W., who told him that when they first went to the Gilberts it was impossible to find a single 'good' girl in any of the villages. He then entered another hundred words or so about the lodging-house five minutes' walk from the dock run by a half-caste and his native wife, adding laconically 'On these three notes I constructed a story called "Rain" '.

An American writer of French roots, Wilmon Menard, who got to know Maugham in his last years through the kindness of Max Beerbohm, discussed his South Seas and other travels with him. Because Menard knew the region well himself, his father having lived there, he found Maugham unexpectedly forth-coming about his voyages. Menard went on to discover among the dwellers in the South Seas citizens of close parallels in life for Maugham's characters and situations: all the elements in his most famous story were données presented by life to Maugham on a plate. Yet who but Maugham could have turned them all into 'Rain'! Not only that, Menard even discovered that the tart on the run was actually called Miss Thompson and that her name appears on the passenger list of arrivals from Los Angeles and Honolulu on November 14, 1916 along with those of Somerset Maugham and E. G. Haxton.[8]

In Apia they met the administrator of the island. The man in charge, the source of power, authority and decision, always had a deep fascination for Maugham and the instant verdict on this one was that 'one can guess that he runs his island competently but with an exaggerated insistence on insignificant details. He measures everything by the standards of the public school-boy.'[9] It was another administrator, according to Menard, Dick Williams on Savaii, the largest island of W. Samoa, who pro-vided him with the prototype for his most tyrannical white ruler, the brutal Mackintosh. And yet another whose alcoholism inspired 'Before the Party'.

Maugham told Menard that he and Gerald were fond of having aperitifs on the high seaside verandah of the Moana Hotel about three miles from downtown Honolulu. In such places as this when the winds of gossip began to blow among the drinkers the precious seeds of future stories were scattered, to germinate months or years later in Maugham's fertile brain.

Because of his stammer, and his shyness, Maugham was not a good mixer but Gerald was a brilliant one; if one had to find a single word in which to sum Gerald up that would be the one to choose. As Maugham acknowledged after Gerald's death: 'His gift for getting on friendly terms with all sorts of people had been of inestimable use to me. But for him I should not have got the material for many of the stories I wrote.'[10]

Maugham and Gerald explored Savaii, Apolima and then went back to Apia to depart for Suva in Fiji—'not the blitheness of Samoa'—and from there to New Zealand. It was thus on the second leg of this long trip that Maugham had his first sight of Gauguin's island. It came as readers of *The Moon and Sixpence* will remember as a sharp contrast to the trim neat south coast seaport look of Wellington. 'Nothing for mortal man,' Maugham said, 'was nearer to the golden realms of fancy than the approach to Tahiti. Murea, the sister isle, comes into view in rocky splendour, rising from the desert sea mysteriously, like the unsubstantial fabric of a magic wand. With its jagged outline it is like a Montserrat of the Pacific and you may imagine that there Polynesian knights guard with strange rites mysteries unholy for men to know.'[11] When Maugham arrived in Papeetee, whose subtle French character he noted, Gauguin had been dead for twelve years. The scent however was still warm. He was soon in conversation with the widow of a chief who told him that there were pictures by Gauguin in a place not far from hers. A boy took him to a house in which the painter had been ill and the first things Maugham saw were paintings by Gauguin on the glass panels of the doors. Two had been so picked away by children that they were almost ruined but one —of Eve—was still in fair condition and Maugham rapidly made the owner an offer for the whole door. A deal was clinched at two hundred francs. 'I thought,' Maugham said, 'I had better take the picture before he changed his mind, so we [Maugham and Haxton] got the tools from the car in which I had come, unscrewed the hinges and carried the door away. When we arrived back at the chiefesses' we sawed off the lower part in order to make it more portable, and so took it back to Papeetee.'[12] From there it eventually found its way to Maugham's writing-room.

[4.]

Critics have noted the many points where *The Moon and Sixpence*, avowedly suggested by the life of Gauguin differs from the facts. Most importantly perhaps there was a lot in Gauguin's blood, his extraordinary grandmother, his childhood in Lima, his years with the merchant navy, that suggests that he was not going to be permanently happy working on the *Bourse*. Yet the more we learn about him, the more we come to study the deeper meaning of his work, the more remarkable in its insights and in its impact does Maugham's novel seem. It is somehow truer than the truth.

This novel is Maugham's contribution to a dialectic about the nature of genius and its role in relation to society, and the laws governing society, that had been going on ever since the collapse of the Victorian moral code. That code did not make exceptions; the possession of universal genius did not confer special privileges on an individual. Dickens was forced to lie publicly about the state of his marriage and to keep Ellen Ternan a secret; modern biographical research has revealed similar concealments in the lives of many Victorian men of genius. The crunch came with the arrest of Oscar Wilde in 1895 when genius was put on trial and what had previously been hidden was made public. Genius was sent to prison for infringing the accepted moral code. A decade later Joyce, writing in Dublin out of a specifically Irish situation, put genius in the balance against the whole moral weight of the Catholic Church and its doctrine of Hell which he had mastered so vividly from his Jesuit teachers. He made his dash with Nora Barnacle. 'Welcome, O life! I go to encounter for the millionth time the reality of experience and to forge in my soul the uncreated conscience of my race.'[13] In May 1912 D. H. Lawrence eloped with Frieda Weekley, the aristocratic German-born wife of Ernest Weekley, a teacher of languages at Nottingham University. In the letter which Lawrence wrote to Weekley at the time and which was read out in the divorce court, he implied that the growth of an individual to his or her full potential was a supreme good more important than all the mutual ties and responsibilities of child-rearing that arise out of marriage. 'Mrs Weekley is afraid of being stunted and not allowed to grow, so she must live her own life . . .'[14]

The gospel of self-fulfilment was thus being given a widespread airing when Maugham pondered the career of Gauguin, its most celebrated exponent. In all the above instances the pattern was of family or spouse departed from, or abandoned, for some other person, a Bosie or a Nora, whom the genius compulsively needed in order to gain that condition of fulfilment out of which his art may flourish. It was not just for *her* sake, as he so charmingly put it to her husband, that Lawrence ran away with Frieda. With Gauguin we have an instance of an artist departing solely in pursuit of his own genius; in fact this was really true of Joyce, too, because although he left with Nora whom he later married it was the repudiation of (a) his family and (b) the Dublin of Lady Gregory and Yeats and the Irish Literary Renaissance that was the significant break he had to make for the sake of the development of his art. In the fictional instance of Maugham's Strickland he goes alone because of a genius he *might* have—he has absolutely no proof of it at the time—a genius that he senses will eventually, given the right conditions and the requisite amount of hard work, emerge. In other words he takes a Pascalian gamble on himself as Maugham had done after the publication of *Liza*.

Maugham's own position was however by now ambivalent. No one believed more whole-heartedly than he in the gospel of self-fulfilment, that was the whole point of breaking with family tradition and embracing the literary career but Maugham also had a very important social role to fulfil; he was a fashionable playwright and a fashionable presence; he was the elegant Jester wearing the top-hat, cravat and spats of the Kelly portrait. He was shockingly cynical, of course; and some of the things that the characters in his plays said and did were quite outrageous, but this did not put him outside the pale of society and condemn him to a tiny readership of disciples and intellectuals relying for his livelihood on the generosity of patrons and publishers. On the contrary it gave him a wide and ever-widening following, and a handsome, ever-handsomer income; it gave him what he often afterwards described sardonically as notoriety. Towards the end of his career as a playwright Maugham wrote three or four plays that he wanted to write but reckoned would be too sombre to please. His supposition was only half right; at least two of them were quite successful at the box-office but even if all four had flopped it would not really have mattered because by then, the mid-1930s, he was capable of earning vast sums of money outside the theatre notably as a writer of short stories. The truth was that after *Lady Frederick* Maugham did not have it in him to be unsuccessful even if he had tried. He was the very opposite of the hero of Henry James's story *The Next Time*[15] whose firm intention to write a popular commercial success was always being foiled by the purity of his gift. Maugham's power of arousing and sustaining the reader's curiosity in anything he did was so strong that he even became comparatively popular in that Cinderella of literary forms, the essay, when he turned to it in his declining years.

And yet Maugham was shrewd enough to realize that popularity becomes a form of servitude, a restriction on that divine freedom which is itself a justification for the arduous self-immurement of the literary career. He was in one role the Artist with his godlike power to pursue his vision in his own time and his own way, and in another more immediate role he was the professional producer of books and plays at the mercy of the whims of a paying public and the treacherous swiftly veering winds of taste and fashion. This double role is reflected in the whole scheme of *The Moon and Sixpence*, written in 1917 after he had married Syrie, in which a pleasing irony arises through Maugham as he is in reality in confrontation with an ideal Maugham, pursuing an original vision in solitary splendour and who identifies with his own hero, Charles Strickland. The first restriction he has to overcome is the changing conception of the novel in this period.

When Maugham came to write *The Moon and Sixpence*, the elegant Edwardian landscape of fiction, the world of Court Leys and his own early novels had begun to be shattered by a bombardment as severe as anything that had taken place at Ypres and on the Somme. Lawrence had published his first novel three years before the war and was currently embroiled

in legal battles with the Director of Public Prosecutions over
The Rainbow and *Lady Chatterley*. Maugham was quick to sense
the dawn of a new age for fiction in England (in the theatre the
revolution was to be delayed, luckily for him, until 1956) with
a new style and a new outspokenness. He was too old and too
reluctant a dog to learn new tricks and therefore had to justify
the traditionalism of his approach. The early scenes of his novel
occur in the drawing-room of an ambitious Colefaxian hostess,
Strickland's wife, to which Maugham-as-he-is in the figure of
the narrator is bidden. He comments defensively to the reader
on the change in the moral climate compared with that of his
own youth: 'I do not remember so crude a promiscuity as seems
to be practised in the present day' and he likens himself to
George Crabbe surviving into the age of Wordsworth and
Byron. 'I am on the shelf. I will continue to write moral stories
in rhymed couplets. But I should be thrice a fool if I did it for
aught but my own entertainment.'

These early scenes of *The Moon and Sixpence* anticipate the
great short-story writer that Maugham was soon to show
himself to be. The departure of Strickland from the safe prosperous respectability of his home, the effect of this on the
character of his wife and the military gentleman her brother, on
the Edwardian social system in fact, is handled with consummate irony. Maugham is accurate and generous enough to show
how well-fitted the system is to overcome this shock to its
complacency and to repair damage done to its tissues. He pays
a notable tribute to the strength of character of the abandoned
wife who comes to support herself by adopting the same career,
running a typing bureau, as Rhoda Barfoot in Gissing's *The
Odd Women*.

But all this is merely the most piquant starter to the main
meal. If the soup and the hors d'œuvres are served in London,
for the entrée we go to Paris where Maugham is bidden first
of all in an ambassadorial capacity on behalf of the wife, and
later at his own behest, to write a play and to pursue the
Bohemian life. It is in his second colloquy with Strickland that
the narrator who has spent the intervening years 'in hard work
and ... little adventure ... the gradual acquisition of the
knowledge of books and of men' goes to the heart of the matter

and the two sides of Maugham's nature the professional entertainer and the dedicated artist try to find an area of common ground:

> I had the feeling that he worked on a canvas with all the force of his violent personality, oblivious of everything in his effort to get what he saw with the mind's eye; and then, having finished, not the picture perhaps, for I had an idea that he seldom brought anything to completion, but the passion that fired him, he lost all care for it. He was never satisfied with what he had done: it seemed to him of no consequence compared with the vision that obsessed his mind.
>
> 'Why don't you ever send your work to exhibitions?' I asked. 'I should have thought you'd like to know what people thought about it.'
>
> 'Would you?'
>
> I cannot describe the unmeasurable contempt he put into the two words.
>
> 'Don't you want fame? It's something that most artists haven't been indifferent to.'
>
> 'Children. How can you care for the opinion of the crowd, when you don't care twopence for the opinion of the individual?'
>
> 'We're not all reasonable beings,' I laughed.
>
> 'Who makes fame? Critics, writers, stockbrokers, women.'
>
> 'Wouldn't it give you a rather pleasant sensation to think of people you don't know and had never seen receiving emotions, subtle and passionate, from the work of your hands? Everyone likes power. I can't imagine a more wonderful exercise of it than to move the souls of men to pity or terror.'
>
> 'Melodrama.'
>
> 'Why do you mind if you paint well or badly?'
>
> 'I don't. I only want to paint what I see.'
>
> 'I wonder if I could write on a desert island, with the certainty that no eyes but mine would ever see what I had written.'
>
> Strickland did not speak for a long time, but his eyes shone strangely, as though he saw something that kindled his soul to ecstasy.
>
> 'Sometimes I've thought of an island lost in a boundless sea, where I could live in some hidden valley, among strange trees, in silence. There I think I could find what I want.'
>
> He did not express himself quite like this. He used gestures instead of adjectives, and he halted. I have put into my own words what I think I wanted to say.

'Looking back on the last five years, do you think it was worth it?' I asked.

'He looked at me, and I saw that he did not know what I meant. I explained.

'You gave up a comfortable home and a life as happy as the average. You were fairly prosperous. You seem to have had a rotten time in Paris. If you had your time over again would you do what you did?'

'Rather.'

'Do you know that you haven't asked anything about your wife and children? Do you never think of them?'

'No.'

'I wish you weren't so damned monosyllabic. Have you never had a moment's regret for all the unhappiness you caused them?'

His lips broke into a smile, and he shook his head.

'I should have thought sometimes you couldn't help thinking of the past. I don't mean the past of seven or eight years ago, but further back still, when you first met your wife, and loved her, and married her. Don't you remember the joy with which you first took her in your arms?'

'I don't think of the past. The only thing that matters is the everlasting present.'

I thought for a moment over this reply. It was obscure perhaps, but I thought I saw dimly his meaning.

'Are you happy?' I asked.

'Yes.'

I was silent. I looked at him reflectively. He held my stare, and presently a sardonic twinkle lit up his eyes.

'I'm afraid you disapprove of me?'

'Nonsense,' I answered promptly. 'I don't disapprove of the boa-constrictor, on the contrary, I'm interested in his mental processes.

'It's a purely professional interest you take in me?'

'Purely.'

'It's only right you shouldn't disapprove of me. You have a despicable character.

'Perhaps that's why you feel at home with me,' I retorted.[16]

Maugham's love-hate for his own creation, for himself, for the double way of life involved in being both a serious artist and a commercially successful one is finely poised here. In bifurcating his own personality in this way he considerably over-simplifies the attitude of the historical Gauguin who unlike Strickland retained an atavistic longing to return to the bosom of his family ('Art is my business, my capital, the future of my children . . .', 'I hope to see you here one day with the children[17] . . .') and was by no means indifferent to the marketing of his work and longed for recognition in his own lifetime. The truth is that no artist however dedicated to his art in however pure a spirit remains completely indifferent to the claims of the living. Even a self-styled hermit like T. H. White (who resembles Strickland at many points) invested all his emotional resources in his dog and when she died was heart-broken. Certainly this classic dilemma of the artist must have greatly exercised the mind of a novelist who had himself just formed an attachment to another human being that was to last as long as that person's death and was himself now married to a woman of great social gifts.

We have seen how in *Of Human Bondage* Maugham identified with the vulnerable partner in a passionate affair and this particularly strong empathy saturates the next section of *The Moon and Sixpence* which concerns Strickland's catastrophic involvement in Paris with the Dutch painter Dirk Stroeve and his taciturn English wife. Here again we have a self-contained story of leisurely suspense leading to sudden melodrama shot through with a cruel irony. Stroeve was suggested by Gauguin's friend and colleague Emile Shuffenecker. There is a picture of him and his wife and two daughters in the Jeu de Paume that must be one of the most witheringly contemptuous portraits of a friend and fellow-artist ever limned. It shows the painter in an obsequious grin washing his hands in a nervous gesture while his family, isolated from him, sit proudly in the foreground. 'If ever a man was born to be cuckolded,' writes Wayne Anderson in *Gauguin's Paradise Lost* 'it was [Shuffenecker]. In his relationship with Gauguin he was a truly passive Christ-figure, or more accurately, a willing disciple prepared to die for the master because the master spoke true. He admired Gauguin's art without qualification, and he knew that his own art would never equal it. Out of some martyred sense of decency—imagine this civilized quality extended to fanatic lengths—he underwent numerous humiliations and a great deal of trouble and expense to do what he could for a man who consistently demeaned him.' Maugham seems aware of all this in his living source material and as so often encompasses it in his novel, so adroitly that truth and fiction seem to merge inextricably together.

He dwells on the ludicrous aspect of Stroeve with his short stature, his red face and his gold-rimmed spectacles, 'the absurd little man' as Strickland puts it, and we remember Maugham's own physical shortness and stammer. As we all know genius at close range is a killer and it is Blanche who, after she has cuckolded her husband with Strickland, must die because she is a woman, and as such jealous of the ideal. Far from feeling the slightest remorse at Blanche's death Strickland regards it as a blessed release:

> 'Do you remember my wife? I saw Blanche little by little trying all her tricks. With infinite patience she prepared to snare me and bind me. She wanted to bring me down to her level: she cared nothing for me, she only wanted me to be hers. She was willing to do everything in the world for me except the one thing I wanted: to leave me alone.'[18]

Away from London, away from the adventuresses and the coolly complaisant wives of Maugham's society comedies, women are a drag and a bore. Yet the sexual problem remains even for Strickland. What he needs is not so much a wife as a female slave who can both satisfy his physical needs and provide him with a suitable model whenever he wants to paint an Eve. He finds her in the person of the thirteen-year-old Tahitan girl, Ata.

The shocking candour of this solution is made acceptable through the skill with which Maugham in the final Polynesian section of the novel transforms his hero from a prickly and tiresome human being into the incarnation of a myth. Charles Strickland becomes 'the Red One'. He suffers his private Calvary of creative dedication dying a leper's death (Gauguin had syphilis) in his remote hut on the mountainside attended at the end only by his faithful Ata. The man whose invariable reaction to every human obstacle in his way was to tell it to go to hell now passes through a hell of the mortification of the flesh while his spirit is liberated in the form of ideally beautiful paintings which he then in a final act of purity destroys. The literary technique by which Maugham works this transformation is one of skilful pseudo-hagiography in which the personality of the One is re-created through the recollections of the Many. The novelist claims never to have seen Strickland again after his departure from Paris and as his hero moves away from the centres of civilized cosmopolitan life towards the more authentic existence of the exotic, he relies on hearsay and research, an old but effective trick to secure credibility. A transitional chapter set in Marseilles (based on borrowed material) shows Strickland's involvement with all manner and conditions of men after which Maugham makes his first use of the various types he encountered on his Pacific tour to play variations on the theme of the slowly comprehending norm to the presence of the exception: men in various states of semi-servitude realize now that for a while they were in the presence of genius, and some of them, like the generous merchant Cohen, actually possess the relics of genius which have acquired a worldly value never enjoyed by their creator. Maugham is surely very true here to the spirit of Gauguin's last years, and his final pictures dense with religious symbolism, even if he is miles away from the actual historical man dabbling in local politics and journalism and making a thorough nuisance of himself to the French colonial administration on the spot and to his few remaining friends and well-wishers in Paris.

Strickland was a more ruthless portrait of the Artist than anything comparable in fiction at the time when Maugham created him. Consider the sunny urbane figure of Henry James's Rowland Mallett or on a more profound creative level Proust's Bergotte: in neither case is there the same social incompatibility, the impatience with life as it is. Maugham says that he made Strickland an Englishman because he did not feel confident that he could manage a Frenchman, or any foreigner, as a main character, and yet in his cruelty and refusal to compromise there is something very un-English about him just as there was about Maugham. Imagine a Henry Moore or Graham Sutherland behaving remotely like Strickland; the figure of Joyce Cary's Gully Jimson with his bibulous, sensual, good-humoured, tolerant anti-bourgeois pragmatism is perhaps much closer to what one might call the English spirit in art.

The Moon and Sixpence was widely reviewed and praise for its technical accomplishment was fairly unanimous. Most reviewers jibbed at Strickland, unable to see the artist for the monster and quite a few had no idea that he was anything to do with Gauguin. The critic in *The Saturday Review* called him a 'crypto-Monet' and then went on rather splendidly to miss the point: 'The question which Mr. Maugham asks and answers in these pages is how would the primitive man, who acknowledges no obligation to God, man or woman, who accepts no creed or code of ethics, bear himself to his fellows in his passage through life?'[19] One of the most distinguished reviewers was Katherine Mansfield who had just begun a spell of book-reviewing for *The Athenaeum* of which her lover, J. Middleton Murray, had recently been appointed editor. She too never seems to have heard of Gauguin: 'If Strickland is a real man and this book is a sort of guide to his works it has its value; but if Mr. Maugham is merely pulling our critical leg it will not do.'[20] But she was nonetheless touched to the quick by the image of the artistic temperament presented in the novel and with her direct know-ledge of the, in some respects, Stricklandish figure of D. H. Lawrence, she reacted with violent antipathy. The main tenor of her criticism was summed up in her title 'Inarticulations'; she wanted much more knowledge of what went on in Strickland's mind and consciousness and presumably much less of the narrator's. She is wrong but she raises an interesting point. Maugham never does go 'inside' in the way of either Henry James or D. H. Lawrence. For him motivation is sub-sumed in action and a novel, like a play, consists of a series of external actions. He is not prepared to penetrate the conscious-ness of the exceptional individuals, Strickland or Larry, Mackintosh or Salvatore, around whose lives he builds his novel or story. Hence these figures have always an ultimate remote-ness and inscrutability; they are like icons, both worshipped and interpreted.

Katherine Mansfield says in her governessy way of Maugham's hero: 'If you have to be so odious before you can paint bananas—pray leave them unpainted.' Strickland is what he is and Time will pardon him (and Gauguin) for painting well. Because of her feminine sense of life as it is lived on the real practical level she saw a menacing threat in the attitude to which Maugham clearly subscribes in this book and she articulated her fear most eloquently:

> The one outstanding quality in Strickland's nature seems to have been his contempt for life and the ways of life. But contempt for life is not to be confused with liberty, nor can the man whose weapon it is fight a tragic battle or die a tragic death. If to be a great artist were to push over everything that comes in one's way, topple over a table, lunge out right and left like a drunken man in a cafe and send the pots flying, then Strickland was a great artist. But great artists are not drunken men; they are men who are divinely sober. They know that the moon cannot be bought for sixpence, and that liberty is only a profound realisation of the greatness of the dangers in their midst.

Maugham was surely well aware of the truths stated here. He had a sense of life that was full of wonder, and an admiration for its inconsistency, and its openings upon adventure, and for the development of individual gift, but for him all this was wholly incompatible with domesticity and family solidarity. As he says in *A Writer's Notebook* family life was an invention of Judaism; the Greeks believed that the world was a battlefield, and life a contest open to everyone to test his skill.

As Maugham is often accused with some justification of being anti-female, it is worth pointing out that the view of woman as the enemy of the creative life that we have seen emerge so harshly in *The Moon and Sixpence* was one which he shared with most of the major fiction-writers of Edwardian England. It was the realistic complement to the sentimentalizing of women by Barrie with his nauseous 'beautiful mothers' and the idealizing of them as a race of St. Joans by Shaw. If one recalls the role of women in relation to the creative gifts of the men in *New Grub Street* and *The Whirlpool* of Gissing, or the damning indictment of Agnes in Forster's *The Longest Journey*, or the truly terrible view of women and their cruelty in personal relations that emerges when the stunned reader has reached the labyrinthine end of Ford Madox Ford's *The Good Soldier*, in this context Maugham seems the child of his time, and he was an accurate enough observer to realize that a completely new idea of the role of women was emerging. He sketched it in plays such as *The Constant Wife* with its women lib-like insistence on parity of esteem and parity of earning capacity.

[5.]

In presenting his challenging portrait of an essentially male genius the figure of Maugham-as-he-is became fixed as we have seen in a posture of bemused detachment, chary of offering any definitive interpretation of the strange behaviour he relates. This now becomes the norm for the novelist-narrator in his stories and it is just as true of him when he is pursuing his more active role in the stories that have survived from Maugham's wartime career as an agent in which he takes the name of Ashenden. These were not published in book form until 1928 and the final one based on his experience as a TB patient very different in mood called 'Sanatorium' is joined to them in the Penguin edition of 1963. Here in geographical terms is Maugham's war: Switzerland, France, Italy and then the ten-day train journey on the Trans-Siberian railway from Vladi-vostock to Petrograd (a sort of Dr. Zhivago in reverse) to be present at the flashpoint of the revolution. The background to this final story (in the original volume) may be found in those extraordinarily interesting pages of *A Writer's Notebook* which describe Maugham's secret mission to Russia in 1917.

After Maugham's marriage to Syrie, apparently in 1916, in New Jersey on his return from the South Seas, her divorce from Wellcome having come through, he was approached by an old friend of the Maugham family, Sir William Wiseman, who was ostensibly the head of the British Purchasing Commission in New York and in fact running the Secret Service. He had an extraordinary proposal to make the newly-wed writer:

> The long and short of it was that I should go to Russia and keep the Russians in the war. I was to be provided with a lot of money half of which was supplied by the United States and half by Great Britain: with this I was to enable the Mensheviks to buy arms and finance newspapers in support of their plans. Four Czechs were to

come with me and, on my arrival in Petrograd, besides giving me any help I needed, were to put me in touch with Masaryk who controlled sixty thousand devoted Czechs.

I told Wiseman that I did not think I was competent to do the sort of thing that was expected of me. He answered that it had been decided that I would do as well as anyone else.[21]

Maugham's intelligence mission happened to coincide historically with a time when Russian fever was starting to sweep through the drawing-rooms of the London literary world and he was able to check his excursions into Russian fiction against the realities of life along the Nevsky Prospekt. Kerensky, whose Democratic Convention he attended, struck him as a sick, weak man who had at least one thing in common with Charles Frohman 'the quality of exciting in others the desire to do things for him'. These passages in the Notebook in which Maugham gives us his considered reflections on the Convention, the Russian character and the novels of Tolstoy, Dostoevsky and Chekhov, fill in the background to 'Mr. Harrington's Washing' in which Ashenden accompanies the puritanical Philadelphian businessman, John Quincey Harrington, into the strife-torn streets of Petrograd. Maugham uses the occasion to give us both an unforgettable portrait of the American conscience in action and also to poke fun at the English Russophiles with their talk of the intelligentsia ('difficult to spell but easy to say') and this prevents a highly amusing and entertaining story from being a great one. Maugham becomes enchanted by the rigour-in-adversity of his hero who contrives to look spruce all through the hazardous train journey and is then killed in a bout of street-fighting while in pursuit of his laundry. For Maugham the psychology of a bore was always more important than the rationale behind a revolution. Maybe among the fourteen unpublished Ashenden stories that Alan Searle says Maugham destroyed on one of his 'bonfire nights' because he thought they contravened the official secrets act, there was a masterpiece of historical insight making use of this same material.

Mr. Harrington minding his own business while history was in the making, is but one of a clutch of characters who dominate each of these stories, and whose heroism the conditions of war serves to expose: the English governess who dies with her secret still unspoken, the Mexican adventurer 'a gentleman —or rather a man of honour' who risks all to kill the wrong man, the Italian dancer on whom monstrous pressure is exerted to betray her Indian lover. By this time Maugham has developed his short story technique to a point where it may be likened to a piece of stretched elastic that is pulled and pulled until it snaps. A secret agent starts from the supposition that everyone around him has something that they wish to conceal and Maugham finds a perfect accord here with his own fictional method. In the case of the Caypors, the Englishman with a German wife, the heroic quality has become inverted and turned into a pathetic treachery although Mrs. Caypor behaves well during her husband's ordeal and Ashenden's relation with her as her pseudo-pupil is an interesting one. It is only in 'His Excellency' that we have a variant on the favourite theme of the mis-mating and the world well lost for a professionally suicidal passion. Here in a long *tête à tête* in the residence over the brandy, Ashenden hears the concealed part of the life of a haughty and aloof member of the diplomatic service. We are miles away from war and espionage in that area of servitude to a degrading passion and surviving the degradation that Maugham understood so well.

The foundation of a whole fictional literature about intelligence—the putting on and penetration of masks in the zone of danger—lies in these Ashenden stories, reaching out in our own time to Ian Fleming, Len Deighton, John Le Carré. Maugham established for all time the peculiar relation between the agent (Ashenden) the chief R here (only a partially characterized figure) who manipulates him, and the victims whom he in turn tries to manipulate. The agent is a worldlywise fellow who can be relied upon not to be swayed by emotion particularly when in the proximity of human suffering. When he is blackmailing Giulia to lure her lover into captivity: 'He felt his relation to her as impersonal as a doctor's in the presence of a pain that he cannot alleviate. He saw why R had given him this peculiar task; it needed a cool head and an emotion well under control.' He shares something of his creator's scepticism and cynicism about women and when he meets the famous harlot, Rose Auburn, by whom the young diplomat Byring has become ensnared to, 'it was somewhat astonishing to Ashenden to discover that she differed so little in air and manner from the smart women of Mayfair with whom, through his books, he had become more or less intimately acquainted'. At times Ashenden himself has for security reasons to conceal himself behind the mask of an army officer when he becomes Major Somerville, yet another Maugham *persona*. As for R he remains pretty much in the background but whenever he does emerge Maugham cannot resist the malicious implication that he is not quite quite. There is a hint in *Giulia Lazzari* of some secret love-affair in the life of R about whom Ashenden knows more than he suspects. It was left to Fleming, a later master of the genre, to make the chief an invulnerable father-image of his subordinate.

When they appeared in 1928 the Ashenden stories were accepted as a fairly substantial contribution to the art of story-telling. Gerald Gould, now reviewing fiction for *The Observer*, summed it up by saying that it was not Maugham at his best or profoundest but it had a firmness of texture and was hard to put down. Edward Shanks in the *London Mercury* found the collection satisfyingly 'enigmatic'—a word that has dogged Maugham's work ever since. Thus, if 'the intelligentsia' were not exactly ecstatic neither were they damning, except perhaps in one instance and that was a review which appeared in *Vogue* by D. H. Lawrence. In this, his only direct confrontation with Maugham, Lawrence proved himself to be a supple and spontaneous reviewer adept at seizing the point:

[Ashenden] is almost passionately concerned with proving that all men and all women are either dirty dogs or imbeciles. If they are clever men or women, they are crooks, spies, police-agents, and tricksters 'making good', living in the best hotels because they know that in a humble hotel they'll be utterly *déclassé*, and showing off their base cleverness, and being dirty dogs, from Ashenden himself, and his mighty clever colonel, and the distinguished diplomat, down to the mean French porters.

If, on the other hand, you get a decent straight individual, especially an individual capable of feeling love for another, then you are made to see that such a person is a despicable fool, encompassing his own destruction. So the American dies for his dirty washing, the Hindu dies for a blowsy woman who wants her wrist-watch back, the Greek merchant is murdered by mistake, and so on.

It is better to be a live dirty dog than a dead lion, says Mr Ashenden.
Perhaps it is, to Mr Ashenden.

But these stories, being serious, are faked. Mr Maugham is a
spendid observer. He can bring before us persons and places most
excellently. But as soon as the excellently observed characters have
to move, it is a fake. Mr Maugham gives them a humorous shove
or two. We find they are nothing but puppets, instruments of the
author's pet prejudice. The author's pet prejudice being 'humour',
it would be hard to find a bunch of more ill-humoured stories, in
which the humour has gone more rancid.[22]

This from the man who had just published *Lady Chatterley's Lover*
and *The Woman Who Rode Away*—but is it in fact true? Time
has leant more reality to John Quincey Harrington and Chandra
Lall than it has to Mellors. Maugham certainly never tried to
prove anything in his life about human beings; his attitude was
one of the most intense scepticism but it is interesting to see him
being thus branded as a cynical puppeteer by the darling of the
intelligentsia as early as 1928. Certainly you could not say that
the pair of tubercular lovers in 'Sanatorium', who are prepared
to advance the date of their own deaths in order briefly to enjoy
life together as a married couple, were in the opinion of Ashenden
despicable fools. They seem to have his unstinted admiration.
This story, which reveals how in a closed, imprisoned community adult human beings easily revert to childishness, is
somewhat more Chekhovian in style than the rest of Maugham's
tales. It was suggested by Maugham's own stay as a TB
patient at the end of his stint as an agent at Nordrach-on-Dee
in Scotland. The patch on the lungs which he had contracted
during the severe Swiss winter of 1915 had worsened now after
improving during his Pacific trip. As one might expect
Maugham was not the man to let being a patient interfere with
his literary career. Not only did he observe his fellow patients
and store away material, he also turned out original work. 'I was
sent to bed every day at six o'clock,' he tells us, 'and an early
dinner gave me a long evening to myself. The cold windless
night entered the room through the wide-open windows, and
with mittens on my hands so that I could comfortably hold a
pen, it was an admirable opportunity to write a farce.'[23]

CHAPTER SIX

Mainly Heroines

[1.]

THE FARCE THUS written was called *Home and Beauty* in England and *Too Many Husbands* in the United States. Maugham never saw the original production in London in 1919 but it was a great success with Gladys Cooper in the main part. The war, intelligence work, TB, marriage, Haxton, none of this prevented Maugham from writing plays. In Rome in 1915 he had written *Our Betters*; then as we saw *Caroline* in Geneva, *pace* the Swiss police, presented in London in 1916. In 1917 he wrote a play for Marie Löhr called *Love in a Cottage*, and in 1918 *Caesar's Wife*. With such work Maugham enlivened a wartime theatre that was booming, drawing huge numbers of men in uniform.

'It was commonly said in the trenches,' reports St. John Ervine, 'that the War Office was subsidizing the performance of appalling twaddle in order to make the soldiers glad to go back to the Front. Ten days of West End plays, the authorities said, and the men will go quietly to the trenches.'[1] Inevitably a wartime theatre will do a roaring trade in escapism: from 1916 *Chou Chin Chow* ran and ran, but the stage also began to reflect the social changes that the war precipitated in the work of Barrie and others.

Maugham did not dramatize the war directly: he was a sardonic observer of the land fit for heroes. The new England of war-profiteers and fixers peeps wickedly through the merriment of *Home and Beauty*; in *The Unknown* the great gulf between those who went away to fight and the non-combatants of the older generation is revealed; and in *For Service Rendered* the lasting impact of the war on a 'lost generation' is studied in the complacent pastures of rural Kent in the 1930s.

In his plays even more than his novels Maugham had a journalist's eye for good copy and many of them have their origin in some passing mood which they preserve with great zest. Maugham dismissed their chances of survival with a wave of the hand, saying that he regarded the prose drama as 'hardly less ephemeral than yesterday's newspaper'. It is my purpose to suggest that Maugham was an even better dramatist than he was a journalist and that working from his own urbane vantage point within the tradition of Ibsen and Becque he succeeded in dramatizing some of the more significant social tensions of English life in the period between the wars.

Beneath their accurately observed outward occasions, Maugham's plays possess, like all good drama, a subtle sub-conscious appeal. The story—to take one instance—of the returning hero and what he finds in his native land is a myth basic to the human mind, at least as old as Homer. Maugham uses it with intuitive understanding in two of the plays just mentioned, and when one of them, *Home and Beauty*, was given a stylish revival recently by the National Theatre at least one perceptive critic, Frank Marcus in *The Sunday Telegraph* saw the irony in making a farce about new, mercenary, heartless, ruthless England with its honours for the dishonest and its cosseting of the spoiled, a land which the returning heroes repudiate with indecent haste.[2]

Victoria, a delectable creature in spite of her two defecting husbands, is but one of a great gallery of outstanding roles for women that were to come from Maugham's pen in these years. The greatest period of English drama, the Elizabethan and Jacobean, occurred before the arrival on our stage of the actress and hence, with obvious exceptions we can all think of, is weak in strong female roles. The realistic theatre attempted to make up for this deficiency and no one can complain that the plays of Henry Arthur Jones and Pinero lack good parts for women. They tend however to be rather similar women—characters like Mrs. Dane, Mrs. Tanqueray, Mrs. Ebbsmith lack indivi-duality. They are *femmes fatales*. It is more in what they repre-sent for their menfolk in the way of temptation than in what they are in themselves that their importance lies.

Maugham etched his heroines with a sharper and subtler needle than his predecessors. He was indeed God's gift to the great actresses of his day and his success seems inseparable, as he freely admitted, from such stars of the period as Irene Vanbrugh, Gladys Cooper, Fay Compton, Margaret Bannerman and Flora Robson.

If Maugham had shocking views about women, particularly as we have seen about what a mistake it was for an artist, or anyone who wished to lead the creative life, to become involved with them, this misogynistic attitude was combined with the most remarkable empathy with the sex. Maugham understood women much better than any other playwright of this period whether it was women of the political and social aristocracy, the wives of the professional middle-class or the common prostitute. He understood them much better than Shaw, for example, who merely created new stereotypes of his own by giving women many of the qualities of leadership and resourcefulness traditionally ascribed to men. Shaw devoted a lot of wordage in his polemical plays to the plight of women and led the crusade for their liberation from the domestic prison but it was Maugham who dramatized the actual reality of their situation at the time when they achieved their political and social independence.

Maugham captured in all its most elusive forms that frightening new species—twentieth-century woman. He peopled his stage with dissatisfied women, heartless women, competitive women, masculine women, outrageous women, self-sacrificing women, Anglo-American women and one mercy-killing maternal woman. He agreed that the only profession open to most women was that of marriage, and he examined the nature of marriage from a point of view foreign to both Pinero and Henry Arthur Jones, that of women. He set his sights most frequently on marriage among a class whose economic prosperity was as precarious as its values, floundering between what Mrs. Ardsley in *For Services Rendered* called 'the pale shadow that is all you clever people have left me of God' and the as yet unfamiliar new ritual of the analyst's couch. In this historic vacuum marriage was seen as a dry, brittle comedy of the waste land and Maugham's *théâtre* may be put beside Eliot's poem as an expression of it.

Those deceptively casual first-acts with their card-playing and their small-talk give absolutely no indication that we are going to be taken well beyond the permissible limits of taste and candour by the end of the second. No wonder that Maugham became piqued when his careful, witty, moral analyses were rejected by critics because they were too popular, and cross when his view that the theatre should be entertaining was misinterpreted to mean that it should be trivial and superficial. He insisted that failure in the theatre was attributable to bad workmanship, not an indication of superior moral worth. For him success was an indication that the engine was running sweetly and its purring gave him the power to carry through a disturbing proposal such as he showed embodied in his heroine of *The Constant Wife*, Constance when her newly-won economic position enabled her to follow Ibsen's Nora out of the conjugal front door and into the world at large.

[2.]

The wisdom of her behaviour in Maugham's eyes is foreshadowed in an earlier play *The Circle* through the mouth of Lady Kitty whose life of social exile has taught her exactly the same lesson as Constance. She in her turn tries to teach it to Elizabeth, whom she sees as being about to make the same mistake as she did all those years ago:

Lady Kitty: You don't know what it is to have a man tied to you only by his honour. When married people don't get on they can separate, but if they're not married it's impossible. It's a tie only death can sever.

Elizabeth: If Teddie stopped caring for me I shouldn't want him him to stay with me for five minutes.

Lady Kitty: One says that when one's sure of a man's love, but when one isn't any more—oh, it's so different. In those circumstances one's got to keep a man's love. It's the only thing one has.

Elizabeth: I'm a human being. I can stand on my own feet.

Lady Kitty: Have you got any money of your own?

Elizabeth: None.

Lady Kitty: Then how can you stand on your own feet? You think
I'm a silly frivolous woman, but I've learnt something
in a bitter school. They can make what laws they like,
they can give us the suffrage, but when you come
down to bedrock it's the man who pays the piper who
calls the tune. Woman will only be the equal of man
when she earns her living in the same way that he
does.

Elizabeth: (Smiling) It sounds rather funny to hear you talk like
that.[3]

The Circle, constructed across a generation gap in which past
ironically mirrors present, has two heroines, an old and a
young; one of the high-spots of the play is the discussion
between them on the ethics of bolting, from which the above
quotation comes. What they are bolting—or have bolted—
from is the boredom of respectability and responsibility; they are
bolting out of a marriage that gives them social status and
economic security but desperately lacks romance; a union from
which the rainbow has come and gone for good. It is against
the dreary backcloth of such a marriage that the callow young
planter with his classic line at the climax of the great love duet
in act two—'I think you're such a ripping good sort'—seems
aglow with an irresistible attraction to poor Elizabeth, just as
thirty years before the lovable, irascible old dunderhead Lord
Porteous had done to the now raddled but still alert Lady Kitty.

Before she finally bolts Elizabeth is treated in scenes of
superb comedy to a chilling vision of what lies at the other end
of the rainbow, exile, dissoluteness, the company of the
European demi-monde, childlessness and a now elderly lover
whom she cannot stand the sight of, but neither this, nor
Arnold's 'downy' wheeze of removing all resistance to the
liaison, can quell the newly aroused Nora in her. The comedy
ends with her departure from the marital home for the joys of
the Federated Malay States.

As in Becque, these people belong to the world of a professional élite which gives a hidden bedrock of ambitions lost and
won as a base for the comedy. The title means not only that the
wheel has come full circle but that we are here inside a charmed
circle of power and influence whose members are prey to the

pettiest of private motives. Maugham was remembering those
fashionable drawing-rooms in Westminster to which he was
bidden as a guest when he had his first success as a playwright:

> At certain political houses I frequented they still talked as though
> to run the British Empire were their private business. It gave me
> a peculiar sensation to hear it discussed, when a general election
> was in the air, whether Tom should have the Home Office and
> whether Dick would be satisfied with Ireland . . . I could not dis-
> cover in the eminent statesmen I met there any marked capacity.
> I concluded, perhaps rashly, that no great degree of intelligence
> was needed to rule a nation.[4]

Yet within *The Circle* there is an agreeable geniality tempered
by the wisdom of maturity. In spite of all the awfulnesses,
Maugham is saying, and all the degradations, if you do give up
all for love, the world *is* well lost. Bicker as they must, Lady
Kitty and Lord Porteous have an affection for each other that in
the end is indissoluble and that makes her want Elizabeth to
bolt even though she has put the case against doing so with
such unanswerable force. The heart has its reasons and in the
final moments of the comedy they prove to be stronger than
reason itself.

The spectacle of a woman attempting simultaneously to
satisfy the demands of a lover and a husband was standard fare
in the French theatre ever since *La Parisienne* in 1885. In
England extra-marital affairs had to be hinted at rather than
directly presented. Caroline in *The Unattainable* had a husband
who was permanently absent and was therefore able to enjoy
the devotion of the leading barrister she had ensnared in a
happy state of indefinite balk, as far as ever marrying him went.
A report of her husband's death upsets this equilibrium and
provides Maugham with his basic situation for a comedy. He
shows us with a merry plausibility how as they look upon the
wide ocean of choice that has suddenly opened before them
neither Robert nor Caroline wishes to embark for the distant
shore of marriage. His point is that these two people are perfectly happy, as happy as any two human beings who have been
exclusive to each other for ten years can be expected to be, so
long as they are not required to enter into the marriage contract. He likes his house; she likes hers; neither wants to move;

it is as simple as that. The thing will founder on the dominant feminine will incarnate in Caroline which is, when it comes to it, stronger than that of Robert: and yet all the social pressures in the form of Caroline's hideous women friends are driving them inexorably towards marriage and only the eleventh-hour reappearance of Caroline's husband provides them with a blessed reprieve. The situation is teased out beautifully in Maugham's best nonchalant man-of-the-world manner and in the course of it the motivations behind the institution of marriage are thoroughly spelled out by Robert:

> My dear, I have a large experience of the reasons for which two people marry. They marry from pique or from loneliness, or fear, for money, position or boredom; because they can't get out of it, or because their friends think it'll be a good thing, because no one has ever asked them before, or because they're afraid of being left on the shelf; but the one reason which infallibly leads to disaster is when they marry because they want to.[5]

Almost fifteen years separate Caroline from Noël Coward's *Private Lives*: the line of succession may be clearly traced from the almost forgotten frolic to the more famous comedy.

In the mordant, scabrous play he wrote next, *Our Betters*, Maugham turned to the society marriage market at its most sordid, a world where grotesque and formidable American millionairesses married into the effete European aristocracy and used their wealth to further their social ambitions. It is a corruscating caricature of the world of Henry James with two young American innocents, the enchanting Bessie and Fleming Harvey, her beau, adrift against the Bakst colours and cushions of Pearl Grayson's Grosvenor Street drawing-room; there Pearl entertains her lovers and her rivals like Minnie, Duchesse de Surennes (*née* Hodgson, Chicago—'a woman of opulent form, bold, self-assured, outrageously sensual. She suggests a drawing of a Roman Emperor by Aubrey Beardsley...') and the sweeter-natured Princess Flora della Cercola (*née* Van Hoog). Their men friends are a grim lot: sexual athlete Tony Paton and the ineffable Virginian snob Thornton Clay—forerunner of Eliot Templeton in *The Razor's Edge*—who called more countesses by their Christian names than any man in town and

Pearl's immensely rich and immensely vulgar lover Arthur Fenwick (founded on Gordon Selfridge) who calls her 'girlie' and explains that 'they laughed when I first came over here'. It is through a heavy subsidy from him and the complaisance of her absent husband that Pearl maintains her position as London's top hostess.

This play in its London production of 1923 came as an absolute revelation of Maugham's genius as a playwright to Desmond MacCarthy when he became the first dramatic critic of the *New Statesman*. He likened it to 'an exposure in the manner of Maupassant of one luxuriant corner of the social jungle'.[6] English society is here in an advanced state of deliquescence. Pearl's conquest of it is based on her discovery very early in her career that the English can never resist getting something for nothing. Whatever is fashionably 'in' from Kreisler to a new dancing-master you will find it laid on for you at Pearl's. Marriage is a mockery, a mere means to personal aggrandizement. In vain may the shocked Fleming talk of honour and decency and self-restraint. Maugham determines to shatter this young man's illusions. He does so in Pearl's country place where the plot explodes. She is spotted on a moonlit assignation with Minnie's lover in the summerhouse and the curtain goes down on her saying to him, 'You damned fool. I told you it was too risky.'

The line achieved a gasp of horror in 1923 when it proved a bit too much for the Lord Chamberlain who insisted quaintly that the discovery of the lovers should not be made by Bessie but by the young Etonian peer, Lord Bleane! Maugham however has a more serious point to make. He sees these American ogresses as examples of the new woman who has become cut off from her traditional duties and in an intoxication of freedom goes to pieces, rather like an African country when the natives take over. 'English women,' the unfortunate Princess explains, 'in our station have duties that are part of their birthright but we strangers in a strange land have nothing to do but enjoy ourselves.' Or again, as Bessie protests, when like Isabel Archer she turns down her peer:

Don't you see that we're not strong enough for the life over here?

It goes to our head; we lose our bearings; we put away our code, and we can't accept the code of the country we've come to. We drift. There's nothing for us to do but amuse ourselves, and we fall to pieces. But in America we're safe. And perhaps America wants us.[7]

As this big satirical play pursues its stately course like some great Atlantic liner this is one of many revelations that it churns up in its wake in a foam of wickedly funny lines. It is time it had a re-launch.

[3.]

From Pearl Grayson's drawing-room at the hub of smart social London to the British Consular Agency Residence in the Cairo of the Khedive was the leap that Maugham made in his next play. The authenticity with which both these milieux are created is evidence of his acute powers of observation at this time, but in *Caesar's Wife* he had a more ambitious aim than merely to observe an aspect of the complicated chessboard of Middle East politics. He wanted to show the nobility of character in both men and women that had been so conspicuously absent from his theatre up to now and to rebut the view that he only achieved his triumphs by putting thoroughly unpleasant people on the stage. If marriage was a prison, the sentence could be served with dignity. He had recently read Madame de la Fayette's novel *La Princesse de Clèves* with its depiction of the sacrifice of passion to honour and he thought it 'would be interesting to treat this theme in a modern way'. What impressed Maugham particularly about the original was the manner in which although the emotion is deep and true the tone 'is never raised above that seemly to persons of good breeding'.[8] At the risk of displeasing some critics who found the play slow-moving this is exactly the tone that Maugham succeeds in sustaining in *Caesar's Wife*. 'A triumphantly tactful evening,' said *The Times* critic of the first night in March 1919. The play is punctuated by silences; circumstances cruelly wrench her secret from the lips of Violet Little. She loves her husband's secretary and nobly begs that he be sent away from

Cairo to a perfectly acceptable job in Paris, but the stern Agent refuses to do this. The Khedive needs a new secretary and handsome charming Ronny is, he insists, ideally suited for the job. The safety of the Empire, it seems, depends upon Ronnie staying in Egypt; and even when Violet actually confesses her passion for this young man to her husband, in a marvellously tense scene in the second act, he remains irremovable in his resolve. Anyone but Sir Arthur Little, K.C.B., K.M.G. would, one feels, have packed the blighter straight off and no nonsense, but he goes out of his way to ensure that he remains; thus they are all put to a severe moral test which needless to say they all come through, honour undimmed.

Like some glinting glass prism this play can be turned different ways to reveal new beauties of construction: not the least of these is the manner in which other women apart from the heroine are made to suffer a testing involvement in her situation. Here is a society in which, although the ostensible role of women is social, their greatest influence may be as hidden persuaders in the workings of the administration. It is Ronny's sister who first of all moves heaven and earth to get him sent to Paris and the irony here is that she herself has been in love with Little for years and is nonetheless secretly exerting her influence to save his marriage from probable disaster. As the female pressures pile up on Little, one is reminded of that other sorely extended administrator in foreign parts, Shakespeare's *Othello*. But Little though perplexed in the extreme never loses his cool and he is rewarded by the respect and loyalty of his wife after his life has been preserved by none other than Ronny in a plot hatched by the emergent nationalist, Osman Pasha.

One critic found Little unattractively reptilian: but to me he remains a finely chiselled figurehead of a class whom Maugham understood so well; he is the embodiment of leadership, sinewy, shrewd, courageous, a believer in having it out at once and a very accurate summer-up of a situation, a natural Tory who behaves with openness and good breeding both to the fellers of the opposite camp and to the people in his charge. Hear him as he utters some words of wisdom to a visiting Labour M.P. who is about to make a journey up the Nile into Upper Egypt:

You may learn a good deal that will surprise you. You may learn
that there are races in the world that seem born to rule and races
that seem born to serve; that democracy is not a panacea for all
the ills of mankind, but merely one system of government like
another, which hasn't had a long enough trial to make it certain
whether it is desirable or not; that freedom generally means the
power of the strong to oppress the weak, and that the wise statesman gives men the illusion of it but not the substance—in short a
number of things which must be very disturbing to the equilibrium
of a radical Member of Parliament.[9]

This is a very rare instance of straight political utterance in the
Maugham canon and it is one which unfortunately time has not
rendered either obsolete or irrelevant, unlike some of those by
his more overtly political contemporaries, Shaw and Wells.

[4.]

Caesar's Wife with its ambience of political tension and its
interest in the behaviour of English people in positions of
responsibility abroad has more in common with the short
stories than with most of Maugham's plays. On the whole in
the theatre he preferred to dramatize the behaviour of the
English at home. In *Love in a Cottage,* a comedy that he wrote
for Miss Marie Löhr in 1917, he did stray as far as the shores of
Lake Como, but after the Egyptian piece he produced *Home and
Beauty* (1919), *The Circle* (1919) and *The Unknown* (1920), all
firmly rooted in the old country. Meanwhile Maugham continued to travel extensively himself. Throughout the 1920s he
went to China, Australia, the Malayan Archipelago, Central
and South America. *The Trembling of a Leaf,* set in the South
Seas, his first book of short stories since the youthful *Orientations,* appeared in 1921 and a year later *On a Chinese Screen,* a
sequence of thumbnail sketches about China which also provided material for the play, *East of Suez.* This was an attempt
to provide Basil Dean with something spectacular that he could
mount at His Majesty's. It opens with a colourful street scene
without any dialogue and music specially written by Eugene
Goossens, followed by the story of a Eurasian woman who is

married to one Englishman and in love with another. Agate
swooped on it like a hawk, accusing Maugham of insincerity
and evasion in his handling of the situation:

> Daisy [he wrote] is defeated not because she is a Eurasian, but
> because she is Daisy. Yet both plays [he made a comparison with
> *The Second Mrs Tanqueray*] set out to prove that if the class is 'not
> nice', you cannot afford to have anything to do with it. Touch pitch
> and you will be defiled. Both plays prove a particular case from
> which we are to deduce an unwarrantable conclusion.[10]

And so he might have added did *A Man of Honour*; yet for all
that Daisy remains no less convincing a female than the new
women of the London plays.

By the early 1920s other hands than those of Maugham had
tried to shape his work for the stage. In 1922 two American
journalists approached him for permission to make a play out
of the story *Rain*. Maugham agreed somewhat reluctantly as
he didn't think that there really was a play there. Yet the work
proved to be one of the most successful of all 'his' plays. 'The
long promised downpour took place on Tuesday evening,' wrote
Agate, 'and proved a very handsome affair.' In 1925 Edith Ellis
made an adaptation of *The Moon and Sixpence* which had a
success when it was performed at the New Theatre with Henry
Ainley as Strickland.

Maugham's next original play seems to have been something
called *The Camel's Back*, a comedy about a repressive husband
which has not survived and need not detain us. Then came *The
Road Uphill* which has never been either published or produced.
Set as it is in Chicago at the end of the war it is an ancestor of
The Razor's Edge and may conveniently be discussed when we
come to consider that major novel. It was in 1926 that Maugham
took the lid off modern marriage yet again in his most mature
view of that much maligned institution, *The Constant Wife*. It
was given first in New York with Ethel Barrymore as Constance
where it was something of a wow. 'Deft, clever and altogether
delightful, said *The New York Post*, while 'has a great many
lines of high comedy and not a few of wisdom' confirmed Robert
Benchley in *Life*; but Basil Dean's London production the following year was a disaster, Maugham's mini-Guy Domville as

it were, at which the groundlings barracked the play on the first night. There was some muddle over the demarcation of the Pit from the Stalls and the Pitites had been forced to give up a whole line of their seats.[11] St. John Ervine felt that because of this fracas the play could not be properly judged. However, Agate gave his verdict unequivocally: he was not amused; 'the characters,' he declared, 'were all patient plodding tillers of the conversational soil—they gave us no action, and we gave up expecting any.'

What Agate failed to point out was that the play was a restructured and remotivated version of the first successful marital comedy *Penelope*, in the light of Maugham's own experience of marriage. Like Penelope the heroine is married to a busy and successful medical man who is having an affair with one of his patients, but instead of the gay, dotty, golightly mood of the earlier play with its belief in non-resistance as the cure-all for infidelity, we have a more serious probing of the different standards of sexual conduct currently applicable to meo and women. Constance's mother represents the old-fashioned view:

> I have my own ideas about marriage. If a man neglects his wife it's her own fault, and if he's systematically unfaithful to her in nine cases out of ten she has only herself to blame . . . No sensible woman attaches importance to an occasional slip. Time and chance are responsible for that.[12]

On the other hand when it comes to *women* straying down the primrose path Mrs. Culver has a quite different attitude:

> Of course I believe in fidelity for women. I suppose no one has ever questioned the desirability of that. But men are different. Women should remember that they have their homes and their name and position and their family, and they should learn to close their eyes when it's possible they may see something they are not meant to.[13]

Maugham sets up his experiment designed to modify this old-fashioned view. He introduces a gentleman from Constance's past who during that time has remained somewhat improbably both unmarried and in love with her. It is all set up now for her to pay her husband back in the same coin. This she seems reluctant to do.

Then suddenly her friend's husband bursts in, with *her* husband's cigarette case which he has found on his wife's pillow. Agate said contemptuously that the banality of this device was enough to make poor Scribe turn in his grave. But the point of it is the way in which the whole potentially explosive and destructive situation is completely defused by Constance whose finest hour this is. The tissue of lies that Constance pours out to the irate husband is so monstrously implausible that it becomes credible. She behaves like a true woman of the world, showing at this point all the qualities that Maugham most admired in people, courage, tact, patience, urbanity, the ability to take risks and bluff one's way through a delicate situation. Constance's unlosable cool is not however like that of Penelope, a strategic feint it is based on the fact that she regards marriage not as a sacrament but as a profession, the only decent one open to a woman of her class:

> In the working-class a woman cooks her husband's dinner, washes for him and darns his socks. She looks after the children and makes their clothes. She gives good value for the money she costs. But what is a wife in our class? Her house is managed by servants, nurses look after her children, if she has resigned herself to having any, and as soon as they are old enough she packs them off to school. Let us face it, she is no more than the mistress of a man of whose desire she has taken advantage to insist on a legal ceremony that will prevent him from discarding her when his desire has ceased.[14]

On the other hand she will not as she explains to her prospective lover contemplate any violation of the marriage contract while she remains dependent upon her husband.

> It all comes down to the economic situation. He has bought my fidelity and I should be worse than a harlot if I took the price he paid and did not deliver the goods.[15]

It is not difficult to see why—pit-muddle or no pit-muddle— such frankness should have proved too much for London audiences of 1927 and that the play should have had its first success in the States where the economic liberation of women took place earlier. Only after Constance has earned enough money will she go on an experimental holiday abroad with her lover. In this way she can reconcile her infidelity with her 'most endearing quality', her constancy. Herbert Farjeon who reviewed the comedy in *The Graphic* wondered whether 'even the glamour surrounding Miss Fay Compton will entirely blind audiences to the ethical questionability of her stage conduct.'[16] Unlike Mr. Farjeon many of them must have recognized that after this play one of the great social hypocrises of English life had been given a most searing exposure. Of all the heroines of Maugham's marriage comedies, Mrs. Dot, Penelope, Caroline, Victoria, to name the most memorable, Constance is the one who serves as the working-model for the future for English women in real life. Indeed, after he had written it Maugham had more or less said his say about the marriage-prison. It was Noël Coward who went on to find rich seams of material for comedy in the values underpinning a modern marriage and to introduce a new kind of heroine, the Amandas and Elviras whose attraction was not combined with any obvious desire for economic independence. As for Maugham, he had begun in his mind to phase himself out of play-writing. The process was a gradual one, continuing until the early 1930s. He still had several plays in him, such as *The Letter* adapted from the short story of that name which had first appeared in magazine form in 1924. A strong drama involving a mask of feminine falsehood it provided Gladys Cooper with a splendid vehicle.

[5.]

After this success there were at least two plays which never saw the light of day or night and then the famous four final plays of which the first in 1928 was *The Sacred Flame*.

Maugham's passion for metaphysical speculation that had been awakened by Kuno Fischer in Heidelberg all those years ago had found an outlet in an early play *The Unknown* (1920) in which John comes back from the war (like the protagonist in *The Hero*) at odds with his family and fiancée; his experiences on the battlefields of France and Belgium have turned him into a free-thinker. His father—like the Vicar of Whitstable—is a believer whose faith appears to crumble in the face of his own imminent death and his fiancée is a girl of strong character and unyielding conformity. Maugham neatly pin-points irreconcilable attitudes among his main characters:

Col. Wharton: The Christian doesn't fear death. His whole life is but a preparation for that awful moment. To him it is the shining gateway to life everlasting.

John: I should be sorry to think that life was nothing but a preparation for death. To my mind death is very unimportant. I think a man does best to put it out of his thoughts. He should live as though life were endless. Life is the thing that matters.

Sylvia: Doesn't that suggest a very base materialism?[17]

Soon the colonel's orthodoxy will have to face the test of a death sentence pronounced on him by his own doctor whose quiet professional scepticism is pitted against the brash Christianity of the local vicar. Maugham said that when the play was produced after the war the circumstances of the time helped it to a certain success. This was due in no little part to the irruption of a bereaved widow played by Haidée Wright who had lost both her sons in the war and demanded shrilly who was going to forgive God. The final act in which Sylvia tricks John into taking Communion by concealing the fact of his father's death is, as Maugham afterwards recognized, weak, and spoils the play as a whole.

It leads, however, to *The Sacred Flame* (written in 1928) which turns the story of Oedipus inside out. Here is a mother who kills her favourite son out of pity for him. Mrs. Tabret lived for many years while her husband was alive in India and it seems to have given her a belief in involuntary euthanasia. 'What I vaguely divined,' she says, 'was too stupendous to fit into the limits of any creed of men.' Nurse Wayland represents the Christian position and Stella the errant unfulfilled wife whose husband (like Clifford Chatterley) is paralysed from the waist down: she is the unthinking, beautiful, modern Isolde (she does in fact go off to hear Wagner's *Tristan* with her lover at the end of act one) torn between the claims of two brothers.

What gives the play its power is the smouldering scenes of suspicion after Maurice's death in which the naked emotion and passion bursts through the rationally-minded surface and swamps it. Maugham provides us with a remarkable combination of detection and metaphysics. The doctrine of the transmigration of souls hovers strangely over an Agatha Christie plot; the soul of the dead man, we are told, may be reborn in the child of his brother out of his wife's womb; and there is an attempt to delineate three distinct states of feeling on the part of the women—comradeship, pity and passionate love. If we compare Mrs. Tabret with the Edwardian Miss Ley as a source of wisdom we see how Maugham has moved to a new twentieth-century enlightenment tinged with oriental mysticism. In her farewell to Nurse Wayland, the self-interested defender of the faith, we can observe the displacement of one scale of values by another:

> Mrs Tabret: How ungenerous it would have been of me to resent the passion that bound him to Stella and the tender comradely habit that bound him to you. God bless you for the kindness you showed my poor Maurice and for the unselfish love you bore him.
>
> (She takes Nurse Wayland's hands and kisses her on both cheeks)
>
> Nurse Wayland (with a sob): I'm desperately unhappy.
>
> Mrs Tabret: Oh, my dear, you mustn't lose your admirable self-control. No one can make an omelette without breaking eggs . . .[18]

Love may take many different forms as Maugham hints in the quotation from Coleridge from which the play takes its title:

> All thoughts, all passions, all delights,
>   Whatever stirs this mortal frame,
> All are but ministers of Love
>   And feed his sacred flame.[19]

Maugham said that in this piece he tried to break out of the limitation of dialogue based on colloquial speech. He felt that the extreme colloquialism of Noël Coward and others represented a threat to the continuance of prose drama. 'I thought,' he explained, 'I would try to make my characters speak not the words they would actually have spoken, but in a more formal manner, using the phrases they would have used if they had been able to prepare them beforehand and had known how to put what they wanted to say in exact well-chosen language.' The passage of time has not rendered much of the experiment audible to the naked ear. The characters mainly talk just like other Maugham characters. Only when Mrs. Tabret is trying to explain the philosophical position behind her actions does the language become at all high-flown and then not for long. At any rate the experiment was not a success and it was not repeated when he came to write *The Breadwinner* in 1930.

There was nothing either mystical or metaphysical about this scintillating work. It is a straightforward comedy of 'men's lib.' that still holds the stage today whenever it is revived. Charles Battle, a stockbroker with a grown-up family and a mansion in Golders Green, has had enough. The threat of 'hammering' on the Exchange gives him a taste for freedom; as always in Maugham it is misfortune that brings liberation. The women surrounding him are forced for once to react to male initiative. Maugham makes each of them (wife, wife's friend, daughter and daughter's friend) find it impossible to accept the fact that she is not the cause of Battle's revolt. He seals it with the symbolic gesture of jumping on his top-hat in the middle of the second act. The comedy received better reviews in England than it did abroad even though objection was taken to the heartlessness of the mercenary young people in the first section and particularly to the daughter's line about the market for prostitution being ruined by amateurs, which in later performances had to be cut. Maugham's scathing treatment of these youngsters may be seen as his riposte to the bright young things of Noël Coward.

The actor, William Fox, who appeared as one of them in the original production of *The Breadwinner* tells me that when Maugham was approached to secure his agreement to the omission of a line or two he said, 'You've b-bought it. You can d-do what you like with it.' Unlike some playwrights Maugham was never stage-struck and unlike Anouilh, for instance, he never put the theatre itself into his plays. One of the very few utterances about the theatre on the stage does in fact come in this play when Battle's daughter confesses to him that she wants to be an actress. He tells her to be natural and when she replies that that ought to be easy he goes on to say:·

> It isn't. It's the result of infinite pains. It's the final triumph of artifice. And remember that society only looks upon you as a freak and the moment you're out of fashion drops you like a hot potato. Society has killed more good actors than drink. It's only your raw material. Let the footlights, at least spiritually, always hold you aloof.[20]

This remark is slightly out of context for Battle and we may be sure that it represents the considered view of the author. Certainly Maugham remained completely aloof from his public. He was not one of those playwrights who haunt the theatre while their own plays are being performed, savouring each laugh. If he happened to be in London he would more likely be found in the Garrick Club playing bridge of which he was an avid if middling player who hated losing. It is just worth pointing out, in our look at Maugham in the theatre, that his work as a playwright coincides with the rise and dominance of bridge as a game throughout Europe and America. Bridge first made an appearance on the stage in Maugham's *Smith* before the First World War where, as we saw, it became a kind of symbol for the indifference of the bourgeoisie to the plight of the unfortunate; it reappears continuously throughout his plays along with patience, bezique, piquet and chess. It is not too fanciful perhaps to see bridge as a kind of paradigm of the principles of construction on which his plays are based. In act one hands are hidden and bidding establishes a contract between playwright and audience; in act two play begins, the fall of the cards brings its surprises, the positioning of the trumps is intriguing and unexpected; in act three the inevitability of the previous play emerges as the playwright makes his contract with several tricks to spare.

How beautifully he finesses in *The Sacred Flame* using the intransigence of Nurse Wayland gradually to force the opponent's ace, the mother-murderess, in the last few moments of the drama and what classic roughing with Battle in *The*

Breadwinner as each of the women who try to weaken his resolve is trumped.

[5.]

In the few remaining hands that Maugham had to play in the theatre his skill remained as great as ever. It is hard to think of two works that better illuminate the mood of the ugly 'thirties in Britain than *For Services Rendered* and *Sheppey* with which the master left the table. If up to now he had shown us women who asserted the supremacy of their wills in affluent drawing-rooms he turned in these plays to paint a picture of women trapped in a social enclave where once again he who pays the piper calls the tune. *For Services Rendered* is a perfect illustration of Maugham's favourite doctrine that suffering does not ennoble but makes people bitter and ungenerous. On the surface all is serene in the little world of Leonard Ardsley, respected solicitor in rural Kent; the not so young people play their tennis and take their drinks while he sweats it out in his office. Then Maugham proceeds to rip that surface to shreds; he summoned the spirit of Strindberg to haunt the green pastures of English country house comedy. Mrs. Ardsley still clings to 'the pale distant shadow that is all you clever people have left me of God'. Her daughters and the other women do not even have this shadow with which to cling, only the men of straw to whom they are married or committed inescapably: an ex-naval lieutenant in financial trouble with his local garage business, a coarse-grained farmer whose officer style cracks under the strain of the empty peace. The son of the house is in worse plight having been blinded in the war and addresses himself to his tatting and games of chess with an embittered dignity; hovering in the background is a lecherous local plutocrat.

Among such menfolk what hope for the women? Gwen must put up a brave front knowing that Wilfred may bolt; Ethel a braver one as her husband's inferiority complex bursts out anti-Barrie like when he is in liquor ('The King made me a gentleman. His Majesty. I may only be a farmer now, but I've been an officer and a gentleman. And don't you forget it.'); Eva a yet

braver one still as she slowly goes out of her mind at the thought
of a life of servitude at the behest of her blind brother. Flora
Robson had a sensational success in this part, culminating in her
cracked mad rendering of *God Save the King*. Lois, the youngest
and prettiest, has a shabby escape-route open to her, that of
bolting with Wilfred, which she shabbily takes.

Agate's criticism that it did not seem proven that the war
could be blamed for such a concentration of ill-fortune among
one Kentish circle does not appear nearly so relevant now. The
play was a much truer expression of its period than
contemporaries were prepared to admit.

It had a disappointingly short run and Maugham said contemptuously afterwards that any dramatist could see how by
sentimentalizing it in a series of sugary happy endings it could
have been turned into a success. 'But,' he added, 'it would not
have been the play I wished to write.'[21] He also complained at
this time to an interviewer in *Theatre World* of the elaborate
mystique of the theatre and the ballyhoo surrounding it in the
newspapers. He looked forward to a time when plays that
lasted only an hour could be produced in simple unfussy sets so
that from the author's point of view the whole thing was more
like a short story.[22] He was unconsciously anticipating TV
drama. The last two works for the theatre to come from his
own pen were certainly not of this order; one was an adaptation
of Chiarelli's *The Mask and the Face*, about a supposed crime
passionel on the shore's of Lake Como that like his earlier play
with this setting remains unpublished. Originally produced in
New York by the Theatre Guild it never crossed the water to
the West End. The other, his theatrical swan-song, was
Sheppey: the nickname of a London barber who in 1933 wins
one of the residuary prizes (worth £8,500) in the Irish Sweep.
With his roots in Kent and his home in Camberwell, with his
professional pride and his empathy with human misery, his
lucky contentment and modesty of ambition, we have in Sheppey
the first fully rounded working-class character Maugham had
drawn since Liza. He stands within sight of the frontier of
middle-class life which his ghastly daughter has already crossed
in her mind in her intended marriage to a council schoolmaster:
but like the clerk in the early story in *Orientations* Sheppey has

had a revelation; his contact with outcast London has acted on him like 'a great white light' and determined him to spend his fortune Christ-wise among the poor and needy.

Desmond MacCarthy, who had a high regard for *Sheppey*, admired the way in which at the end of the first act the audience were totally mystified about how the play would develop and what effect his newly-acquired wealth would have on the hero; but once the secret was out several other critics led by Agate were disappointed. He talked of 'sentimental Galsworthy'. The work of Galsworthy's that has the closest parallel to *Sheppey* is *The Pigeon* (1912) in which a bourgeois artist called Wellwyn —the pigeon of the title who lets himself be plucked—invites down-and-outs back to his London studio. The play draws attention to the fact of spontaneous charity as a power of more positive good than religion, science or sociology. It is not without its humorous moments but it totally lacks the savage irony, the larger resonance of Maugham's bitter comedy.

Wellwyn has a daughter who is deeply opposed to his charitable activities: so has Sheppey and it is her hostility that becomes the mainspring of the final two acts. She is the modern girl in all her grisliness, the counterpart of stockbroker Battle's selfish kids in Golders Green. Maugham's most withering moment is when she prays aloud that her father may be certified as 'potty'. Her exchanges with Bessie Le Gros, the prostitute whom her father shelters under his roof, are full of superbly cutting innuendoes. Here are two devastating final portraits in Maugham's theatrical gallery of women.

The mistakes most critics made with *Sheppey*, which did not have a very long run, was to see it as the tragedy of a saint, when in fact it was the comedy of a philanthropist. True, Maugham followed Galsworthy's pattern in showing how the ingrained habit of crime is too strong for the thief to be rehabilitated, and the tart to be happy away from the streets, and that Sheppey is betrayed by most of those closest to him, but the defects are in him as much as in them. Maugham was content to leave the glory of a full-scale play about Christian theology to George Moore whose *The Passing of the Essenes* was also performed in 1933. Only Charles Morgan of the overnight critics was on the right tack; writing in *The Times* he said:

Mr Maugham has not written a play about a saint; he has written a play about the world's reluctance to part with its money, and has written it with fluency, judgment and wit—with everything, indeed, except that supreme devotion that might have exchanged success for a masterpiece.[23]

At the end of the play Sheppey dies in his own armchair and his devoted wife comments: 'He always said 'e was born lucky. He died lucky too.' She means that he was lucky not to have to suffer the further disruption to his peace of mind and status that his new wealth would impose. Several critics felt cheated by this easy way out and what they objected to even more was the way that Maugham, permitting himself a little *avant-garde* experiment, made the prostitute turn into the figure of Death and in a colloquy with the barber recite the old Arabian Night's tale of the merchant who had an appointment in Samarra as he pleads with her for stay of execution. No modern audience would turn a hair at this mild excursion into symbolism but it incensed Agate and totally baffled the first-nighters in spite of a fine performance by Ralph Richardson in the title role.

[6.]

It seems fitting that Maugham should have ended his career in the theatre with the appearance of a transfigured harlot as easeful maternal death. In these bitter last plays it has been the elderly maternal women, Mrs. Tabret, Mrs. Ardsley and Mrs. Miller, Sheppey's wife (who unlike her daughter meekly accepts all that her husband wishes to do) who have stood out as exemplars of charity, disinterestedness and goodness, almost but not quite obscured by the heavy concentration of egoism among which they dwell. It is as if he was saying that women when they have passed beyond their sexual nature are the beneficent force that holds society together. Mrs. Wilcox and Mrs. Moore have similar roles in E. M. Forster's novels.

After *Sheppey* Maugham wrote no more for the theatre though other writers, S. N. Behrman in *Jane* and Guy Bolton in *Larger Than Life* were to make successful plays from his work. He did, though, ponder the hazards of the business and the

qualities required for success in it. The fruits of these medita-
tions were given in the prefaces he wrote to the collected
edition of his plays and in *The Summing Up*. In spite of the
changes that have occurred in the theatre since Maugham's day
no would-be playwright can afford to neglect the opinions of the
old master; here is the basic grammar of stagecraft succinctly
and sardonically stated. One of the most far-reaching points he
made was that the kind of play he wrote was doomed very soon
to die the death:

> . . . I do not mean for any such foolish reason as that I have ceased
> to write. Realistic drama in prose is a form of art, though a minor
> one, and a minor art, responding to a particular state in civilisation,
> is likely to perish with a change in that state.[24]

He was wrong about this. Terence Rattigan's *French Without
Tears* first saw the light of the Criterion Theatre three years
after *Sheppey*; the spirit of dramatic insouciance that had
informed so many of Maugham's plays still had some life in it,
as was proved by the careers of Noël Coward and John Van
Druten among others. After the interregnum of poetic drama in
the post-war years realism had a renascence with a new liberty
of invective and oriented away from metropolitan moneyed
people. Yet as I write the old forms, and the old conflicts of
class even, seem to be returning to haunt the theatre like ghosts.

Watching the plays of his younger contemporaries Maugham
began to feel his age. The clipped conversational staccato of
Coward's dialogue made his seem almost ornate in its insistence on completed sentences. His characters had often behaved
in a manner that was deliberately shocking but the behaviour of
the new generation he found beyond any conceivable threshold
of shock. Under such conditions comedy became impossible.

Some years after he had retired from the theatre Maugham
amused himself by rewriting the plot of *The Second Mrs.
Tanqueray* to suit the moral ambience of the mid-1930s. Paula
has long since committed suicide. Aubrey Tanqueray's daughter
Ellean now has a son who is engaged to a respectable neighbour's daughter. He takes after his grandfather in that he has
had an affair with a high-class call-girl. Her stepmother decides
that this fact must be broken to Honor who greets the news

with this reaction: 'I was as pleased as Punch when I found out
. . . You see, darling, you can tell me if he's all right in bed.'
This was in the novel *Theatre* (1937) into which Maugham put
all that he had learned about the back-stage world of the
theatre just as he had put all that he had observed of the back-
stairs world of literature in his earlier and more famous novel
Cakes and Ale (1930). I would like now to turn to these two
works.

CHAPTER SEVEN

Bicycling Down Joy Lane

[1.]

'I HAVE NOTICED that when someone asks for you on the telephone and, finding you out, leaves a message begging you to call him up the moment you come in, as it's important, the matter is more often important to him than to you.' With this sentence Maugham begins his satirical-romance masterpiece, *Cakes and Ale* (1930). It is a style that conforms with the utmost quiet and decorum to Dryden's definition of good prose as the conversation of gentlemen, giving off that peculiar ironic bouquet that the vintage Maugham expert will be sniffing appreciatively until the stuff begins to run out in the 1950s. When he comes to open later bottlings he will find that the 'I have noticed that . . .' will more often than not give way to the mellower, fruitier flavour of 'I have a notion that . . .' to introduce a gnomic observation both obvious enough in itself, and pertinent to the story, but somehow hitherto unformulated in the mind of the reader.

The whole tone of it is too intimate, too even-tempered, too essayish for the theatre, but writing so many comedies for the stage has given the Master a perfection of humorous timing that he was never to lose, as we see in the next sentence: 'When it come to making you a present or doing you a favour most people are able to hold their impatience within reasonable bounds.' Then he gets down to business:

> So when I got back to my lodgings with just enough time to have a drink, a cigarette, and to read my paper before dressing for dinner, and was told by Miss Fellows, my landlady, that Mr Alroy Kear wished me to ring him up at once, I felt that I could safely ignore his request.

'Is that the writer?' she asked me?
'It is.'

It is all here, donnée, suspense, characters, viewpoint, relation-
ships, life-styles, all planted firmly in well under a hundred
words. Maugham tells us, in one of the various prefaces he
wrote for the book, that,

> It was as a short story, and not a very long one either, that I first
> thought of this novel. Here is the note I made when it occurred
> to me: 'I am asked to write my reminiscences of a famous novelist,
> a friend of my boyhood, living at W.[hitstable] with a common
> wife, very unfaithful to him. There he writes his great books.
> Later he marries his secretary, who guards him and makes him
> into a figure. My wonder whether even in old age he is not slightly
> restive at being made into a monument.' I was writing at the
> time a series of short stories for the *Cosmopolitan*. My contract
> stipulated that they were to be between twelve hundred and
> fifteen hundred words, so that with the illustration they should
> not occupy more than a page of the magazine ... I thought this
> story would do for this purpose, and put it aside for future use.
> But I had long had in mind the character of Rosie. I had wanted
> for years to write about her but the opportunity never presented
> itself; I could contrive no setting in which she found a place to
> suit her, and I began to think I never should ... It suddenly struck
> me that the little story I had jotted down offered me just the
> framework for this character that I had been looking for. I would
> make her the wife of my distinguished novelist. I saw that my
> story could never be got into a couple of thousand words, so I
> made up my mind to wait a little and use my material for one of
> the much longer tales, fourteen or fifteen thousand words, with
> which following upon *Rain*, I had not been unsuccessful. But the
> more I thought of it the less inclined I was to waste my Rosie on
> a story even of this length. Old recollections returned to me. I
> found I had not said all I wanted to say about the W. of the note,
> which in *Of Human Bondage* I had called Blackstable. After so
> many years I did not see why I should not get closer to the
> facts. The Uncle William, Rector of Blackstable, and his wife
> Isabella, became Uncle Henry, vicar, and his wife Sophie. The
> Philip Carey of the earlier book became the I of *Cakes and
> Ale*.[1]

Undoubtedly we feel the constant pressure of real, that is lived through, experience behind this novel, as we did in the earlier book, but in a much less painful manner. The ghosts of humiliation have been laid, and the evocation of his childhood world by the I-narrator, Willie Ashenden, a professional writer, is both agreeably nostalgic and acute. Whether the narrator is dwelling upon the calculating and ambitious men and women of the world of letters in which he now lives and has his being, or remembering those care-free, good-humoured, full-bodied, spontaneous characters of a now golden Edwardian era, Rosie and 'Lord' George Kemp, he never loses his own poise; and his shrewd play of mind full of witty asides and confidences is one of the delights of the novel.

During the decade and a half that has elapsed between *Of Human Bondage* and this book, Maugham has not merely read Proust more than once, but he has seen how what Swann called 'la terrible puissance recréatrice de sa memoire' could be made to work in a fresh patterning of his own life. If *Of Human Bondage* was in its structure a Victorian three-decker born after its time, *Cakes and Ale* resembles a pocket-sized Anglo-Saxon *Swann's Way*. The stultifying Murdstoneish prison of Blackstable vicarage, with its vulnerable deformed hero, has now turned into a lost paradise akin to Combray; and it has its own unforgettable Princesse de Guermantes, in the ample form of the local barmaid (whose original Mr. Calder identifies as the second daughter of Henry Arthur Jones, with whom Maugham had his great pre-marital affair).[2]

On one of his visits to Blackstable Willie Ashenden strolls down a road we have never been in or even heard of before. This is Joy Lane which he recalls as a rambling open prospect; now it has been developed and covered with houses and seaside bungalows. He hires a Daimler to take him out to Ferne Court where the second Mrs. Driffield lives and when he is inside the car he experiences, towards the end of the book, his most Proustian moment. The car has exactly the same aroma as 'the old landau which my uncle used to hire every Sunday morning to go to church in', and this scent acts on him like the madeleine. He is transported back in his memory to the front pew of Blackstable church and hears his aunt saying to him:

'Now, Willie, mind you behave nicely today. You're not to turn round, and sit up properly in your seat. The Lord's house isn't the place to loll in and you must remember you should set an example to other little boys who haven't had your advantages.'[3]

Cakes and Ale is an essentially humorous novel, the humour being of a peculiarly inbred kind. It belongs to the tradition of fiction about the profession of letters that begins with *Pendennis* and continues so scathingly with *New Grub Street*[4] and the tales about authorship by Henry James and Beerbohm. The concern in all these works is professional and personal integrity. Gissing makes the point, epitomized by his hero Jasper Milvain, a triumphant literary maid-of-all-work, that success can only be attained by a complete surrender of an individual's precious essence of honesty to the market forces boosting inferior work, and he makes the corresponding point, exemplified by the denizens of Grub Street, who are so accurately depicted in the book, that failure and the preservation of integrity are synonymous. It was a point, alas, that Gissing saw exemplified in his own career, as many another failed author has done after him but with much less justice, usually. Maugham's position was completely different: no author can have been less soured by failure than he was when he wrote *Cakes and Ale*. He was at the height of his post-First World War fame. The Kelly portraits and the photographs of him at this time show a brisk, moustached, military-looking, middle-aged man, alert and in command. He had purchased the Villa Mauresque at Cap Ferrat in 1928, so that after separating from his wife, he and Gerald could live out of England in style when they were not on their travels.[5] His plays were being performed and revived all over the world; his short stories were appearing regularly in Hearst's *International Magazine* in America and Nash's in England. Translations of his books into foreign tongues were spreading the Maugham gospel far and wide. Critical appraisals of his fiction were beginning to appear in French and in Finnish. Whatever his motive in attempting to blow the gaff on the literary racket, it could hardly have been a sense of failure. The view from the terrace of his newly-acquired villa was a rosy one as far as his own future as a writer was concerned.

[2.]

If he had become a permanent expatriate it was nonetheless in an essentially insular English context that he presented his findings about the mechanics of reputation-making. He uses his new Proustian freedom to modulate not only between past and present, innocence and experience, but also between London and Whitstable. In both places the same social configurations, the same class prejudices and snobbish taboos, that were, as we have seen, such a feature of Maugham's early work, remain; and the idea that somehow subsumed them all, that of the conduct proper to a gentleman, provides Maugham with his motivation once again. 'Gentleman' is the key-word in the book and the one which, admirers of it will remember, it so brilliantly ends.

Maugham had examined gentlemanly conduct in the social world and along a vast frontier of private life; in his tales he was to examine it still many times wielding authority in tropical climes. Here in *Cakes and Ale* he focuses upon its operations in the intrigues of literary life. Hence the choice of Hugh Walpole —and I suppose after all the fuss and Maugham's contradictory denials and admissions we had better agree that it *was* Walpole —as the model for Alroy Kear, the smoothest operator in the business. Walpole was born into the purple. His father was a distinguished cleric and academic. Maugham gave Kear a comparably illustrious background ('. . . *o.s.* of Sir Raymond Kear, K.C.M.G., K.C.V.O., *q.v.*, and of Emily, *y.d.* of the late Major-General Percy Camperdown, Indian Army'). By contrast, Ted Driffield was a Blackstable local, son of a bailiff, raised in the parish but with that mysterious, authentic, creative gift that Maugham always delighted to find flowering in the most unexpected places.

In the closed society of Blackstable gentility, *circa* 1890, he was clearly a highly undersirable companion for the vicar's nephew and, for this reason alone, one of powerful attraction to the boy. Willie's first encounter with him shows Driffield more in the character of H. G. Wells (justifying Maugham's statement that he was a composite portrait) than Hardy. Willie had taken his new bicycle along to Joy Lane to learn how to ride it where, as it happened, the Driffields were engaged in the same pursuit. The whole atmosphere of light-hearted fun is pure Wells, reminding one of his jolly novel, *The Wheels of Chance*. Driffield offers to give the lad a cycling lesson. Though reluctant because conscious of the social gulf, Willie finds that he is 'unable to withstand his friendly violence'. Under Driffield's guidance he pedals away furiously,

> ... and Mrs. Driffield ran into the middle of the road with her arms akimbo shouting: 'Go it, go it, two to one the favourite,' *I was laughing so much that I positively forgot all about my social status.*[6] (My italics.)

It is thus by breaking out of the social pale in Blackstable that young Willie finds the father and mother substitutes that eluded Philip Carey until he met the Athelneys in London. Among Maugham's great harlot characters, Liza, Mildred, Sadie Thompson, Bessie Le Gros, Rosie is in a class by herself for abundant warmth and spontaniety, realized in a series of masterly portraits throughout the book, that remind one of paintings by Wilson Steer and Matthew Smith. Later on, when Driffield has reached his lonely eminence as the grand old man of English letters, she will have become the skeleton in the cupboard for his biographer, Alroy Kear. In the event it is a skeleton richly endowed with human flesh as Willie discovers when, in seedy Sickert-like London lodgings, he achieves the ultimate Oedipal satisfaction of sleeping with her.

Before that, however, he must suffer several more rude shocks to his inherited system. The first of them is when at the end of his holidays he goes back to boarding school in Tercanbury and the Driffields are there at the station to see him off. As the train is leaving Driffield presses a small package into his hand. It consists of two half-crowns wrapped in a piece of toilet-paper. 'I blushed to the roots of my hair . . . he must see how impossible it was for a gentleman to accept a tip from someone who was practically a stranger.' The youth swallows his rage as he covets the extra five shillings. 'But I assuaged my wounded pride by not writing to thank Driffield for the gift.' In Whitstable, later in the holidays, he suffers a sense of isolation in the Verdurin-like little circle of army and clergy and other local worthies when they discuss his new friend and his books.

'Can he write?' asked Mrs. Encombe.

'You can tell at once that he's not a gentleman,' said the curate, but when you consider the disadvantages he's had to struggle against it's rather remarkable that he should write as well as he does.'[7]

Maugham has fun showing the purely literary implications of this kind of social prejudice, how it influences judgements about Dickens's writing, but he goes on to demonstrate that there is some truth in it. Soon after this the Driffields *do* behave in the most ungentlemanly way, outraging the entire community of the town: they shoot the moon, upsticking with all their belongings, leaving their creditors to whistle for their money; it was a not uncommon practice of members of the Edwardian working-class, intolerably crippled by debt. Marie Lloyd's famous song, 'My old man says follow the van . . .', is about a woman absconding *à la* Driffield.[8] The episode comes as a nasty jolt to young Willie. He learns from it that people who lift one out of oneself onto a plane of pure enchantment nearly always let one fall to earth with a sickening thud. 'I was much more shocked than Mary-Ann [the maid]. I was a very respectable youth. The reader cannot have failed to observe that I accepted the conventions of my class as if they were the laws of Nature . . .'[9]

If the ethics of their social conduct provide one shock to the lad, their sexual morals produce another. 'Lord' George, 'exuberant, flashy, loud, and boisterous', with his brown bowler tilted rakishly back on his head, is a second father-figure, standing for everything liberatingly antithetical to the values of the vicar of Whitstable. It is when Willie observes that his affair with Rosie continues *after* her marriage to Driffield that another blow has been struck against the conventions of his class. Later he recognizes that though they may have been unreliable and immoral, these people had a life-enhancing vigour and a generosity that has been lost during the years that he has come to manhood. Certainly it is completely absent from the

drawing-rooms of the London literary world in which Driffield
in his years of fame and eminence gained acceptance.

The whole process of that acceptance involving the
manœuvres of Mrs. Barton Trafford, the literary hostess—a
development of a type first sketched in Mrs. Strickland—is one
of the great satirical joys of the book. Behind her genteel
exterior Mrs. Trafford commands all the resources of the
modern public relations firm. Her lionizing takes the form of
lion-making and lion-taming and it is as a caged beast (but one
ready to spring to liberty when the moment is ripe) that
Driffield now appears to the narrator. He experiences that
delectable Proustian shock of encountering someone known only
in a past context in a present one that is completely different
and trying to discover if there is any connection between the
figure then and the one now.

Considering that *Cakes and Ale* has no less than three
novelists as major characters Maugham manages remarkably
well to give us an idea not only of their totally different personalities but also of their work. He praises Driffield for his
portraits of rustics confessing to a great distaste for the kind
of novel he wrote. That, clearly, is founded on the work of
Hardy, but then the picture is fudged deliberately by the
remark that his style took on more life when he began to dictate
his books, which must refer to Henry James. In the suggestion
that his final apotheosis was brought about neither by the
strenuous efforts of Mrs. Barton Trafford, nor those of his
second wife, but merely through his own longevity (something,
says Maugham, that the English can never resist, though they
did partly resist it in his own case) we are presumably back to
Hardy.

Towards the end of his own long life Maugham seemed to go
out of his way to make the kind of revelations about himself that
Kear was determined to avoid in his life of Driffield. But in the
1930s he could not have anticipated the degree of frankness
about the most intimate details of the private life to which the
art of biography and autobiography has reached today, when
the son of two pillars of the literary establishment has written a
book showing how both his parents were homosexuals, and how
well the marriage worked in spite of that, or when the nephew

of the queen of Bloomsbury has described with utter frankness the attempts made by his father upon the virtue of his aunt, it is hard to imagine what all the fuss was about over the first Mrs. Driffield.

But fifty years ago the view still persisted that a writer's life should be in as good taste as his work, and therefore the disreputable aspects of Driffield's early Blackstable years represented a very real problem for Alroy Kear in writing his life. Ashenden and Kear discuss the difficulty in a conversation that goes to the heart of the novel:

> '. . . I don't want to say anything that's untrue, but I do think there's a certain amount that's better left unsaid.'
>
> 'Don't you think it would be more interesting if you went the whole hog and drew him, warts and all?'
>
> 'Oh, I couldn't. Amy Driffield would never speak to me again. She only asked me to do the life because she felt she could trust my discretion. I must behave like a gentleman.'
>
> 'It's very hard to be a gentleman and a writer.'
>
> 'I don't see why . . .'[10]

If Alroy Kear ever finished his biography of Driffield one can imagine the beautifully bland and discreet job he made of it, comparable to those early lives of Dickens containing no mention of Ellen Ternan. In fact this whole skeleton-in-the-cupboard theme in *Cakes and Ale* is itself part of the satire; it is a parody of the kind housemaid's trash novelettes that Mary-Ann and her like enjoyed, and it is also a brilliant device for keeping the reader on his toes while Maugham pursues his main Proustian objectives, the nature of the literary life and the resurgence of character across the intervals of time. In his essay on *War and Peace* Maugham admired the way Tolstoy gave a new dimension to the perfunctory epilogues of the older novelists by telling us what really happened to the principal characters after the story proper is over, 'Natasha, who was so sweet, so unpredictable, so delightful, is now a fussy, exacting, shrewish housewife.'[11] In the same way he tells us what happened to Rosie years after all the other characters have given her up for dead. Lord George, her great love, had in his latter days struck it rich with Tammany Hall in New York and left her comfortably off. Ashenden rediscovers her as a white-permed, bridge-playing matron in Yonkers, still capable of drawing admirers even in her seventies.

Rosie seems thus to be one of those people who have the power of continual renewal. Age does not wither her. Maugham implies through the reflections of Ashenden that this is one of the great rewards of authorship, too, rather than the fashionable and ephemeral reputations created in the Barton Trafford ambience. As a young man he suggested that the life of medicine gave its practitioner great personal freedom but now, when he returns to Blackstable and recognizes a man he had been at school with who is the local doctor, he reflects:

> His life was over. I had plans in my head for books and plays, I was full of schemes for the future; I felt that a long stretch of activity and fun still lay before me; and yet, I supposed, to others I must seem the elderly man that he seemed to me.[12]

The other reward of the literary career in Maugham's eyes is one that I have already mentioned, catharsis. Maugham tries to show it in action, as it were, in *Cakes and Ale*. Unlike other mortals a writer has the power to transmute the bitter dross of life's miseries into the pure gold of literary art. Throughout the book there are references to a major novel of Driffield's called *The Cup of Life* that occupies the same place in Driffield's œuvre that *Jude the Obscure* does in Hardy's. It has a very harrowing scene in it, parallel to the Father Time episode, where a child dies in hospital, and we are to suppose that this incident had an original in life, based on the death of a son that Rosie had by Driffield. (Could Maugham have known anything, or guessed anything, about Hardy's wild oats days in Dorset?) Rosie's immediate reaction to the death was to go to Romanos with an old friend, eat a jolly good meal and then make love. The whole thing is the *locus classicus* of Maugham's view of how an artist stores up the wounds of life and then regurgitates them. Driffield 'used' the episode for his book and Maugham makes several points that tell one a lot about his own practice as a novelist: first, that Driffield guessed at Rosie's behaviour and got it right in essence but not in detail; second, that the episode was never discussed or even referred to by either party;

third, that Driffield behaved afterwards with infinite kindness
and tact; and fourth, that by objectifying the incident in a novel
he was released from it for ever. Maugham emphasises what he
was to reiterate often later that because he possesses this power
of self-absolution the writer is the only free man. *Cakes and Ale*
is one of the wisest, wittiest and wickedest books ever written
about authorship.

[3.]

As someone who was endlessly fascinated not just by the
creative process but by what happens to people who adopt it as a
profession, and how it affects the private self, it was inevitable
that sooner or later he would write a novel about an actor or an
actress. In fact he waited until 1937, when he published
Theatre. Against all those Maugham heroines described in the
last chapter one must put, as a kind of pay-off to them, Julia
Lambert who might during her triumphantly successful career
have impersonated any one of them. Now, in the more intimate
form of fiction, Maugham penetrates behind appearance and
shows us the inner woman manipulating the actress. This use
of a matinée idol as a figure of what one may call the aesthetic
dilemma, the inroads made by the creative life on personal
integrity, was not new to Maugham. In that fine subtle treatment at the turn of the century by Henry James, *The Tragic
Muse*, he says of his heroine Miriam Rooth, the exotic
adornment of the *Comédie Française*:

> As soon as she stepped on the boards a great and special alteration
> usually took place in her—she was in focus and in her frame; yet
> there were hours too in which she wore her world's face before the
> audience; just as there were hours when she wore her stage face
> in the world.[13]

There are a great many hours when Maugham's Julia wears her
stage face in the world. The question is simply whether she ever
wears anything else, whether after she has become a household
name she has any other face at all. There is an exquisitely
amusing episode in which, conscious of her failing powers of

attraction, she decides to reward an old and loyal flame by at long last allowing him to sleep with her, only to discover that this is not what he wants at all. Maugham gives us a brilliant account of her bearing throughout this most distressing evening, how she begins by modelling herself on Romney's portraits of Lady Hamilton and how at the moment of truth ('Christ, he doesn't want me. It was all a bluff') she turns a gesture of welcome into one of renunciation. For most of the book Maugham shows us Julia's sexual needs creating entanglements in her career. She is seduced by a fellow-passenger on the blue train to Nice in a way that is somewhat similar to the account in Mary MacCarthy's later story, 'The Man in the Brooks Brothers Suit', while her main affair as a relief from her magnificently handsome, gentlemanly, but unfortunately impotent husband, is with a young accountant whose one ambition is to be a gentleman.

Theatre is not a novel for the stage-struck. It reflects accurately Maugham's disillusioned aloofness from the theatre, but the interesting thing about this aloofness is that it does not preclude a passionately held belief in the theatre as a process of absolution. It is this aspect of the novel, Julia's creativity alongside her hypocrisy, that gives it a significance more lasting than a dozen similar stories about sex-mad actresses. Maugham analyses her skill at creating character in a passage where one feels he is closely identifying with her:

> She was not aware that she deliberately observed people, but when she came to study a new part vague recollections surged up in her from she knew not where, and she found that she knew things about the character that she had had no inkling of. It helped her to think of someone she knew or even someone she had seen in the street or at a party: she combined with this recollection her own personality, and thus built up a character founded on fact but enriched with her experience, her knowledge of technique and her amazing magnetism . . . It often seemed to her that she was two persons, the actress, the popular favourite, the best-dressed woman in London, and that was a shadow; and the woman she was playing at night, and that was the substance.[14]

Julia's theatrical education and upbringing is analogous to Maugham's literary one. Like Lily Langtry she was born in

Jersey and became bilingual in English and French. Before
going to R.A.D.A. she had lessons from a *sociétaire* of the
Comédie Française and heard tales of Bernhardt, Coquelin and
Mounet-Sully; then she did her stint in the hard school of
provincial rep. during the period of the naturalistic play—
'Ibsen, Shaw, Barker, Sudermann, Hankin, Galsworthy'—and
met her future husband while he was Oswald and she was
Regina in *Ghosts*. Years later, at the height of her fame when
things in London had got too much for her, Julia returns to her
relatives, now in St. Malo, where she discovers that her cele-
brityhood is an embarrassment rather than an asset and she
muses upon the provincial tedium of the life led by her mother
and aunt:

> The strange thing was that they were content. They knew neither
> malice nor envy. They had achieved the aloofness from the common
> ties of men that Julia felt in herself when she stood at the footlights
> bowing to the applause of an enthusiastic audience. Sometimes she
> had thought that aloofness her most precious possession. In her it
> was born of pride; in them of humility. In both cases it brought one
> precious thing, liberty of spirit; but with them it was more secure.[15]

Like Maugham Julia finds a compensation for the frustrations of
a disorderly private life in the creative act—we now see what
Charles Battle meant when he advised his daughter, who
wanted to become an actress, to remain aloof behind the footlights—and like Maugham, too, Julia remains highly competitive in her aloofness, as we learn hilariously in the most famous
passage in the novel when she steals the scene from an up-and-
coming young actress in the post-Pinero play *Nowadays* by
waving a red scarf about during all her most important lines.
(This was supposed to be founded on an episode in the career
of Marie Tempest, but the same story has been told of half a
dozen famous actresses.) After all her sexual humiliations Julia
ends the book a happy woman: she makes a great intellectual
discovery as she dines alone on a juicy steak in the Berkeley
grill after the performance; it is that when she brings to life a
fictitious character on the stage she has created something more
real than reality: 'Thus Julia out of her own head framed anew
the platonic theory of ideas' and thus she points the way to one

of Maugham's future lines of speculation in both his fiction and his more personal writing.

It is easy to tire of a character such as Julia, despite Maugham's wit, when one has to live with her throughout an entire novel. He was only too aware of the problem himself, which is why he had turned ten years earlier to the short story again. He had written 'Rain' at the age of 46, and he had had great difficulty getting this work accepted by a magazine. Eventually it was bought by H. L. Mencken and published in *The Smart Set* in 1920. After that Maugham went on to write story after story until he gave up some time after the Second World War. 'I liked the form. It was very agreeable to live with the personages of my fancy for two or three weeks and then be done with them. One had no time to grow sick of them as one easily may during the months one has to spend in their company when writing a novel.'[16] Let us see now who these personages were and the kind of lives they led.

CHAPTER EIGHT

Streaks of Yellow

[1.]

AT THE END of *The Circle* Teddy and Elizabeth bolt for the
Federated Malay States. It is, we saw, the happy ending to the
perfect comedy; after reading those stories that Maugham
actually set in the Federated Malay States and the South Seas
in *The Trembling of a Leaf* (1921), *The Casuarina Tree* (1925)
and *Ah King* (1933), with their riveting accounts of what the
happy couple were in for when they got there, one can only
mutter, 'God help them.' Did Elizabeth discover, for instance,
like the newly-wed wife in 'The Force of Circumstance', that
Teddy had a native mistress by whom he had already had three
children and when she complained that she could not bear to
think 'of those thin black arms of hers round you', did he explain
disarmingly in the words of Guy: 'I wasn't in love with her, not
even at the beginning. I only took her so as to have somebody
about the bungalow.' Or did she find, like Millicent Skinner in
'Before the Party', that he was an alcoholic of such magnitude
that the Resident had told him to find a wife on his next leave in
England and snap out of it or else? Or was she shown, like Mrs.
Hamlyn in 'P. & O.', the spectacle of his faraway native mistress's spell working on him so that he hiccuped to death before
the dismayed eyes of the callow young ship's doctor? Or did she
find, like Anne Torel in 'The Door of Opportunity', he was
afraid to go out and quell a rising of coolies, making her the
laughing-stock of all the other white women? Or that, like Mark
in 'The Book-Bag', he had been having an incestuous love-affair
with his sister who promptly committed suicide on her arrival?
Or did it work the other way and like Olive Cartwright in
'Footprints in the Jungle', did *she* become enamoured of a

gentleman down on his luck to whom her husband offered a job and who shot her spouse dead one day when he was returning home with the coolies' wages with her connivance? Or like Violet Moon in 'The Back of Beyond', did she plan to bolt with a fellow-planter friend of her husband's but at the eleventh-hour did he shilly-shally on discovering she was pregnant and kill himself on the boat on the way home?

The mind boggles at the thought of what might have happened to them in that Maugham country he called Malaya. What kind of resemblance, if any, did it bear to the place where so many of Maugham's countrymen spent happy and fruitful working lives between the wars? Let us listen for a moment to the words of one who knew the place intimately:

> There is no unrest in Malaya, [stated Cuthbert Woodville Harrison in his *Illustrated Guide to the Federated Malay States*, third impression 1920]. The country is perfectly quiet and the people contented. The object of all classes in British Malaya is not to covet other men's goods nor to desire other men's possessions in life, but still to labour truly to get their own living. Neither Malays nor Chinese are of a litigious nature. The Malays especially have a strong contempt for the hedge-lawyer, and, as Muhammadans, sedition is especially abhorrent to them. It is a very rich country, full of valuable mineral deposits, and also one of those gardens of earth which when tickled laughs itself into harvest. The people in it are either connected with the tin industry or the planting industry. If they are foreign to the soil their object is to make a fortune from it and retire home; if they are native Malays their object is to continue in that state of peasant proprietorship in which they have always so far found sufficient happiness. There is no street in any town which is not perfectly safe for Europeans who conduct themselves properly, but, as elsewhere, if people insist on prying into the dark and unsavoury places which exist all the world over in every considerable town, and there get in to trouble, they will have only themselves to blame.[1]

Happy, happy land! But wherever he went in East or West Maugham spent a great deal of his life prying into 'the dark and unsavoury places which exist all the world over', particularly those within the hearts of middle-class English men and women. For him Malaya and Borneo and the South Seas were arenas in which to observe people's characters determining their destiny;

for him as for Kipling and Conrad the isolated Outstation was a Great Good Place where the real man emerged. In his Introduction to *A Choice of Kipling's Prose* he acknowledged his debt:

> ... in his discovery of the exotic story [Maugham wrote] he opened up a new and fruitful field to writers. This is the story, the scene of which is set in some country little known to the majority of readers, and which deals with the reactions upon the white man with his sojourn in an alien land and the effect which contact with peoples of another race has upon him. Subsequent writers have treated this subject in their different ways, but Rudyard Kipling was the first to blaze the trail through this new-found country, and no one has invested it with a more romantic glamour, no one has made it more exciting and no one has presented it more vividly and with such a wealth of colour.[2]

For Maugham it meant that he was able to examine far greater extremes of behaviour than might occur within the confines of a London drawing-room. Such *crimes passionels*, apparently so foreign to the English temperament, as wife killing lover, lover killing husband, could be made to seem not merely possible and probable but even inevitable in the harsh light of a tropical sun. He needed, as we saw from the notebook entry on 'Rain', to be given only a hint from his own or other people's experience (mined for him as often as not in bibulous conversation among planters or officials by Gerald) to fashion a classically proportioned drama of moral failure. Let us observe him setting about his task with the episode of the Bore.

In Borneo they talked about the Bore meaning not some tiresome superior in the administration but a huge tidal wave that by reason of the peculiarity of the lie of the land surged up certain rivers. In 1922 Maugham and Gerald Haxton were travelling up the Sarawak River when the Bore suddenly came upon them. 'It was a great mass of water,' the novelist recorded later in his *Notebook*, 'eight, ten, twelve feet high, and it was quite plain at once that no boat could weather it.'[3] The boatmen who were prisoners from the up-country jail lost control of the boat and both they and the English travellers were tipped out into the water. They clung onto the side of the boat as the waves dashed over them, praying for the Bore to pass. Instead the boat upturned, swung round and round like a wheel, making it extremely difficult to keep hold of. Maugham was physically the weaker and he began to tire first. Gerald stayed by him and tried to give him a hand but there was not much he could do against the fierce swirl. The crew, who were also clinging on, noticed Maugham's exhaustion. A thin mattress floated past. They rolled it up somehow and gave it to Maugham as a life-belt. He clung to it with one hand and with the other struck out for the shore some forty or fifty yards away. Gerald followed and two members of the crew swam with them, one keeping close to Maugham. Gerald touched bottom first; they both waded through the mud and slithered onto the bank. They were covered in black mud from head to foot. Then Gerald had a heart attack. Maugham, wearing his dripping shirt as a loin-cloth, thought his friend was going to die. But he recovered and they were both taken by canoe to a Dyak long-house where they spent the night.

The Bore reappears in a story published three years later entitled 'The Yellow Streak'.[4] Two men, a planter and a mining engineer, Campion and Izzart, go off together up-country by boat and they encounter the Bore in all its fury just as Maugham and Haxton did. The external description is an almost word for word transcript of the onset of the Bore as it appears in the *Notebook*. But what of the two men's reactions? Maugham analysed his own emotions after the event and was surprised to note that at no time during the whole thing had he been at all frightened. 'I suppose the struggle was so severe that there was no time for any emotion.' In the story, however, he makes Izzart terrifield to the point of utter funk and when he hears Campion calling for help he pretends he has not heard; he clutches at a floating oar and swims to the shore, saving his own skin. He imagines that Campion has been drowned. He is horror-struck when he sees him coming ashore later. For the rest of the story we watch Izzart's character fall apart under the stress of believing that Campion will betray his moment of cowardice. Izzart's shame forces to the surface of his mind something that has slowly been dawning on us through a series of subtly planted clues, notably his over-zealous adoption of the gentlemanly mask, it is the fact of his mixed native and white blood. It is this he feels, rationalizing his shame, that must have been responsible for the cowardly manner in which he acted. Meanwhile Campion behaves with unchanged sang-froid, not having realized that there was anything unworthy about Izzart's conduct, and only through his companion's extraordinary subsequent behaviour, realizing that his nature contains what he calls 'a yellow streak', as he bids him at the end of the tale, 'Have a cheroot, dear boy.' It is a neatly wrought reversal: the common little man turns out to be the gentleman, the Harrovian to be the cad.

In his plays, which be it remembered were being written and produced concurrently with these exotic tales throughout the 1920s, Maugham used comedy in its traditional role of uncovering the basic assumptions of a society and putting forward alternative ones in striking antitheses of character and attitude. In his short stories he performs the same feat, even at times working on the same antitheses. The degree to which drama and short story might be interchangeable may be seen in the comparative ease which he himself was able to adapt 'The Letter' for the stage and others were able to make such a vastly successful play out of 'Rain'. Both these stories have the same structure of a man or a woman weakening under pressure until we peer into the inmost recesses of the soul, the outward mask stripped away. In both it is the relentless pressure of a person's sexual energy that endangers his social mask. Maugham inherited this story pattern of the steady attrition of an individual's resolution from his master Maupassant, who loved to show how the pressure of time could weaken the stoutest resolve (as in 'Boule de Suif', for instance). The short story has the inestimable advantage over the novel that the whole span of time in which this process occurs may be conveniently encompassed by the mind of the reader. In the much longer form of the novel you live through a great deal of time but you have difficulty at the end of it seeing the process as a single whole. Whereas at the end of 'The Yellow Streak' we have in our minds an absolutely complete picture of the pattern of Izzart's degeneration, just as we do that of Cooper in 'The Outstation', Leslie Crosbie in 'The Letter', Mackenzie's in the story to which he gives his name,

Gallagher in 'P. & O.', Lawson's in 'The Pool'. (In the latter the protagonist is a man of culture whose degeneration occurs after he has married a half-caste and he quotes from 'The Hound of Heaven', a poem with the Christian pattern of last-minute regeneration after a relentless pursuit through time.)

The fact that in so many of these stories degeneration begins through sexual contact with women of the native population, or through an attempt to defy the rigid paternalistic code of the white ruling administration, is not likely to endear Maugham to the modern liberal-minded reader. It is of course a fact that some members of the administration did have native mistresses. They were not all saints and celibates. But did this involve them in inevitable catastrophe, as Maugham implies? Not according to one historian at least, writing about Sarawak in the 1920s. Steven Runciman says in *The White Rajahs*:

> The 'unprintable' things seem merely to have been the possession by several of the officials of local mistresses drawn from the indigenous people. This was, in fact, far less dangerous to the well-being of the country than the growing tendency amongst the newly come wives towards a 'Mem-sahib' attitude with regard to non-Europeans, whom they tried to exclude from their Club. Such behaviour ran counter to the whole tradition of Sarawak and was kept as far as possible in check.[4]

It is this latter sort of social nuance, to which E. M. Forster was so alive in the Indian context, that Maugham passes over in his fixation with inter-racial sex. Several of his stories turn on the passion of a white man for a coloured woman and in none is the outcome a happy one. One of the most skilful is *The Force of Circumstance* where the native woman is barely seen but her presence is felt throughout the whole story preying upon the mind of the English wife. Guy's affair with a half-caste woman was purely circumstantial in origin, yet in the end it proves more durable than his marriage.

There is a comparison to be drawn between Guy's situation and that of the hero of a story of Kipling's Maugham enormously admired called 'Without Benefit of Clergy',[5] about an Indian girl of 16 who had become the wife of a young district officer. There can never have been a more enchanting heroine for a story than Ameera with her archaic love-talk and her joy at presenting her lord with a son. She comes vividly alive as a human being caught up in the awful mechanism of fate just as much as her husband—and so do the more minor native members of the household, Pir Kahn, the grey-haired janitor, her covetous old mother, little Tota the apple of his parents' eyes; even Mian Mittu, the parrot. Love between members of different races may be doomed but here and now, until the cholera strikes, they are all *dans le vrai*. What destroys them is a blind natural force stemming from the indifferent and inscrutable Powers to which all are subject and against which propitiation is of no avail. The paradoxical impression left by the tale is one of affirmation.

It serves among other things to show up one of Maugham's limitations, to which he freely admitted, as a historian of the latter-day colonial scene. He was capable of identifying only with the ruling caste; the nearest he gets to Ameera is Daisy in *East of Suez* (and for that he needs the help of a Meggie Albanesi) or perhaps Waddington's Manchu mistress in *The Painted Veil*. He does not grant his native characters fictional parity of esteem with his white ones: they are either sinister, shadowy figures in the background, like the blackmailing Singapore lawyer's clerk, Ong Chi Sen, who fixes up the deal in 'The Letter', or they are mere agents of the white man's degeneration with occult powers to help them sometimes. Maugham formed his view of what such a relationship would inevitably lead to during his first visit to the South Seas and gave expression to it in 'The Pool', where the cultivated hero Lawson makes the fatal mistake of allowing his sense of a life more natural than any he had known before trap him into a marriage with a beautiful half-caste Samoan girl. As a crude down-to-earth mining-engineer comments:

> He was a darned fool to marry her. I said so at the time. If he hadn't, he'd have had the whip hand over her. He's yaller, that's what he is, yaller.

Lawson takes his lovely wife back to Scotland with him but the chill local waters (where she shatters the locals by bathing by herself) prove no substitute for the idyll of the pool and, when he follows her back to Samoa, he has lost so much status as to be of no consequence in the eyes of his fellow-whites and is horribly exploited by his native in-laws. It is a retelling of the expulsion from the Garden of Eden, the moral being—don't try to do a Gauguin if you lack his ruthless genius. The vision gained and lost appears again in 'Red': where an obese American sailor returns to Samoa to hear from a white settler the story of how a handsome young seaman fell in love with the beauty of the island, and had an affair with a native girl: we discover at the end of the recital that this revolting old soak is himself the one-time Red. The squat, bulging woman his former love has turned into fails to recognize him.

Contact with native blood through sex leads always to disaster, so does the presence of it in the individual himself— as in a much later and very nasty story 'Flotsam and Jetsam' set in Borneo. Norman Grange is a crypto-white man; he has been born and bred in Borneo and this gives him a hopeless sense of isolation from his fellow-whites and turns him into the sort of cross, disagreeable fellow who would shoot his wife's lover and then continue to live with her in a Zolaesque hell. The Granges' one consolation (since their rubber estate is barely successful enough to enable them to make both ends meet) is to read a lot, Grange's preference being for writers like Lamb and Borrow.

This seems to be the other fatal thing, to be at all intellectually or literary-minded. That was the trouble with the appropriately-named young D. O. Alban in 'The Door of Opportunity' in the collection *Ah King*. He was a brilliant linguist in Chinese—but he refused to play football. His wife put reproductions of Gauguin and Marie Laurencin on the walls of their bungalow and at night they would listen to Alban playing Debussy on the piano and reflect on the characters of the other administrators and planters in a very superior way:

> At fifty they had the outlook of hobbledehoys. Most of them drank a great deal too much. They read nothing worth reading. Their ambition was to be like everybody else. Their highest praise was to say that a man was a damned good sort. If you were interested in the things of the spirit you were a prig. They were eaten up with envy of one another and devoured by petty jealousies. And the women, poor things, were obsessed by petty rivalries. They made

a circle that was more provincial than any in the smallest town in England.

Alban's attitude, so bitterly resented by the other white men, proves to be hubristic. When he has to quell a riot in his district among the Communist-inspired Chinese coolies he holds back out of a kind of arrogant caution rather than real cowardice, but this is enough to break what promised to be a brilliant career. Maugham's technique here of telling the story in the form of an extended playback is seen at its most masterly. It starts with their arrival at Tilbury and everything is implied in the first sentence: 'They got a first-class carriage to themselves.' Then we flash back to the moment when Alban did not go through the door of opportunity and while Anne thinks back over it all we slowly realize that the end of this particular journey means the end of her loyalty. It is this last blow that really proves too much for him. The brilliant intellectual and scholar turns into a sobbing rejected child as his wife rushes blindly out of the room for good. Alban's degeneration is complete.

It is interesting that Maugham should share with Kipling and other popular writers of his generation this contempt for the intellectual in the world of action. Is it at heart a form of self-contempt? If he had gone into the colonial service he would have been like Alban, possessing many of the same accomplishments. When he presents us with these simple character-equations, native blood = yellow streak, literary and artistic sensitivity = yellow streak, Maugham emerges as an absolutely typical member of his class and background, the archetypal old boy of The King's School, Canterbury, as it was in the bad old days of *Of Human Bondage*. The reassurance that he gave to the prevailing climate of prejudice about categories of people may explain some of his popularity. It was beyond Maugham's imaginative scope to show how a crippled literary intellectual may manifest more moral courage than a games-playing bully, as E. M. Forster tried to do in *The Longest Journey*.

Maugham's most memorable portrait of a bully—and one to whom he appears to give his unstinted admiration—is in a story called *Mackintosh* where a swinish administrator, Walker, lords it over one of the larger islands in the Samoan group. He gazes scornfully at his new assistant's books after they have been unpacked to reveal an edition of Gibbon and *The Anatomy of Melancholy* and asks him: 'What in Hell have you bought all this muck for?' The character equation here in the assistant is slightly more complex: reader of books = compassion and humanitarianism when dealing with the natives instead of the requisite degree of merciless authoritarianism. Walker's paternalistic nature compels him to rule the native Kanakas with a rod of iron, utterly fearless of threats to his own life, riding roughshod over anything that stands in the way of his manic obsession, the building of a road right round the island. In the end his extreme provocation proves too much for his book-loving assistant, who connives at his murder. When the terrible old man at last dies, saying: 'Forgive them. I've loved them, you know, always loved them,' he shoots himself in an access of remorse. The author's (and the reader's) admiration here is all for the awful Mackintosh. The Biblical quotation does not seem blasphemously inappropriate on his lips. The story-teller's art has given him an air of being larger than life, a mythical prepotence compounded of exceptional courage, self-belief and indifference to the opinions of others, the characteristics of Maugham's heroes and heroines from Liza onwards.

The one time in these exotic tales when Maugham finds this power, to break with the inherited code and make one's own law, in a person of culture and sensibility, is in the story from the South Seas group entitled *The Fall of Edward Barnard*. The hero of this story belongs to the affluent world of post-First World War Chicago; he is engaged to a society beauty when a change in his family fortunes sends him off to a job in Tahiti. Here through reading, conversation, the influence of a former financial swindler, the overwhelming charm of the place and of the native women, he decides to stay permanently and to renounce all that a return to Chicago might hold. As his ex-fiancée slips off the ring, and pledges herself to his best friend, she comments that Edward always lacked 'backbone'—and this of course is just what, according to Maugham, he does not lack. Maugham succeeds impressively in constructing an ironical antithesis between the values that he chooses to represent by the smart life of Chicago on the one hand and the unsmart back-to-Nature existence of Tahiti on the other. It is an effective story in its own right but many readers will treasure it as the blue-print for the mature reworking of the theme in terms of the teaching of the Bhagavad-Gita years later in *The Razor's Edge*.

By contrast to the bookish yellow-streakers Maugham's white ruling caste includes a high proportion of those whose resoluteness of purpose resulted in the taking of life of their own kind. He was always an avid reader of detective stories and as his own working-life coincided with their great period could hardly fail to be influenced. The big difference between his work and that of the regular practitioners of the genre in its classic phase, is that in a Maugham story about a murder there is never much doubt as to who the murderer is. But if you do not insist on a whodunnit element, tales such as 'P. & O.', 'The Letter', 'Footprints in the Jungle' and 'Flotsam and Jetsam', could go straight into an anthology of Best Murder Stories and have indeed in some cases already done so. What Maugham keeps us guessing about is the precise mechanics as he describes the apparent ordinariness, the simple everyday reality of the soil from which the murder flourishes, and the rapidity and completeness with which a murder becomes assimilated. What he, asks, lies in the past of that comfortable, determined-looking woman with the jutting jaw-line who comes into the Club once a week with her husband and teenage daughter and plays a strong hand of bridge? Simply that she is a kind of Lady Macbeth who, unlike her illustrious archetype, suffers no remorse, no crack-up, no hand-washing, but lives to enjoy the fruits of her crime in successful, hard-working tranquillity as a respected figure of the community. This is the interesting thing about Maugham's murderers: none of them are ever brought to book. They all get off scot-free unless of course they are natives. This was not the result of any desire on Maugham's part to show up failures in the administration which he in fact admired, as he did the vast majority of the administrators and planters, even when they failed to provide him with significant material; it stems from his cold, painterly, dispassionate approach to the task of story-writing. He was simply concerned to isolate those moments when an individual takes the law into his or her own hands and the life of a planter or a district officer in pre-war Malaya offered him more possibilities of observing this phenomenon than elsewhere.

It is the final Malayan collection *Ah King* (1933) that contains his most shattering stories of the hurts done in these ultimate places by white to white. The weeping native servant whose name provided the book with its title is the mutely detached observer of the strange antics his own land has induced in his masters. The Maugham connoisseur will, incidentally, wish to read the stories in their original volumes: *The Trembling of a Leaf* (1921) with its prose poems on the lure of the Pacific as prologue and epilogue and its pervasive *gauguinerie*, its sense of mystery and lost paradise; *The Casuarina Tree* (1926) where the romantic poetic mood has been replaced by a much more realistic and ruthless penetration of the English people who lived in the Malay Peninsula and in Borneo. Cyril Connolly awarded it, with two other volumes of stories, a place in his hundred key books in the Modern Movement (1880–1950) on the grounds that:

> In these Far Eastern short stories (*The Casuarina Tree* and *Ah King*) and in the secret service tales of *Ashenden* (1928) Maugham achieves an unspoken ferocity, a controlled ruthlessness before returning to sentiment with Rosie in *Cakes and Ale*. He tells us— and it has not been said before—exactly what the British in the Far East were like, the judges and planters and civil servants and their womenfolk at home, even as Ashenden exposes what secret service work is really like. That would not be enough without his mastery of form, if not of language. His bloodless annexation of the Far East pays off in *The Casuarina Tree* which includes 'The Yellow Streak', 'The Out-Station', 'Before the Party' and 'The Letter'— about a coward, a snob, a murderess and a blackmailer.[6]

The blackmailer is in fact the Chinese lawyer and therefore not one of the British. But even without him it is a fairly formidable list of iniquities. One quite sees how such stories cannot have endeared him to his erstwhile hosts, even though Maugham was at pains to point out that 'the reader must not suppose that the incidents I have narrated were of common occurrence. The vast majority of these people . . . were good, decent, normal people. I respect, and even admire, such people, but they are not the sort of people I can write stories about. I write stories about

people who have some singularity of character which suggests
to me . . .' etc., etc. The trouble with that is that literature has
the effect of turning the exceptional into the typical; no one
reads C. Woodville Harrison any more but people will continue to read Maugham's stories about the Federated Malay
States. His general picture of the white administrator with his
immense solidarity and the limitations of his essentially
philistine way of life is all there is left of them.

[2.]

The white administrator was the source of all authority and
had the power to impose his will and moral code upon the
natives. Maugham observed him closely in both his judicial and
missionary role. 'Mr. Somerset Maugham, I suppose, has,'
said Graham Greene, 'done more than anyone to stamp the
idea of the repressed prudish man of God on the popular
imagination.' Long before he set foot in the South Seas
Maugham was a confirmed Diderotine; the missionary lady in
'Rain' is a reincarnation of Mary Clibbourn in *The Hero* who, it
will be remembered, had the same difficulty in inculcating a joy-
less standard of rectitude among her village lasses. But if in his
travels in China Maugham was hard on those Protestant
missionaries who retired to the hills in the heat of summer, on
the whole, whether in Spain or in the Far East, he had nothing
but admiration for people dedicated to the religious life; their
uncrackable self-discipline was something which he understood.
He gave the fullest expression of his admiration in his portrait
of the hard-working community of nuns in the plague-spot near
Hong Kong in *The Painted Veil* (1925) where, as in *The Narrow
Corner* (1933), he set aside the short story with an exotic
setting for the short novel. Both these books combine an
atmosphere of fairy-tale remoteness, an Arabian Nights sense
of enchantment, with a highly sensational love story and much
pondering on the question of how ought one to live.

The Painted Veil is the more popular of the two in that it is
an enthralling book to read in which all the contradictory
Maugham ingredients—romance and realism, cynicism and

hero-worship, repartee and purple patches, bedroom farce and exotic description—all somehow jell together as the enthralled reader is carried breathlessly along from one mood to another, watching what nowadays we might call a search for authentic existence. For about the first eighty pages it might be just another far eastern short story about the commonplace adultery committed by a commonplace woman of the British community in Hong Kong with a commonplace Assistant Colonial Secretary. (The name of the city had to be changed just before publication because of libel but now it has been restored as Hong Kong.) Her boring biologist husband discovers them in bed together, after which Kitty realizes that her lover is not a gentleman and has no intention of jeopardizing his career by divorcing his wife. So it all might have ended with Kitty's suicide or departure for England.

Instead Maugham makes the outraged husband offer her the chance, a loaded chance, of accompanying him to the cholera-stricken town thirty miles away where he has volunteered to replace the resident medical officer who has himself fallen a victim to the epidemic. After the shattering interview with her lover she really has no choice but to accept. Maugham thus establishes one of those axes between the point of origin and the point of revelation on which he loved to work. Kitty's commonplaceness, her essential middle-class English 1930s insularity of mind, becomes a dramatic asset. As the bearers carry her through the jungle we wonder how someone so ordinary will fare under the extreme conditions that lie in wait for her. It is a magical vision Kitty has of the cholera-infested town as she stares at it from the eminence of her bungalow (a deceased missionary's) shrouded in the slowly dispersing morning mist. Maugham's late nineteenth-century Pateresque aestheticism pays its final dividend, giving us Kitty's sudden ineffable sense of a beauty that precedes her experience of human suffering and human limitation. Her involvement in the plague is a gradual progress fraught with many delicately sprung surprises. Her encounter with Waddington, the Deputy Commissioner, one of Maugham's most interesting creations, is the first of them; a quizzical, courageous, alcoholic man, he represents a different order of being from the conventional bed and bridge-playing, stengah-swigging set in Hong Kong. He has rooted himself in the indigenous culture to the point where he not only has a Chinese woman as his bed-fellow, and what a ravishing creature she is, but 'perhaps unconsciously he had adopted the Chinese view that the Europeans were barbarians and their life a folly: in China alone was it so led that a sensible man might discern in it a sort of reality'. (Here at least is an educated and civilized man whose psychological make-up contains not the slightest hint of a yellow streak!)

Exposure to Waddington's self-containment and eccentricity is for Kitty the first circle, as it were, of a purgatory—the novel was inspired, Maugham tells us, by Dante's line 'Siena made me, Maremma unmade me'—that leads her to an enlarged conception of herself, her husband, her lover, the whole meaning of life. The book has more organic development than any other Maugham novel with a heroine at its centre; and he is skilful at showing the stabbing sequence of self-revelations that she has to suffer in the plague town. Some chance remarks of Waddington's make her realize the utter worthlessness of her lover, his reputation as a cheap philanderer; the next shock is her first sight of a corpse which 'makes everything else seem so horribly trivial'. But it is only when she goes to visit the convent of French nuns in the middle of the city, in the poorest district, that Kitty arrives at a more positive notion of how to live through the example of the nuns themselves, creatures of tireless work and dedication. In his portrait of the Mother Superior Maugham achieves what is often said to be the most difficult thing a novelist can do, create a truly good, a saintly human being, one in whom are combined aristocratic birth, natural authority, innate courtesy, spiritual insight and complete humility. It is from her that Kitty gains a fresh and frightening perspective on her husband: the nuns discover in him the same fearless and seemingly inexhaustible strength in combating the cholera epidemic as in themselves. They revere him as a saviour and some of the glory brushes off on Kitty herself for accompanying him on such a mission. The novelist's irony was never more acute than in showing here what a difference exists between the face that Kitty and her husband show to the world and that which they show to each other. For her part she gains the thing that she has hitherto lacked, respect for him, but he remains utterly unrelenting and unforgiving. Maugham reveals something very frightening that even the Mother Superior does not suspect, which is that all his good works are motivated by deep, loathsome, vindictive self-pity. It seems appropriate that eventually, when thanks to his efforts the force of the plague has abated, it should carry him off among its final victims, and that Kitty should live. Her work in the convent in the task of child-minding has brought her very close to the nuns and, through conversations with the Mother Superior about the spiritual life, has enabled her to penetrate the 'aloofness' which had initially oppressed her when she met them. She goes back to Hong Kong with the outlook of a mature human being.

Here again the tale might have ended quite satisfyingly but Maugham has another surprise up his sleeve. Waiting to greet her on the dock is the wife of her former lover who, in her hour of bereavement and distress, offers Kitty hospitality and care. She is thus brought back into direct, daily contact with the man who was the cause of her downfall and it is from this proximity that Kitty learns the bitterest lesson of all: that passion may survive disillusion and that the moral sense, even when it has been suddenly discovered, may be just as suddenly set aside when temptation comes again. As the crow flies it is only thirty miles from the city of Hong Kong to the cholera town, but the distance between the Kitty who learned there a new freedom and the Kitty who yields slavishly once again to the Assistant Commissioner is incalculable.

By giving his story a title from Shelley, and an epigraph from Dante, Maugham was making a claim for it as a serious work as well as hinting the source of the plot; but its popular sensational form of torrid passion and tropical sun blinded many reviewers to its depths of insight. *The Times Literary Supplement* was splendidly Grundyish. 'One may doubt,' it pontificated, 'whether it is strictly necessary to the indictment of lust that purely lustful episodes should be described so conscientiously.'[7] You can say that again, in the 1970s. Other reviewers thought that the characters were puppets, the situation was trite, and the ending 'the silliest ever inflicted by a brilliant writer on a brilliant story'.[8] On the other hand the *Nation* and *Athenaeum*

commented that 'the silliness of the main situation only tests
Mr. Maugham's skill as a writer and his power of convincing us
that we are dealing with the momentous problems of a woman's
soul'.[9] In much of this one can detect what Colin Wilson calls
the anti-success mechanism at work. In 1925 Maugham was
even more ubiquitous than usual. 'Rain' was a theatrical smash-
hit; *The Moon and Sixpence* had also been dramatized; stories
were appearing each month in the magazines; *Of Human
Bondage* had, after a decade, begun to establish itself as a
modern classic. Maugham's tireless flow of invention was
intolerable to many a penny-a-lining reviewer. But for all the
jibes *The Painted Veil* continued to be read. In 1931 Lytton
Strachey, the high priest of literary journalism, took it away to
read while suffering from 'flu and pronounced it 'Class II,
division I'; it is a useful coding when thinking of Maugham by
comparison with, say, Dostoievsky and Tolstoy—but what
about a more realistic comparison with a later novel of tropical
sex, *The Heart of the Matter*? Here one would be inclined to put
Greene into Class I, division II and count Maugham's the less
flawed work.

[3.]

In the end Maugham exhausted the seam of exotic inspiration.
A trip to the West Indies in the 1930s at Kipling's suggestion
did not provide him with any inspiration; but the colonial vein
as a whole proved to be wonderfully rich and while it lasted it
could be moulded to suit any length of tale. The briefest were
those written at the request of Ray Long, editor of *Cosmopolitan* magazine, who required stories 'short enough to print on
opposite pages and leave plenty of room for illustration'.[10]
Long, incidentally, was eventually so influenced by the
Maugham mystique that he actually became a real-life Departer
and gave up everything to live the beachcombing life. As an
editor the restrictions of space that he imposed on Maugham's
art inspired many brief studies of some depth, such as 'A Friend
in Need', about a hard-hearted British businessman met in
Kobe, and 'The Four Dutchmen', who were all such amiable

shipmates until a girl came between them. From these tales one may discover fragments of Maugham's itineraries during these *wander jahre*. In the former, for instance, he recalls

the S.S. *Utrecht*, on which I had travelled from Merauke in New Guinea to Macassar. The journey took the best part of a month, since the ship stopped at a number of islands in the Malay Archipelago, the Aru and the Kei Islands, Banda-Neira, Amboina and others of which I have even forgotten the names, sometimes for an hour or two, sometimes for a day, to take on or discharge cargo. It was a charming, monotonous and diverting trip. When we dropped anchor the agent came out in his launch, and generally the Dutch Resident, and we gathered on deck under the awning and the captain ordered beer. The news of the island was exchanged for the news of the world. We brought papers and mail. If we were staying long enough the Resident asked us to dinner and, leaving the ship in charge of the second officer, we all (the captain, the chief officer, the engineer, the super-cargo and I [and Gerald?]) piled into the launch and went ashore. We spent a merry evening. These little islands, one so like another, allured my fancy just because I knew that I should never see them again. It made them strangely unreal, and as we sailed away and they vanished into the sea and sky it was only by an effort of the imagination that I could persuade myself that they did not with my last glimpse of them cease to exist.[11]

That was written in 1928. It was some five years later that Maugham made his supreme effort of the imagination about one of these little islands of the Dutch East Indies, Banda-Neira, and calling it Kanda he set a whole novel in it, *The Narrow Corner*. The title comes from Marcus Aurelius in a quotation suggesting that there is small room for manœuvre in a man's life and the hero (if that's the word for him) is a stoic of a peculiarly Maughamish kind, Dr. Saunders. We met him first in an earlier book of Maugham's about the East, *On a Chinese Screen*: 'He was not on the register . . . But it was evident that he was a very clever doctor and the Chinese had great faith in him.'[12] He is also a missionary-baiter, teasing the protestant who has retired for the hot summer months to the hills about a stranger called Christ who was looking for him. By the time we meet him again he has mellowed a little. 'He took an interest in his fellows that was not quite scientific and not quite human.

He wanted to receive entertainment from them. He regarded them dispassionately and it gave him just the same amusement to unravel the intricacies of the individual as a mathematician might find in the solution of a problem.'[13] In other words he is a latter-day Miss Ley adopting that typical Maugham posture of being ever-present but never involved or committed. He teams up with another character who made a brief but memorable appearance in an earlier book, Captain Nicholls, the dyspeptic sea-dog from the Marseilles section of *The Moon and Sixpence*. The captain has been given the delicate mission of escorting a young Australian killer around the Indonesian islands while things cool off for him back home. Nicholls's function in this book is not merely to provide some coarse comic relief in the form of down-to-earth comments on the rarefied sentiments expressed by the other characters, but also to demonstrate how great courage may be combined with great meanness and brutality. He is a villain of the deepest dye, probably a murderer, but he totally lacks the yellow streak, and that is enough to redeem him in the eyes of Maugham. The only things that inhibit him are his digestion which is bad, and his wife who is worse, and has a way of turning up unexpectedly when he gets to a port.

Nicholls takes Saunders aboard to the dismay of his other passenger, the handsome Fred Blake. The doctor is accompanied by his exquisite Malay servant Ah Kay, whose slender form Saunders watches admiringly as he prepares the opium pipes. Ah Kay (twin to Maugham's own Ah King) represents that rare condition, selfless devotion to another human being.

The book has the same essential structure of a journey to the interior, to the place of revelation as *The Painted Veil*, only here that place is a volcanic island of the Dutch East Indies; Kanda —as Maugham called it—was once a prosperous centre of the spice trade; its fine old fortress is the product of occupation by the Portuguese and the marble pillars of the now largely deserted palatial houses were the status symbols of the mercantile Dutch. Maugham sometimes liked to pretend that he had no gift for descriptive writing but he never succeeded better in portraying a *genius loci*; it is a peculiar combination of derelict grandeur and seedy charm. In this archetypal setting

Dr. Saunders may observe some singular specimens of human nature free to develop unconstrainedly. As the tall, Viking-looking, Danish planter Erik Christessen explains: 'The place is dead. We live on our memories. That is what gives the island its character.'

I said just now that in the Mother Superior of *The Painted Veil* Maugham succeeded in creating a truly good human being. In Christessen, whose name is not given to him without signi-ficance, he tries again but this time in a spirit of irony. It is a dangerously vulnerable kind of goodness that Erik embodies in contrast to the rogueries of Nicholls and the detachment of Saunders, a goodness that is illusioned, untested, unshrewd. He has lived too much in the world of books and not enough in the world of people. His head is chockful of English literature and he is perpetually quoting *Othello* (the Moor's plight is the analogue of his own). He acquired his love of Shakespeare in Copenhagen from Georg Brandes (how fiendishly accurate Maugham always is about this kind of detail) and then romanti-cally made his way East, fetching up on this remote island. Here he came under the influence of Frith. Frith is another great reader. Maugham found men of letters everywhere. As a young man Frith got it into his head that this island was the one place where he wanted to live; when he reached it, although it did not quite come up to his expectations, 'he forced reality to tally with the fancy'—a sign of maturity. He brought an air of Cambridge eccentricity to the place. That hint that there might be a criterion for strange or anti-social conduct in Indian philo-sophy, which was first sounded by Mrs. Tabret in *The Sacred Flame*, blossoms now in Frith who is an authority on the Vedantas. He practises non-attachment and believes in rein-carnation. He spends his time in the interminable task of trans-lating the Lusiads of of Camoens, believing that he may himself embody the soul of the dead Portuguese poet. Frith is one of the most interesting of those Maugham characters who, as we should say, have opted out of the system.

He contrasts strikingly with the old man Swan whose daughter he married. This ruthless and crotchety Swede, 'adventurer in the soulless desert of hard fact', owns the plantation on which they all live. The only female within miles is his granddaughter Louise who, with her ash-blonde hair, young trim figure, looks ravishing when she changes into a green sarong for dinner. Christessen, who immediately strikes up a friendship with the Australian murderer—there are homosexual echoes through this novel—feels a rationalized, protective, reverential love for Louise. He explains:

> She's so sweet. She's so gentle. She's so tender, and yet there is a a sort of aloofness in her that keeps you at a distance. It seems to me very rare and beautiful. I'm not jealous of it. I'm not afraid of it. It's a priceless possession and I love her so much that I regret she cannot always keep it. I feel she will lose it when she becomes a wife and a mother, and whatever beauty of soul she has then it will be different. It's something apart and independent. It's the self which is part of the universal self; perhaps we've all got it; but what is so wonderful in her is that it is almost sensible, and you feel that if only your eyes were a little more piercing you could see it plain. I'm so ashamed that I shall not go to her as pure as she will come to me.[14]

It looks as if this is that same aloof condition that we have observed in so many Maugham heroes and heroines but—and this is the clever psychological perception that precipitates the melodramatic crisis to which this otherwise strangely contemplative story now hastens—Louise's aloof purity emerges as a subjective illusion of Christessen's. He comes to realize this in the middle of the night when he observes the Australian leaving Louise's room where she has slept with him. It is a kind of repeat of the episode for which the boy is on the run, only this time it is Christessen who shoots himself. He commits suicide for a complex of reasons of which his own inability to live without illusions is perhaps the strongest. Christessen's inevitable death is beautifully prepared for by Maugham in the conversations he has with the visitors to the island. It is the hubris of goodness. Christessen's real human passion and attachment was not to Louise at all but to her recently dead mother, another example of the maternal archetype that haunts Maugham's most mature work:

> She was a woman who never read much, but she had a vast fund of knowledge, lying there like an unworked mine, gathered, you

would have said, through innumerable generations out of the time-
less experience of the race, so that she could cope with your book
learning and meet you on level terms. She was one of those persons
who made you feel as if you were saying wonderful things, and
when you talked to her thoughts came to you that you had never
dreamt you were capable of. She was of a practical turn and had a
canny sense of humour; she was quick to ridicule absurdity, but the
kindness of heart was such that if she laughed at you, it was so
tenderly that you loved her for it. It seemed to Erik that her most
wonderful trait was a sincerity so perfect that it glowed all about
her with a light that shone into the heart of all that had com-
munication with her.[15]

After Christessen's death it is time for Saunders and Nicholls
to leave the island and return to Singapore via Bali. At the same
time the narrative leaves the plane of the archetypes and moves
back to the level of a regular thriller about a murderer on the
run. Fred's liaison with a woman in Sydney and the sordid killing it entailed now comes out. But he has served his turn for the
novelist as the instrument of disillusion and he dies at sea in
dubious circumstances, having won all Nicholls's money at
cribbage. Saunders makes his way back to his useful humdrum
life as a dispassionate healer feeling strangely liberated by his
experience. Nicholls goes ashore at Singapore where, to his
horror, he comes face to face with his harridan of a wife. One
murder story encloses another in this unconventionally constructed novel. It can be read as a straightforward, exotic
thriller full of suspense and atmosphere and unpredictability, but
it can also be appreciated on a completely different level, where
you need C. G. Jung at your elbow. It is in his stories of the
Far East that we find the richest sub-text in Maugham's work,
and where we may watch him trying to break out of the confines of realism. Those who have lived and worked in these parts
delight to fault him on points of detail, yet how skilfully he
creates the semblance of exotic reality by seizing upon some
salient feature, such as the empty volcano in *The Narrow
Corner*, or throughout the short stories the chik-chak, a noisy
species of lizard; I take this little creature to be an emblem of
Maugham himself, like Whistler's butterfly. If one tries to
sum up his fictional examination of the white middle-class

European who went to spend his life working among the native population in one of the colonial possessions, the picture is not a heartening one. Few like Waddington seem to survive the experience intact. For many life is a process of degeneration, or of eroded integrity. Those who go out with high ideals like Frith end up as pathetic clowns; those who go to rediscover a lost Eden become degraded by pleasure and sloth; those whom jealousy or greed provoke to the destruction of their own kind may live on unpunished and flourish like the casuarina tree; those who regard the world well lost usually end in poverty and disillusion. The only consolation is the beauty of the land bursting ironically upon the human drama from time to time. If we look for nobility of soul we must make do with one remarkable French Mother Superior, and if we look for someone in this huge world of the Orient, of whom the author seems wholeheartedly to approve, it is a hedonistic, crypto-homosexual, busted doctor with a coldly clinical eye for human suffering and a self-possession that has its frail support in the opium pipe. No wonder names had sometimes to be changed for fear of libel. No wonder Maugham's hosts did not always read the books that his sojourn among them had inspired with undiluted pleasure.

CHAPTER NINE

On the Judgment Seat

[1.]

DO PEOPLE BEHAVE noticeably better when they are at home, or at leisure in a society composed of their own kind, than when they set themselves up to govern native peoples in exotic lands? If we are to judge from the stories that Maugham published in the 1930s and 1940s in such volumes as *First Person Singular* (1931), *The Mixture as Before* (1940) and *Creatures of Circumstance* (1947), the short answer must be—'no'. You cannot of course make a strict chronological distinction between the far and the near in the work of so fertile a writer. You will still in these books encounter the odd D.O. from Borneo in an agonizing marital entanglement during a spot of leave in London, and the miniscule tales of *Cosmopolitans* (1936) span both East and West. But from now on you will be sipping dry martinis rather than gin pahits. You will swan around London, Paris, the French Riviera, Seville, Rhodes, Florence, places where centuries of civilized living have left their mark.

When Graham Greene came to review *Cosmopolitans*[1] he complained that the stories 'had no echo of the general life', being bounded by 'the liner routes and the leisured quarters'. Since he wrote that review Mr. Greene has come to learn how much success isolates an author from the general life, but is it really true, either of that volume, or of Maugham's accidental stories as a whole? As always he approached the general life through the private life and the professional life; in others words, he focused so sharply upon the particular that it came to have a general application. A story such as *Episode*, in which a Brixton postman steals money from the mail he is delivering to keep a girl a cut above him socially in the style to which her mean-minded mother thinks she ought to have become accustomed, chissels through the wall that shuts out the atrocities of suburban working-class life in the years between the war and shows us gradations of snobbery as exclusive and destructive as anything to be found higher up in the social scale. And Maugham moves up and down that scale in his stories with a nimble agility. At the top are characters like Lord Mountdrago, the insolent Tory politician, locked in a love-hate relation with his Labour opponent and at the bottom the young man for whom the innocent Sunday pastime of kite-flying became a way of discovering the distinction between being a son and being a husband. [2]

Both this story and *Episode* came to Maugham from his friend Alan Searle, who had had much experience in helping first offenders in Wormwood Scrubs Prison, and who suggested the character of Ned Preston round whom the tales are told. Would that Maugham had given us more of such stories for they show him at his most compassionate. Mr. Searle told me that when he read *Episode* he was amazed at the accuracy with which Maugham had depicted people he had never actually met. 'I really began to believe in inspiration,' said Mr. Searle. Maugham did a spot of prison-visiting himself when they went to the great French penal settlement of St. Laurent de Maroni in French Guiana to meet the murderer whose trial formed the centrepiece of the novel *Christmas Holiday*, published just before the war. The visit proved fruitful not only on that account but also in providing material for two fine stories of a grim kind, *A Man with a Conscience* and *An Official Position*, in which Maugham was at his most ironic making deductions about nature as a whole from the presence of so many murderers *en masse*, just as he had studied isolated instances of murder in the East. 'I arrived at the conclusion that at the bottom of nearly all these crimes was an economic motive . . . somehow it affected their pockets,' he concluded. The St. Laurent stories have a rather special place in the canon because they show Maugham moving in the spirit of the Dostoievsky of *The House of the Dead*, with the difference that he is a visitor, not an inmate, among men who no longer have any need to wear a social mask: when a man has been tried and found guilty of murder he is wholly known.

In society people conceal their motives behind some kind of front or mask for many different reasons, and Maugham's technique of story-writing is one of penetration. He always mistrusts appearance; he chooses his victims with care, and like Dr. Saunders he judges but he does not condemn. He accepts the social mask at the outset for what it is and reveals it in operation (the beginning); then he shows it faced by some crisis of confidence (the middle), moving to the moment (the end) when it is displaced and/or replaced. By the end everything should have been made plain; no question that the reader might reasonably wish to ask, about the people and situation of the story, should be left unanswered. Maugham was out of sympathy with the stories written by members of the intelligentsia and the world of Bloomsbury because of what seemed to him to be their inconclusiveness. He admired Chekhov but deplored his influence upon writers whose admiration for his work led them to believe that subtle impressionism could be a substitute for organic form.

But though Maugham continued to play by the old rules, the realistic rules of Maupassant, he realized that literature is like everything else subject to fashion. He knew only too well what happened to an artist when the public tired of him. Unlike some successful authors he never took his popularity for granted. He may have pretended in sardonic deference to a luke-warm review, that with each fresh volume of short stories it was just 'the mixture as before', but in fact the mixture was always being changed to take in new places and experience. Maugham's most scathing story about the tyranny of fashion and of public taste on those who aim to make their living by providing entertainment is the one entitled *Gigolo and Gogolette*.[3] Although Maugham never consciously wrote anything with a hidden meaning, one may, perhaps, be permitted to interpret this story, beneath its brilliant surface realism depicting pre-war Riviera life, as a parable of the plight of the professional writer, who with each new book at the behest of his publisher and agent attempts the Dive of Death (through a burning hoop above a swimming-pool). The fickle public watches while eating, hoping secretly that he will come a cropper, but giving generous applause when he lands safely. One day he meets the Human Cannon-ball (a best-selling novelist of two decades ago, now totally forgotten, living meagrely off a beneficence provided by the Royal Literary Fund). He sees a horrible vision of the future. No wonder, he thinks, some of them sometimes lost their nerve.

That fate never befell Maugham. During his long innings as a story-writer, from his forties to his seventies, he was tireless in his quest for fresh material, using his sixth sense, money to trawl life. He observed people both as host and traveller, always alert for the precious few embryonic facts. His energetic out-going approach to his task earned him the label of man of the world. If by that one means the ability to hold one's own wherever one happens to be, it is an apt description, but Maugham was more than just a man of the world, he was a *literary* man of the world. Of all the varieties of men and women he encountered he had a feeling of blood-brotherhood with the literary practitioner. Mr. Searle speaks of his innumerable acts of kindness to young writers. He founded an annual award to help them to find inspiration as he had done in travel, and he ultimately left the residue of his fortune to the Royal Literary Fund to the benefit of those for whom literature had been a less kind mistress than it had to him.

As we might expect therefore, Maugham wrote several stories about literary life and they are among his best. Although stories about authorship appeal to critics and others professionally engaged in literature, the danger for the general reader is that the problems they deal with may seem remote from life and the characters' behaviour hard to accept in ordinary terms. This was what Maugham felt invalidated the stories about the literary world of Henry James:

Take *The Author of 'Beltraffio'*. In that a mother lets her only child, a little boy, die of diphtheria so that he could not be corrupted by his father's books, of which she profoundly disapproves. No one could have conceived such a monstrous episode who could imagine a mother's love for her son and in his nerves feel the anguish of the child tossing restlessly on his bed and the pitiful, agonising struggle for breath.[4]

Whatever subtle problems arising out of the writer's relation to his material that Maugham might deal with, he never made people behave in a completely incredible way. The uneasy relation between literature and ordinary life is exposed with both credibility and glorious irony in *The Colonel's Lady*.[5] Two aspects of pre-war English life, the hearty and the aesthetic, are brought into collision when the colonel of the title, a gentleman farmer—'a jolly good fellow. That was what he wanted to be. He desired no higher praise'—finds a time-bomb planted on him in the shape of his wife's book of poems. From this moment, on page one of the story, we watch literature calling the tune in spite of the colonel's gallant efforts to put it in its proper place of being seen but not heard.

> 'Not much money in poetry my dear,' he said in his good-natured hearty way. So much for poetry. It might have been a discreditable incident that they had silently agreed not to mention.

But literature imposes itself on life. The poems become widely read—here perhaps Maugham *is* stretching probability a little —and the author acquires great popular renown reducing the colonel to the status of 'Colonel Peregrine, E. K. Hamilton's husband, you know.' In the end he is forced to the drastic step of actually reading the book himself to discover that it is the story of his wife's passionate love-affair with a much younger man. The Evie he knows is a mask, what he reads is her real face. At the close of the story, in a talk with his solicitor, who counsels him against legal action, he half sees that it must have taken great courage for her to keep the mask in place so firmly for so long. The story ends unforgettably with the colonel saying: '. . . one thing I shall never understand till my dying day: "What in the name of heaven did the fellow ever see in her?" ' But for all that, the assumptions on which his life was based hitherto have been undermined by his wife's gift.

Poet Evie compares well with Mrs. Albert Forrester in *The Creative Impulse*,[6] who 'had given the world half a dozen volumes of verse, published under Latin titles, such as *Felicitas*, *Pax Maris* and *Aes Triplex*', and who gathers around herself an admiring circle of the literary profession in 'something as near the French Salon of the Eighteenth Century as our barbarous

nation has ever reached'. This scorching piece of literary satire
has its parallel in the Mrs. Barton Trafford scenes of *Cakes and
Ale*. The odious Mrs. F. triumphs in the end over her abscond-
ing breadwinner of a husband when he goes off with the maid by
writing her most successful book about it, a detective story.
This great Somerset Maugham gesture, the turning of life's
ills into art, is something beyond the scope of Humphrey
Carruthers in *The Human Element*. He is interesting in that he
is a distinguished writer of the inconclusive-Bloomsbury-
Chekhov school who despised Maugham's work and whom
Maugham despised. All the more fascinating then, that, when
Maugham encounters him in Rome, he should find him desperately clinging to him out of the need to confide in someone
in his unhappiness. He then proceeds to tell Maugham what is
in fact a typical Maugham story of a great society beauty, with
whom he was in love, whose marriage broke up and with whom
he went to stay in Rhodes only to discover that she was having
an affair with her chauffeur. For Carruthers this collapse of his
idol proves to be traumatic. Maugham's advice to him is that he
should put it all into a story and get it off his chest (as in fact
Maugham has already done). This is something quite incon-
ceivable to Carruthers because Maugham implies he is too much
of a gentleman to be a real writer:

> He paused for a little and I saw him reflect. I saw that notwith-
> standing the horror that my suggestion caused him he did not for
> one moment look at the situation from the standpoint of the writer.
> He shook his head.
>   'Not for her sake, for mine. After all I have some self-respect.
> Besides, there's no story there.'

If you are an artist, in Maugham's sense, you do not confess
your grief to a fellow-artist met by chance in a foreign city, you
re-create it in a fiction for all the world.

Maugham's most complex story and at the same time one of
his most amusing, about the emotion taken from life that is
transformed through artistic recreation, is *The Voice of the
Turtle*.[7] There are three artists involved here: Maugham himself, a young novelist Peter Melrose, to whom he is at first
hostile but to whom he then warms to the extent of inviting him

to Cap Ferrat, and La Falterona, the diva. Melrose needs
material about a prima donna for his next book and Maugham
provides it by inviting a real one to dinner. But the character
had already been sketched out and written up by Melrose
before he met her. All that life does in this instance is to con-
firm the artist in the truth of his fiction. What he sees, Maugham
implies satirically, is something very different from the reality.
And yet when La Falterona reads the book she recognizes herself in it. Right at the end of the story she sings privately to
Maugham the liebstod from *Tristan*. Platonism takes over. Her
singing bodies forth an ideal reality. Maugham, conscious of her
monstrous everyday self, becomes nonetheless deeply touched.
Did Maugham have an ear for music? It is the art that appears
least in his work but it is difficult to see how someone who had
no ear for music could have written either this story or the one
called *The Alien Corn*. Wagner made a great impression on him
as a young man and as a writer he turned to him several times
when he wanted an analogy for a love so pure and so great that
it sweeps aside everything in its path, as in *The Sacred Flame*.

[2.]

It would, though, be misleading to suggest that creativity in
the arts plays any important part in the lives of more than a
handful of the characters in Maugham's stories. Nor are these
people greatly troubled by those ultimate questions of truth,
beauty and goodness that Maugham himself examined in the
closing chapters of *The Summing Up*. What then if anything do
they believe in? You will accuse me—rightly so—of repeating
myself but it all goes back to inherited racial codes of behaviour
of which, since Maugham is mainly writing about his own
countrymen, the most sovereign is that of the gentlemen. This
is the mask so many of them wear and behind which Maugham
is fascinated to discover a swarm of concealments and inconsistencies. Consider Captain Forestier in *The Lion's Skin*[8] who
lives like Maugham on the Riviera. When it comes to a question
of his taking a job in the difficult post-war world rather than
continue to live off his wife's money, he explains to her: 'There

are some things a gentleman can't do, Eleanor. Anything else I'll do gladly. God knows, I don't attach any importance to that sort of thing, but if one's a sahib one can't help it, and damn it all, especially in these days, one does owe something to one's class.' If you wonder whether so complete an adoption of the mask can ring quite true you are perfectly right. Forester is a phony; a former second-hand car salesman who, on coming out of the army, has assumed the patrician manner to perfection; unfortunately for him he is rumbled by a neighbour with a good memory for faces. I imagine that he might have been lurking somewhere at the bottom of Terence Rattigan's mind when he depicted the bogus major in *Separate Tables*, for the two men are in the same plight of aspiring to a gentility they do not possess, but whereas after the unmasking Rattigan's major suffers humiliation, and incidentally enables a downtrodden young girl to discover her maturity, Maugham's major remains imprisoned in his mask. He plunges into the heart of a raging forest fire to save his wife's dog and, when his unmasker tries to prevent him, he fells him to the ground and leaps into the flames with the words: 'You rotten bounder. I'll show you how a gentleman behaves!' The gentleman's mask is a target for some curious sorties by Maugham. If as here he showed it imprisoning its wearer in a self-destructive inflexibility, there were other occasions when it merely slipped for a while, temporarily to undermine the basis of pre-war society. A most delectable instance of this is a story beloved and beautifully interpreted by Glenway Wescott,[9] *The Treasure*.[10] Richard Harengar is the perfect gentleman; he is a civil servant, a collector of fine silver and a giver of select dinner parties in his London flat to which he moved after amicably separating from his wife. His smooth, bland life is in a perfect state of equilibrium, maintained as such by his own calm, perhaps a shade complacent, temperament, and by his invaluable house-keeper Pritchard. 'She had the English servant's instinctive knowledge of social differences and neither rank nor money blinded her to the fact that someone was not a gentleman . . .' She becomes an institution among his friends and an essential prop to his own gentlemanly, cautious existence. Maugham shows us Harengar's mask gradually displaced when he asks Pritchard, in a spontaneous gesture of kindness, to go one evening to the cinema with him. He finishes up in bed with her and the delicate balance is destroyed; to make things worse he hadn't really enjoyed it very much. But Pritchard's perfection is such that she adjusts the displaced mask for him by behaving the next morning exactly as she had on any other morning. 'He knew that never by word or gesture would she ever refer to the fact that for a moment their relations had been other than those of master and servant. Richard Harengar was a very happy man.'

A society ruled by old-fashioned Edwardian notions of station and decorum was a concept that Maugham never abandoned in his stories, and he gave his greatest admiration to those people whose acceptance of their role was such that mask and face had become one. Sometimes he would discover a rare instance of this on his travels. Like treasure Pritchard, Signora Niccolini retains her style as the model English servant under extreme provocation. She lives in a remote village in Asia Minor, married to a Greek and adopting his two sons by another woman. Maugham describes her in *In a Strange Land* when he stays at her little hotel. She thoughtfully provides him with a hot-water bottle. 'She was a pattern of decorum. It was extraordinary that she could have lived for thirty years in this wild and almost barbaric country without its having touched her.' Decorum, the slightly archaic term is very Maughamish, may be shown in the most unexpected places. Some of Maugham's happiest tales are constructed on a kind of three-card-trick principle in which the reader is invited to spot the lady or the gentleman. However carefully you follow the conjurer's deft hands as he slides the cards about he always manages to fool you in the end. In *Mr Know-All*,[11] for instance, he rapidly sketches for us the odious dealer in pearls, who is his cabin-mate on a voyage to Japan. But when a woman's marriage hangs in the balance this dreadful fellow behaves like a true gentleman, swallows his professional pride and pretends that a real string of pearls are cheap artificial ones. Shipboard provided Maugham with many instances of the deceptive mask and on one occasion with a notable double-bluff. Two men who were supposed to be professional card-sharpers came on board, one posing as a wealthy banker, the other as a distinguished mining engineer. Maugham was fascinated by them and put them under the closest scrutiny. Of one during a friendly game of poker, he said: 'His face was expressionless and I wished I could see him at work.' Later he meets them both in the Ritz and he discovers that one was indeed a broker and the other a mining engineer.

Nowhere is more revealing to Maugham in his investigations into decorum than the card-table. He can hardly contain his delight, he tells us in *The Portrait of a Gentleman*[12] (published first as *The Code of a Gentleman*), when he purchased in a second-hand bookshop in Seoul for twenty yen a paper-bound volume, sporting four aces on the cover, called the *Complete Poker Player* by John Blackbridge, actuary and counsellor-at-law, 1879. Maugham infers that the author must have been a Southern American possessed of a full hand of gentlemanly virtues. He 'had personal dignity, rectitude, humour and common sense . . . I am tempted to quote interminably . . . his language is excellent: it is dignified as befits his subject and his condition (he does not forget that he is a gentleman), measured, clear and pointed . . . I will content myself with giving a few of his aphorisms and wise saws chosen almost at random from the wealth of his book.

'Let your chips talk for you. A silent player is so farforth, a mystery: and a mystery is always feared.'

'In this game never do anything that you are not compelled to; while cheerfully responding to your obligations.'

Blackbridge's attitude to poker has great kinship with Maugham's approach to the art of fiction. He believes in applying logic to all the possible fluctuations that occur and abstaining 'from pressing an ignorant or intellectually weak opponent, beyond what may be necessary either for the purpose of playing the game correctly or punishing presumption'.

Here, then, is a complete code of conduct applicable to all the hazards and eventualities of the game set down in black and white. But in most societies the code is not thus set down; it must be inferred from the behaviour of its members. Maugham was a master at making accurate inferences of this kind. One feels that he is batting on almost too easy a wicket when he demonstrates the code of solidarity and family pride of the

Blands, the Anglicized German-Jewish family in *The Alien Corn*.[13] How searingly he shows the mask of English reserve and undemonstrative calm cracking wide open when the son of the household decides to be that ungentlemanly thing, a pianist. I might just as easily have put this famous story under the heading of Maugham's tales about artists and would-be artists, for it is yet another treatment of the artist-gentleman antithesis, but it is to me much more a story about the strength on the individual of the racial and parental code. In a slighter vein Maugham takes an impish delight in telling how a young scapegrace on the loose in Monte Carlo kicks over all the traces of his father's code and gets away with it. *The Ant and The Grasshopper*[14] is another example of how Maugham inverts a traditional fable to favour the happy-go-lucky individual, and in *Princess September and the Nightingale*[15] we have Maugham as a fabulist pointing a very sad moral indeed. It is all a question of *Appearance and Reality*. Maugham borrows this title from Bradley for one of his stories with much ironical apology before going on to probe the sexual code of a Parisian senator, who forces his girl-friend to marry her lover, so that he may have a respectable married woman for a mistress. (Garson Kanin tells how René Clair disliked this story so much that he refused to film it.[16]) In *The Unconquered*[17]—the only extant Maugham story of the Second World War—a young French woman would rather murder her own child than lose her self-respect by marrying the young German who loves her and whose father it is. In Spain it is a harsh code of passion and revenge that Maugham uncovers in such stories as *The Mother*,[18] turning on a woman's murderous love for her son and *The Point of Honour*,[19] a tale echoing Calderón in which vengeance is seen as 'the mainspring of the nobleman's code'. In Italian society in Florence Latin blood runs just as precipitately when in *A Woman of Fifty*[20] a son murders his father when his own English wife comes between them. Maugham indefatigably makes his point that a code destroys those who uphold it for its own sake.

It is only to the humblest characters who possess no code save their own self-possession that Maugham seems to extend his admiration. There are not very many of them. The most

memorable is the Italian fisherman Salvatore,[21] in the story of
that name, who accepts his hideous lot uncomplainingly and
represents 'goodness, just goodness' and among the women one
or two of the servant class like Pritchard and Signora Niccolini.
In our look at Maugham's comedies we saw that he had a soft
spot for the bolters and the constant wives who fought for their
independence in a man's world with the male weapons of money
and initiative; beside them we must put a rather sad sisterhood
from the short stories. At the other end of the human spectrum
to Salvatore is Louise, in the same collection whom Maugham
calls 'the most selfish and monstrous woman I have ever
known'. Because she trades emotionally on suffering no one
had ever penetrated her façade of grief: neither her two husbands nor her daughter, all of whose lives she wrecked; no one
that is until Maugham. 'Perhaps,' he goes on, 'she had an
inkling that I saw the face behind the mask and because I alone
held out, was determined that sooner or later I too should take
the mask for the face.' It is remarkable how deeply into a
character Maugham managed to go in stories that were only a
few pages long. Human egoism, and particularly feminine
egoism, is something on which Maugham rang many changes
throughout his tales, whether it was that of the young suburban
wife Betty, clamping down on her kite-obsessed husband, or the
casual female luncheon guest working her way through the
menu, sublimely unaware of the young writer's straits as he
struggles to make his way in Paris. Surrender to appetite, that
collapse of self-discipline, a sort of yellow streak of the gastric
juices, is a favourite theme, nowhere more maliciously treated
than in that classic story (familiar through the Master's own
recording of it) *The Three Fat Women of Antibes*.[22] One certainly has 'an echo of the general life' here in the case of anyone who likes food and has tried to lose weight as much indeed
as in Mr. Greene's story of the two lesbians overheard in a
restaurant in off-season Antibes.[23] It is the hunger not just for
food but for romance which allows Maugham to penetrate
behind the feminine mask in several brilliantly amusing stories.
As Mortimer Ellis the bigamist explains in *The Round Dozen*:[24]

> No wonder they jumped at me, no wonder they wanted me to go
> back to them. The only one who gave me away was the milliner,

she said she was a widow, my private opinion is that she'd never been married at all. You say I did the dirty on them; why, I brought happiness and glamour into eleven lives that never thought they had even a dog's chance of it again.

Miss Porchester with her ultra-respectable Edwardian background, the perfect gentlewoman to all outward seeming, emerges as the twelfth. What is so enjoyable in this tale is not just the wicked brilliance of the conception but the Beerbohmesque neatness of parody with which it is carried through. Mr. St. Clair's views on literature speak volumes: 'I admire Charles Dickens. But Charles Dickens could never draw a gentleman. I am given to understand that young people nowadays find Mr. Trollope a little slow. My niece, Miss Porchester, prefers the novels of Mr. William Black.' But if one thinks back to Beerbohm and the *fin de siècle* when reading *The Round Dozen* it is in the context of the young Evelyn Waugh and the turbulent 'twenties that one follows the career of another young woman who enters upon a *déclassée* love-affair, Betty Welldon-Burns, only daughter of the Duke of St. Erth, in *The Human Element*, who ends up in the arms of her chauffeur Albert, to the dismay, as we saw just now, of the writer Humphrey Carruthers who is desperately in love with her. Maugham sketches with beautiful precision the career of a fabulous young woman of the Gladys or Diana Cooper kind and her impact upon the public: 'Girls copied the way she did her hair and manufacturers of soap and face creams paid her money to use her photograph to advertise her wares.' Then in this female *galerie* there is that loquacious bore, Miss Reid, who can only be silenced when in *Winter Cruise*[25] the ship's radio officer is ordered by his German captain to make love to her for the honour of the fatherland. After this she shows a silent, self-absorbed face to the world.

But is there not among Maugham's hundred-odd short stories a female Salvatore, a woman who embodies 'goodness, just goodness'? It will come as no surprise to the reader who has followed my quest for maternal archetypes in his work to learn that she is already in her fifties and a widow by the time we meet her. The answer is *Jane*,[26] heroine of the story of that name, and of the successful stage play that was made out of it by the American playwright, S. N. Behrman. To be sure, Jane appears to present a very different face to the world when she is an immense social success and widely sought-after at the end than that of the dowdy, insignificant creature we see at the beginning. But this is merely a question of fashion, not of Jane. At the beginning her 'hair had evidently not known the tongs of Monsieur Marcel', whereas later on it was 'cut very short and clustered round her head in tight curls'. The point about Jane is that 'She managed (as so few people do) to look exactly what she was'. Maugham turns inside out the classic comedy situation of a woman of advanced years who believes she has an irresistible attraction for every man she meets and that her idlest remarks are pearls of wit and wisdom. Jane is simply herself and she speaks only the truth, but these two attributes are enough to render her the wonder and cynosure of the smart London society, to the chagrin of her sister-in-law, who is determined to be smart and have her drawing-room done up in the latest manner even if it means ruthlessly sacrificing 'chairs in which she had comfortably sat for years, tables, cabinets, ornaments on which her eyes had dwelt in peace since she was married, pictures that had been familiar to her for a generation; and delivered herself into the hands of an expert'. (Such an expert at this time as was Syrie Maugham.) For the *dénouement* Maugham sustains his moral paradox with the finessing skill of a very great player: Gilbert does not leave Jane to bring comfort to her envious sister-in-law, it is Jane who leaves Gilbert to find a more suitable mate in an adoring admiral.

[3.]

Like Jane, Maugham claimed that he earned his reputation as a wit by merely telling the truth. In fact, however, Maugham was both a great wit and a cunning apologist for his own moral system, which is that all systems of morality are to be mistrusted and that pleasure is a greater good than any abstract notion of goodness. If one tries to discern his own code from the stories it is precisely not that of a Christian or a gentleman. Within the stories Maugham is in a constant dialogue with this traditional code and he is working to undermine it. As the titles of so many of his stories reveal, he knew his Bible and he knew from having to listen every Sunday of his boyhood to his uncle's sermons, the value of anecdote in moral persuasion. Long after he had escaped from that Sunday influence he worked to uproot it. Maugham wanted to preserve the forms of the rigid Edwardian society in which he grew to manhood while questioning its basic moral assumptions. He once wrote a parable called *The Judgment Seat*[27] in which he challenged the view that there is something ennobling to the character in resisting temptation, and in this context temptation meant the woman to whom one was not married. Maugham assumes the *gravitas* of the recording angel as he sets the scene on the Day of Judgement and tells how throughout their lives John and Ruth denied their passion for each other on account of Mary, John's wife. All three were aware of the situation and by traditional standards all three behaved magnificently. Ruth devoted herself to the sick and the poor; John 'did everything that could be expected of a man who was a Christian and a gentleman' and 'Mary, a good, faithful and (it must be confessed) exceptional wife, never thought to reproach her husband for the madness that had seized him'. Inside though, John hated Mary and Mary hated John with an implacable hatred and Ruth, in performing her charitable offices, becomes domineering, intolerant and vindictive. Yet when the story opens all that is behind them: '. . . grey and drab life had been, but that was passed; they had not sinned and now their reward was at hand.' Maugham's little surprise, as we guess in advance, is that their reward is not at hand, or rather that their reward is complete annihilation. The Eternal extinguishes them utterly. In resisting temptation while on earth they have ceased as human spirits to exist. For all our anticipation the brutality of the end comes as a nasty shock. Uncle Willie steps down from the pulpit with a grim smile on his face. Like all sermons it is heavily loaded in favour of the preacher's point of view and is a justification for his own way of life. What Maugham fails to see is that if you resist temptation merely because you hope for a reward, you will be annihilated more completely than if you succumbed. He cannot conceive how, through resisting temptation, you become more human, more real: here and now in this life. As W. H. Auden says:

'Like everything else which is not the involuntary result of fleeting emotion but the creation of time and will, any marriage, happy or unhappy, is infinitely more interesting and significant than any romance however passionate.'[28] This view of marriage is one to which Maugham did not subscribe.

He made his point again, in a less scriptural manner, in a story called *Virtue*[29] in which Maugham invites a young D.O. on leave from Borneo, at a loose end in London, to meet a respectable middle-aged couple called the Bishops. They go to Ciro's where the young man dances with Margery Bishop and the upshot is that after sixteen years of 'happiness' the Bishops' marriage is completely wrecked. What wrecks it is not that the lovers sleep together but that they do not sleep together. The husband is understanding and the wife behaves like a gentleman (or rather, a lady). The tension engendered by the renunciation drives the husband to drink and an early grave and the lover goes back to Borneo where he does not invite the widow to join him. Maugham discusses the case with a friend:

> '. . . A virtue that only causes havoc and unhappiness is worth nothing. You can call it virtue if you like. I call it cowardice.'
>
> 'The thought of being unfaithful to Charlie while she was living with him revolted her. There are women like that, you know.'
>
> 'Good gracious, she could have remained faithful to him in spirit while she was being unfaithful to him in the flesh. That is a feat of legerdemain that women find it easy to accomplish.'
>
> 'What an odious cynic you are.'
>
> 'If it's cynical to look truth in the face and exercise common sense in the affairs of life, then certainly I'm a cynic and odious if you like.'

The tone here is very typical of the mature Maugham, story-teller, man of the world, mover in society, unshockable observer of the curious behaviour of his friends. It is some way from the impersonality of Maupassant. Maugham is a secret apologist. He is trying to persuade us that hedonism is less harmful to human life than a morality based on trust and loyalty. He has found one area where the old idea of Virtue still obtains and he proceeds to undermine it. It is the old philosophy of 'going lightly'. He is as sharp and amusing an observer as ever but the shadow of Maugham himself falls across his observation, in contrast to the work of his master Maupassant, where the story is observed *en soi*. Take, for instance, Maupassant's story *Happiness*[30] which has Maugham's favourite theme of the world well lost. A group of people sit as the sun goes down outside a villa in the south of France talking about love. Suddenly a confused shape looms up on the horizon. Someone says, 'It is Corsica!' Then the island comes into sharper focus with the contours of its mountains and valleys visible. It is a marvellous image of love—something that is both mysterious and palpable, confused then clear. It is also an image of something we have met already many times in Maugham, the faraway island to which one escapes to find happiness. Then one of the party tells a story of a visit to Corsica some five years before, emphasizing the wildness and remoteness of it and its savage beauty, much as Maugham was to do later with the islands of the Pacific. The traveller meets a very old woman who is looking after her deaf and senile husband. Something in the neatness and severity of her bearing suggests that she is not a native Corsican. It emerges that though she has lived on the island for fifty years she came originally from Nancy and knows the traveller's family. She was Suzanne de Sirmont, daughter of a noble family, who created a great scandal by eloping with a hussar, the son of a peasant.

> I asked:
> 'Have you at least been happy?'
> She answered with a voice which came from her heart:
> 'Oh yes! very happy. He has made me very happy. I have never regretted.'
> I looked at her, sad, surprised, astounded by the sovereign strength of love! That rich young lady had followed this man, this peasant. She was become herself a peasant woman. She had made for herself a life without charm, without luxury, without delicacy of any kind, she had stooped to simple customs. And she loved him yet.

When the man has finished a woman comments:

> 'All the same, she had ideals which were too easily satisfied, needs which were too primitive, requirements which were too simple. She could only have been a fool.'

Another said, in a low, slow voice, 'What matter! she was happy.'

And down there at the end of the horizon, Corsica was sinking into the night, returning gently into the sea, blotting out her great shadow, which had appeared as if in person to tell the story of those two humble lovers who were sheltered by her coasts.

At the end of the anecdote the judgement remains open. The only certain thing that that story tells you about Maupassant is that he was an exquisite artist. This surely is what it means merely to tell the truth. If in the last analysis we put Maugham, mindful of his great gifts as a story-teller and the huge body of work he produced, none of which falls below a high level of excellence, in a class just below that of the greatest international masters of the art, it is because of the ubiquitous presence of himself and the partial view of human possibility that he imposes on his material.

CHAPTER TEN

Don Guillermo and Other Portraits
of the Artist

[1.]

MAUGHAM DID NOT think of writing as a wholly sedentary job, but as one requiring exceptional stamina both physical and mental. For all his stammer he was a very tough and sinewy individual; and in nothing was his toughness more apparent than in his insatiable appetite for travel. He stumped the world to become the best-travelled author of his time, perhaps of any time. Nowadays it is common enough for a famous author to spend much of his working life in travel, hopping on and off aircraft, lecturing and doing special journalistic assignments, and later on to use the material gained in this way in his novels: Graham Greene, Angus Wilson bring the wry comic vision of English fiction to a terrain that is world-wide.

Maugham was the pioneer of the territorial expansion of the English novelist. It was remarkable that one who had grown up at a time when English fiction was dominated by the country house and London society, should have seen how much was to be gained by escaping from them; it was remarkable, too, that someone who believed so implicitly in the conventions of civilized life, and who had constructed such an indomitable routine for his own, should have been so ready to abandon it. But though Maugham was a phenomenal stickler for regular writing hours he had discovered, first of all during lulls in duty behind the front during the First World War, the pleasures of being forced to have nothing to do, and of thus being able to waste time with a clear conscience.

This glorious sense of irresponsibility was what he enjoyed

when he went on his travels and he found great pleasure in an unfamiliar life-style and transient encounters:

> I have slept very comfortably on a mat in a native house in Savaii and luxuriously in an open boat on a Chinese river. I have even enjoyed sleeping in a launch on sacks of copra, and it would be hard to find anything more lumpy. But how exquisite were those starry nights under the Southern Cross! I liked to meet people whom I would never meet again. I found no one boring whom I could expect to see but once in my life.[1]

Above all he enjoyed the sense of escaping from himself, his own literary *persona* and reputation, and finding new material, new patterns. Maugham's travel books are not only interesting for the vivid, witty, shrewd, accurate impressions they give of the countries he visited but also for the glimpses they offer to the admirer of his work as a whole of the author in search of a style. It is instructive to compare the succinct distillations of *On a Chinese Screen* (1922) with the discursive, at times almost garrulous, flow of *The Gentleman in the Parlour* (1930). Admittedly the earlier book was at first intended merely to be off-the-cuff notes for a much longer one that was never written and in it, amidst such poignant sights and sounds as the baby-tower of the infanticides, and the nun's orphanage, and the cry of the coolies as they haul a junk against the current over a rapid, you can still hear the old Maugham giving an airing to his favourite judgement on the drama, that Ibsen only ever had one plot. Yet as a whole the sequences of Oriental sketches has a pared-away impersonality of which his French naturalist masters would have heartily approved; he does genuinely seem to have left himself behind; whereas in the later book we have the emergence of a Maugham who knows he can keep us hooked even when he has no strange landscape to describe, or particular story to tell, merely by the acuity and liveliness of his observations about the craft of letters, and about life itself. Consider the surprising and brilliantly written opening to the book which explains its rather curious title. What is billed as 'a record of a journey from Rangoon to Haiphong' opens with a denigration of Charles Lamb in comparison with Hazlitt whom Maugham has belatedly discovered while travelling up the Irrawady. But what have either Lamb or Hazlitt got to do with

Rangoon or Haiphong, places in which neither of them ever set foot?

The point is simply that in Hazlitt Maugham has discovered an addition to that precious band of writers at whose feet he delighted to sit for long hours to learn the mysteries of his craft, and that this discovery is as momentous to Maugham, more so indeed, than anything he was to see in such legendary places as Mandalay, Bangkok and Angkor.

> I found [he said] a solid writer, without pretentiousness, courageous to speak his mind, sensible and plain, with a passion for the arts that was neither gushing nor forced, various, interested in the life about him, ingenious, sufficiently profound for his purposes, but with no affectation of profundity, humorous, sensitive.[2]

That for a start is no mean attempt at a Hazlittian sentence, as well as being an admirably pithy statement of Maugham's own stylistic aims. On the whole Maugham's prose does not take wing as uninhibitedly as Hazlitt's. It stays closer to the ground and moves with a more measured tread. But not only has Maugham lighted upon a writer after his own heart he has discovered a sentiment, in Hazlitt's essay *On Going a Journey*, that perfectly defines his own pleasure in travel and provides him with an eccentric title for his book; Hazlitt explains what bliss it is

> ... to lose our importunate, tormenting, everlasting personal identity in the elements of nature, and to become the creature of the moment, clear of all ties—to hold the universe only by a dish of sweet-breads, and to owe nothing but the score of the evening— and no longer seeking for applause and meeting with contempt, to be known by no other title than 'The Gentleman in the Parlour!'[3]

Yet as Maugham makes his way through Burma, the Shan States (as they were called then), Siam and Indo-China, he does not truly lose his identity so much as wrestle with it in some bouts of elegant intellectual sparring. He admits that he is often tired of himself and he has a notion that through travel he can add to, and thus change, himself. When he is recording his impression of the pagodas at Pagan or the palace at Mandalay Maugham does efface himself; he gives us some beautiful descriptions of these sights, and of his fellow travellers, but there are also many miles of hard slog by mule or bearer with a monotonous similarity of landscape and it is at such times that Maugham turns inward, and the fascination of the book then becomes to penetrate the mind of Maugham. 'There were a number of subjects I really felt I should come to some conclusion about,' he tells us. Instead of reporting on, say, the evidence around him in Asia of the decline of the British Empire, he prefers to ponder the great conundrums of error and evil, space, time, chance and mutability . . . but the strident ringing of a bell on a recalcitrant mule distracts him, it reminds him of a muffin-seller on a bleak childhood afternoon and forces him to break off from his musings, and wander off on a homelier more professional tack; he invents a character called Blenkinsop who wrote a totally unreadable book that was acclaimed by the London literary world, Mrs. Woolf, Osbert Sitwell, Arnold Bennett, Hugh Walpole . . . and as Maugham witheringly traces the career of Blenkinsop, we are well into the vein that was soon to yield *Cakes and Ale*. Then there is a hiatus in the journey and, as Maugham stops for the night in his bungalow in the jungle, we can observe the familiar pattern of his life reasserting itself. He tries one or more of the seventeen varieties of patience (solitaire) that he knows, settling at length for Canfield. Bedtime brings the novel that he has kept for this particular moment. It is *Du Côté de Guermantes* of which he limits himself rigidly to thirty pages . . . and so on and so on, all the way through Siam and Cambodia and Indo-China to places like Saigon and Hanoi, familiar in another, bloodier context to the contemporary reader. Little did he realize the irony that time would lend to such remarks as 'Hué is a pleasant little town with something of the leisurely air of a cathedral city . . .' Finally, he arrives in Hong Kong where he meets one of those people of no particular importance but who makes for Maugham a definitive remark; it is the obnoxious Elfenbien who gives him his opinion of the human race: 'their heart's in the right place but their head's a thoroughly inefficient organ.' Books, places, artefacts, metaphysics, odds and sods, these are the sources of renewal for Maugham and on each of his travels he goes back to them all.

[2.]

The English writer who finds inspiration abroad usually has one country with which he nurtures a lifelong relation, a land that seems to radiate a benificent influence over his entire work. With George Gissing, although he loved France where he lived at the end of his life, it was Greece; with E. M. Forster, although he loved Italy in which his first novel was set, it was India; with Maugham, although he wrote with admiration of Italy, France and India, in all of which he set major work, it was Spain. He first went there when he was twenty-three and afterwards he wrote *The Land of the Blessed Virgin*; of that youthful effort he wrote later: 'My feelings were genuine enough, but they were the feelings of the travellers who had gone before me. I saw what Borrow and Richard Ford, Théophile Gautier and Merimée had seen.'

Thirty years, and some dozen visits to Spain later, Maugham published *Don Fernando* (1935). One of the lines of thought that occupied him for the whole of his life, both creatively and speculatively, was the strange partnership between fate and the human will; in Paris and London he showed us Philip Carey weaving the pattern of his fate by the exercise of his will; in Spain he reveals a deep current of fatality guiding the actions of his own life, particularly in his relation as a writer with his subject-matter. The book pulls the reader into it inescapably, with the striking instance of the operation of fate with which it opens. The Don Fernando of the title is a tavern-keeper in Seville who also deals in curios. He insists that Don Guillermo —which is how he addresses Maugham—should purchase a certain ancient book. Maugham is most unwilling, but eventually, after three or four refusals, Don Fernando's insistence wears him down. He goes away with the book. The text is in sixteenth-century Spanish and is difficult to read, but after a little patience Maugham succeeds in mastering it, and as he reads it is clear that the volume has, like Hazlitt's essays, or Blackbridge's *Complete Poker Player*, the force of a revelation.

It tells the story of a young man called Inigo in the service of the Duke of Najera who behaves with the greatest gallantry at the siege of Pampluna where he is wounded in the leg. Hooked first by the story of the purchase of the book, we are hooked now by the story *in* the book of chivalry and battle; then for those readers who are ignorant of such things, the trap is sprung: Inigo is St. Ignatius Loyola of whom the book in question was one of the earliest Lives. But now that we have been told what happened to him the narrative breaks off. It is time for some topography. Maugham takes us on a conducted tour of Pampluna—'on the rampart behind the cathedral you may still see the rope-makers making rope in the same way as they have for centuries, oiling their shuttles from oil in a cow's horn, and the makers of espadrilles sewing as though for dear life: which indeed they are'—and then to Loyola, Azpeitia and Manresa, all of which he himself is visiting for the first time, inspired to do so by the book. In Manresa Maugham sees the cave where according to tradition the Saint wrote the first draft of the Spiritual Exercises. As a lifelong practitioner of the written word Maugham has a sense of 'awe' in the face of a work that was such an 'efficacious instrument' in the maintenance of 'ascendancy'. Thus we are led to consider a second book, that of the Saint himself. Maugham deals conscientiously with the circumstances of its composition and the question of borrowings before he goes to the heart of the matter, what the Jesuit founder actually said:

> The title is impressive: *Spiritual Exercises for over-coming oneself and for regulating one's life without being swayed by any inordinate attachment.* A noble aim! It must be a dull mind that is not curious to see what plan this strange man devised to effect so difficult a process.[4]

In Loyola Maugham, the agnostic, has found a blood-brother. Here is someone who, by a combination of intellect and supreme effort of will, has turned vulnerability into a source of endless strength. The Saint is 'an artist who forms living souls to his own image'. But Maugham was never satisfied with mere theory. He tries out one of the exercises and it makes him feel sick. This momentarily abates his admiration.

Admiration is, however, what binds the whole of *Don Fernando* together; it shows Maugham discovering in the golden age of Spain a code and a culture to replace his inherited one of the well-bred English gentleman and the now detested one of Wilde and Pater. The only other imaginative writer of our time to have formed such a close attachment to the Spanish code of honour was a Frenchman, Henry de Montherlant. Both men saw in Spain evidence of that spirit of ascetic dedication they brought to the literary life; both were concerned to write in a style as pure and muscular as possible about the triumphs and failures of the human will; both identified with those whose greatness of soul set them apart from their fellow men and both saw in women a threat to the fulfilment of such greatness. Perhaps one day some student of comparative literature will undertake the task of evaluating them together. It could prove rewarding.

Having thus brought Loyola infinitely closer to us, whatever our own religious belief or lack of it, than a dozen works of Catholic piety, Maugham pauses in his narrative to explain what exactly it is in this book that he is at. Uniquely among his works this is a book about a book that he never succeeded in writing. Over the years his admiration for Spain was such that he had for long been preparing some work of historical fiction in which he could weave together the rich golden strands of the period, territorial conquest, picaresque novelists, extravagant poetry, counter-reformation, the theatre of Lope de Vega, mysticism, sainthood, portrait painting. He toys with a number of heroes—Ponce de Leon the discoverer of Florida, the poet Garcilasco de la Vega at the court of the Duke of Alba, Augustin de Rojas, a strolling player—but for one reason or another none of them quite fills the bill. At length he seems to settle for a traveller from our own shores, 'a young Catholic Scot who had come to seek his fortune under the King of Spain, or the kinsman to an ambassador accredited to the court of Madrid by the aged Queen Elizabeth'. Such a young man would suffer exposure to all the manifold influences abroad at the beginning of the reign of Philip III. Maugham set about his task with a will, but in the event he never wrote the book for the simple reason that he was much more interested in the reality than the fiction. He has far too many hares he wants to chase: a consideration of the Spanish language with its power of forthright expression, and of Spanish literature, with its fantasticated poetry, and its profusion of picaresque novels, that leads him to make distinctions between the waywardness of the amateur writer and the pertinence of the professional, the originality of outlook that reveals talent and the universality of appeal that reveals genius. All this brings us up to Cervantes ('It is unnecessary for me to say anything of the merits of Don Quixote. They shine like the sun at noon. Don Quixote is the most human and most lovable character that the mind of man has invented') and to Maugham's choice as the pick of the picaresques, *Lazarillo de Tormes*. He tilts at the historians who say that it was occasioned by social change, and suggests that it was in fact written for fun. 'I should have thought that the author . . . thought it would be amusing to write the autobiography of a young scamp, and having got hold of a good idea, did what authors do in such a case, wrote it.' Maugham's own rule of fiction-writing, arousing curiosity, then satisfying it with the greatest thoroughness he applies now to this wealth of historical material. The result is a masterpiece of mediation. Maugham relishes the paradoxes thrown up by his subject, the squalor and the magnificence, the brutality and the politeness; he considers in turn all the major figures in the period, and he manages to discover an arresting contradiction relevant to each of them. Out of a very poorly constructed play—'It must be one of the worst plays that was ever written . . . Scenes follow one another with no sequence. Probability is flouted . . .'—Tirso de Molina gave us one of the immortal human types in Don Juan. Cervantes, creator of the supreme exponent of chivalry, lived off the immoral earnings of his wife and sisters. This prompts Maugham to suggest, in a keenly felt digression, that the artist's work must not be judged by his life, and that character in fiction, good and bad, must have its roots in the personality of the artist. Next, in one of the longest sections, he attempts to penetrate the character of El Greco. He cannot accept the conventional view of him as 'a man of an austere temper, indifferent to the things of the earth, who went his lonely ascetic way intent only on expressing his rapt vision'. On the contrary, 'he dwelt in a large house with a display that was thought ostentatious, and he had musicians come from Venice to play to him while he was at dinner. Nothing of this is surprising for it is an error to suppose that the artist lives in a garret from choice ... El Greco had a keen eye on the profits of his trade. He made a great deal of money ...' Maugham notes the suggestion, 'made in a ribald spirit', that El Greco was a homosexual:

> When you survey possibilities it must be admitted that there is in this one a good deal that saves it from being wildly improbable. El Greco spent his childhood and youth in places where he can have conceived no instinctive aversion to that idiosyncrasy. I should say that a distinctive trait of the homosexual is a lack of deep serious-ness over certain things that normal men take seriously. This ranges from an inane flippancy to a sardonic humour. He has a wil-fulness that attaches importance to things that most men find trivial and on the other hand regards cynically the subjects which the common opinion of mankind has held essential to its spiritual welfare. He has a lively sense of beauty but is apt to see beauty especially in decoration. He loves luxury and attaches peculiar value to elegance. He is emotional, but fantastic. He is vain, loquacious, witty and theatrical. With his keen insight and quick sensibility he can pierce the depth, but in his innate frivolity he fetches up from them not a priceless jewel but a tinsel ornament. He has small power of invention, but a wonderful gift for delightful embroidery. He has vitality, brilliance, but seldom strength. He stands on the bank, aloof and ironical, and watches the river of life flow on. He is persuaded that opinion is no more than prejudice. In short he has many of the characteristics that surprise us in El Greco.[5]

Not to mention several that surprise us in Somerset Maugham. Illuminating snatches of self-revelation on the part of the author are one of the pleasures of reading *Don Fernando*; the most interesting insight is connected with the work of another Spanish painter Maugham greatly admired, and about whom he later wrote a separate essay, Francisco de Zurbaran. It was fate operating through a painting by Zurbaran that in the end pre-vented Maugham from writing the book that he had originally planned. It all began when Maugham was in the museum at Cadiz studying the portraits by this artist designed for the monastery in Jerez of the different holy men whose piety illustrated the Carthusian order. Maugham was completely spell-bound by the picture representing the Blessed John

Houghton, the English martyr of the order who had refused to take the Oath of Supremacy and was hanged in 1533 by command of Henry VIII. Zurbaran's portrait of him had been painted some hundred years later and Maugham believed that the features and whole tenor of the face were such that the sitter must have been an Englishman, presumably some obscure English monk resident in the Carthuja when Zurbaran came there to paint. At any rate the face with its ascetic distinction, its restless eager tension, haunted Maugham night and day; he could not get it out of his mind and he came to realize after two or three years of brooding that this man about whom nothing was known would have to be the hero of his novel.

Unfortunately on closer examination it became clear that he was totally unsuitable for the role. He was far too fastidious and, from the worldly and fleshly point of view, too remote a character to undergo all the variety of sensual and other robust adventures that Maugham had planned for him. And yet the power of this putative monk over Maugham's imagination was such that it was quite impossible for him to turn to any other model for his hero. The only course open to him was to abandon that book and to use the material differently, in the book that became *Don Fernando*. If Maugham has a hero in *Don Fernando* it is the Spanish sea-captain of Columbus's time who sent word to an Armenian monk who begged him for a lift: 'I will take him in my ship; but tell him that I go to range the universal sea . . . We go to rove the world and it is not possible for us to tell where the winds will carry us.' Although of an earlier period than that of which he is writing, this man epitomizes for Maugham the sense he has acquired in his wanderings through the Golden Age of Spain of belonging to something greater than the self, that he could corroborate from his own experience as an artist, but without surrendering to the Christian God. He discovered a belief in Man. 'It is not in art that they excelled, they excelled in what is greater than art—in man. But it is thought that has the last word.'

Don Fernando is still not as widely read as it ought to be, and there are many, I suspect, who count themselves lovers of Maugham's work who do not even know of its existence. Yet when it appeared in 1935 its merits did not go unrecognized.

Graham Greene called it 'Maugham's best book';[6] and Osbert Sitwell, reviewing it in the *London Mercury*, said that it had,

> ... the curious, controlled easiness, the limpid effortless phraseology, that have given Mr Maugham his great public, and have at the same time, tended to make those persons to whom the difficulty of a work constitutes its virtue underrate his value as a writer ... The reviewer of this book has often travelled in Spain, and stayed many months there. To him, at any rate, Don Fernando brought back a thousand incidents he had forgotten, and explained a thousand small happenings he had not understood.[7]

The haunting of Maugham by the Houghton painting gives us a fascinating glimpse of how he approached the task of creating character. It was a fatalistic process in which the characters appeared to create themselves, willing their existence upon his conscious mind, and having their tangible origin in an already existing work of art or in some actual individual whom Maugham had observed in real life. What has struck me in my systematic reading of Maugham is how often he found a vivid analogue for a character, or a place, in the visual arts. If literature was Maugham's profession, the activity that above all else he believed in and trusted, the visual arts were his consuming passion. His lifelong friendship with Gerald Kelly was a marriage of true minds; Maugham was a connoisseur of impeccable taste and immense knowledge. He acquired his fine collection of English eighteenth-century theatrical portraits, which he donated to the National Theatre, by another accident of fate that caused him to buy one or two when he had first begun to make money out of the theatre, but his real taste can be seen in the collection of Impressionists and post-Impressionists that adorned the walls of the Mauresque and were sold at Sothebys in 1962, dating from his Lion de Belfort days in Paris with Gerald Kelly. Maugham had, it would seem, a Socratic humility in his discussion of literature with his friends, posing as a plain, ordinary reader who liked to skip the boring bits, and who enjoyed a good story, but he could be quite sharp at times when it came to painting. At least this is what Garson Kanin found one day when he was standing by a picture of a nude man wearing a hat polishing a stone floor, when Maugham appeared, saying:

'You don't know . . . a damn thing about pictures, do you?'
'No, I don't. But how would you know that?'
'I could tell . . . from the way you were looking at that one.'
'Really?'
'Yes. Just as one knows when . . . Kenneth Clark looks that he knows all about pictures.'
The subject of my ignorance does not vaguely interest me, so I make pass-the-time conversation.
'Who painted this?' I ask.
'Kenneth Clark didn't ask. He knew at once.'
'No doubt.'
'It's a . . . Toulouse-Lautrec, actually.'[8]

Scattered among Maugham's writings there is so much understanding and description of painting that one feels he could easily have been a critic or an art historian himself had he not been a creative writer. At the beginning of his career he had felt the need to compensate for his sense of limitation as a descriptive writer by borrowing from 'ready-mades', and the habit once formed then became a necessary stimulus in the creation of character. The earliest version in his work of the Sibyl, Miss Ley in *The Merry-Go-Round* was, we saw, based on a portrait bust of Nero's mother Aggripina in the museum at Naples, and in *The Explorer* the heroine was a Furse. In *Cakes and Ale* Lord George looked 'like some jolly rubicund merchant in an old Dutch picture' whereas the high street at Blackstable 'looked like a picture by Samuel Scott'. Blanche Stroeve in *The Moon and Sixpence* was seen by her husband, admittedly a painter, 'bending slightly over the table in the gracious attitude of Chardin's *Benedicte* . . .'; the lovely Sally in the story *Red*, 'reminded him of the Psyche in the Museum of Naples,' whereas what made Laura, the heroine of *A Woman of Fifty* attractive, 'was the odd mingling in her appearance of the Madonna in an altarpiece by one of the later Italian painters and a suggestion of sensuality'. Julia in *Theatre* is by turns a Botticelli and a Romney and has her portrait painted by McEvoy. In the play *Caesar's Wife* Violet resembles 'a Gainsborough portrait rather than a drawing in a paper of Paris fashions'. The criminal lawyer who defends Berger in *Christmas Holiday* 'reminded you, I hardly know why, of one of those mysterious figures

in a Longhi picture'. Elliot Templeton's costume for the party
he never attended was 'a copy of the gorgeous dress worn
by Philip II in Titian's portrait at the Prado, and when Elliot
told me it was exactly the costume the Count de Lauria had
worn at the wedding of the King of Spain with the Queen
of England I could not but think he was giving rein to his
imagination'.[9]

Once Maugham had hit upon a work of art that gave him a
pre-existing visual impression of the character or the scene,
then he gave rein to his own imagination every bit as freely as
the preposterous and generous Elliot. He goes into this whole
vexed question of portraits from art and life in *The Summing Up*
which continues and develops themes adumbrated in *Don
Fernando*. Maugham cites Turgenev in support of the view that
'it is only if you have a definite person in your mind that you
can give vitality and idiosyncrasy to your creation'.[10] But once
you begin to try to put the person down on paper imaginative
processes take over and the chance of the fictional character
resembling the real one at all exactly is remote. Quentin Bell
has an interesting footnote on this in his life of his aunt,
Virginia Woolf:

> Mrs Maxse [Kitty Lushington] was certainly the original of Mrs
> Dalloway, but I do not think that novel provides, or was meant to
> provide, an exact portrait. Lord David Cecil, who knew Mrs
> Maxse, does not see any close resemblance. Virginia comes
> closest to exact portraiture when she loves her model. She did not
> love Kitty Maxse.[11]

Moreover, there may well be more than one original for a
character. According to Proust's biographer George D. Painter,
Alfred Agostinelli, Colette d'Alton, Mlle. Bauche, Marie de
Chevilly, Marie Finlay, Hélène d'Ideville, Louisa de Mornand,
Albert Nahmias, Marie Nordlinger and Henri Rochat all went
into the making of Albertine.[12] How many people have told
one that they know who the original of Widmerpool is, each
with a different answer? I have avoided positing originals for
Maugham's characters in the present book but for those readers
who enjoy detecting possible models from the life I would refer
them to the work of Robert Lorin Calder. If Mr. Calder is right

in suggesting that Elliot Templeton was prompted by 'Chips' Channon[13] then it is surely of interest to note that the Templeton-type is already firmly established in Maugham's work in *The Hero* and in Thornton Clay in *Our Betters* long before Maugham ever met Chips.

[3.]

Maugham was in his mid-sixties when he published *The Summing Up*. He was at the height of his powers and ready to stake his claim as a serious writer. Rightly or wrongly he was conscious of never having read a just assessment of himself from the critics. In a quiet, even-tempered, modest yet authoritative tone he offers a self-assessment. It is a masterpiece of a kind rare in English, a self-portrait that contains an investigation of literature as a craft whose principles may be formulated and argued about. I once wrote to Evelyn Waugh asking him if he would care to comment on an interview with a distinguished fellow novelist that we had printed in the Sunday newspaper by which I was employed at the time and I received the following reply: 'I am sorry to say that it does not provoke comment and I am too old and too English to want to expatiate my views on fiction.'[14] Maugham suffered neither from such premature senility nor from such native reticence. He was continental enough to enjoy the *causerie*, and with more than forty years of published work behind him, he was ready to take the reader into his confidence, and to tell him about the trials and tribulations as well as the rewards and joys of the trade.

In *The Summing Up* it is, as it were, open day in the Master's work-room. He bids us welcome and shows us in, while he points out all his various pieces of equipment, expounding the precise function of each and recalling the uses to which it has been put. He is courteous, frank and detached about many of his attitudes, to marriage for example; naturally he is not going to give us his love-letters to read but if at the end of our visit we would care to take a seat for a moment he will open up to us about the ultimate questions of truth, beauty and goodness which he has in his layman's way long pondered.

The Summing Up is a book to be read and re-read rather than read about. I have never met anyone who, once having read it, did not admire it, and I have heard many people say that it is Maugham's best book. It certainly makes the view that some still hold, that Maugham succeeded as a story-teller by means of a superficial cynicism instead of a mature attitude to life, seem hopelessly out of touch. Combined with the story-teller was the brilliantly original self-taught thinker and critic, a formidable example of that literary type we sometimes call in English a sage, who begins to show himself fully in *Don Fernando* for the first time, and now has a free rein to give us his mature reflections on all the main literary forms he has used and on the language he has striven so hard to make a delicate instrument at the service of his subtle play of mind.

He puts himself under the most searching scrutiny trying to define the kind of writer he is and to answer some of the charges that have been laid against him; this leads to speculation upon such matters close to his heart as the qualities required to live in the world of imagination rather than the world of action, on the pleasures and difficulties of working with actors and on the degree of collaboration which a playwright may expect from an audience, on the art of the short story and the stage it had reached at the interesting point in time when he began to practise it, on the need in England for a critic with the dedication, the range of Saint Beuve, on Hazlitt again who he now discovers could at times be 'unduly rhetorical; and sometimes his decoration is as fussy as Victorian Gothic', and on a dozen other questions that although literary in origin become of the greatest general interest as Maugham discusses them, each discussion being cunningly interwoven with strands of autobiography and recollection marking the various phases of Maugham's triumphant career.

The declared intention is to trace and round off that mysterious 'pattern' formed by the totality of Maugham's life and work. It is a splendidly nebulous concept, this 'pattern' meaning everything and nothing. Maugham strove as hard as anyone who has ever written in English for formal perfection, and he wanted now to discern a perfect formal pattern in his own career. He followed his nose, his nose for a good story that is, and at the end of the day he called his immense achievement a pattern. The whole concept of pattern was a reversion to the ninetyish aestheticism, to Miss Ley's cult of beauty, that he thought he had outgrown. But if the pattern was formed by the conscious mind, ordering the experience retained by the memory, Maugham believed in the constant renewal of that experience through outgoing contact with other human beings just as much as inward communing with books and works of art. The importance of books, and of what is called culture, in this whole process to Maugham can be assessed not only by the catholic range of his own library, part of which is now at The King's School, Canterbury, but also in the books of essays that he was himself to take so much trouble over and publish during and after the war: *Books and You, Great Novelists and their Novels, The Vagrant Mood, Points of View*. The tension in his temperament between the love of cultural life and the need for 'real' life is one that Maugham confesses to the reader with a candour worthy of respect:

> I have put books aside [he tells us in a passage devoted to his youthful reading] only because I was conscious that time was passing and that it was my business to live. I have gone into the world because I thought it was necessary in order to get the experience without which I could not write, but I have gone into it also because I wanted experience for its own sake. It did not seem to me enough only to be a writer. The pattern I had designed for myself insisted I should take the utmost part I could in this fantastic affair of being a man. I desired to feel the common pains and enjoy the common pleasures that are part of the common human lot. I saw no reason to subordinate the claims of sense to the tempting lure of spirit, and I was determined to get whatever fulfilment I could out of social intercourse and human relations, out of food, drink and fornication, luxury, sport, art, travel, and as Henry James says, whatever. But it was an effort, and I have always returned to my books and my own company with relief.[15]

A similar tone, though one tinged by economic necessity and creative unsuccess can, I think, be detected in a book published thirty-five years earlier than Maugham's. Listen for a moment to this:

I had in me the makings of a scholar. With leisure and tranquility of mind, I should have amassed learning. Within the walls of a college, I should have lived so happily, so harmlessly, my imagination ever busy with the old world. In the introduction to his History of France, Michelet says: 'J'ai passé a côté du monde et j'ai pris l'histoire pour la vie.' That as I can see now, was my true ideal; through all my battlings and miseries I have always lived more in the past than in the present. At the time when I was literally starving in London, when it seemed impossible that I should ever gain a living by my pen, how many days have I spent at the British Museum, reading as disinterestedly as if I had been without a care![16]

This comes from Gissing's *The Private Papers of Henry Ryecroft*, a work that has the same texture of a tapestry made out of a writer's own life and his reflections on his career. It was writers like Pater and Gissing who were in retreat from life, who tried to give some positive force to that retreat whom Maugham saw as an awful warning. He loathed Pater with a loathing that strikes one by its intemperateness. Gissing he never mentioned though probably he had read him. Yet for all Maugham's protestations he, too, is by temperament at least half a recluse. Like Ryecroft and Gissing, Maugham was in certain respects unfitted for life. They were all aloof. This characteristic which we have seen Maugham define in his creative work in so many different ways he now applies to himself. It is his greatest value if something so negative can be described as such, and it is precisely this quality of aloofness that Graham Sutherland instinctively analysed and brought out so brilliantly in his famous portrait.

And yet the aloof artistic recluse is also a man of the world, intent on pursuing his personal pattern in the world. This is the paradox at the heart of Maugham. He is aware of all the dangers inherent in the cult of beauty and yet does he not believe that words alone are 'certain good'? He is contemptuous of culture, when as in the case of the French, it becomes an exclusive priority over the practical necessities of life, and he is always ready to see the correlation between culture and the yellow streak, a cheerful murderer will gain from him the admiration that he denies to a failed poet.

[4.]

A cheerful murderer was at the centre of Maugham's next book, a novel called *Christmas Holiday* (1939). He was a young man whose trial Maugham had attended in Paris and whom he had gone to St. Laurent de Maroni expressly to meet. He called him Robert Berger and suggested that although he had economic motive for his killings, they were really the result of a perverted creative instinct, or urge for self-fulfilment. It is a dangerous doctrine and Maugham does no more than flirt with it. But then *Christmas Holiday* is a novel full of dangerous doctrines which are what it is all about. Maugham is aware of the gathering storm that was about to burst upon Europe, and he found a way of expressing the unease through the consciousness of one young Englishman whose long weekend on the loose in the French capital gives the book its title. He comes from a family as firmly rooted in English soil as the Maughams, the Masons. It is a nasty moment for them when young Charley, just down from Cambridge, wants to become an artist and a great relief when, after thinking it over, he sensibly agrees to go into his predestined berth in the offices of the family estate like his father before him. As a reward for his good sense his father treats him to a jaunt in Paris, giving him a knowing leer as he sets off.

It is his intellectual, social, moral and political virginity that Charley loses, everything indeed but his sexual one, and when he eventually returns home 'the bottom had fallen out of his world'. Maugham takes a keen delight in shattering the cultivated insularity that Charley has inherited from his parents. ('It was a happy accident that they liked Debussy better than Arthur Sullivan and Virginia Woolf better than John Galsworthy.') The shattering comes mainly through a former Cambridge friend of Charley's who is now working in Paris as a journalist, and who has become a fanatical right-wing revolutionary; into this character of the potential police chief Maugham has put his sense of the totalitarian threat. Simon is a frighteningly ruthless figure who even now sends a shiver down the reader's spine; he is the antithesis of Larry in *The Razor's Edge*.

Philip Carey's initiation into adulthood in Paris spanned quite a time; Charley's is rapid and traumatic, through the demonic impact of his former friend and the world of pimps and crooks and tarts that he inhabits, while Maugham with his incorrigible connoisseurship reminds us of the older Paris. He works into the story a scene where the hero, in that very human way Maugham was so good at catching, takes time off to go to the Louvre with the murderer's White Russian wife. Charley knows the collection well, having been to see it several times already, during earlier visits to Paris in the company of his parents. 'After all, it's part of a gentleman's education to have done the great galleries of Europe,' his father told him, and he recalls tramping round the different rooms with his mother and her comments on many of the famous pictures. She quoted Pater by heart as she stood in front of the Giaconda! Only Maugham, one feels, with his passion for painting, could take time off in the middle of a novel about sex and murder to check up on his own pictorial responses and define the generation gap between his characters through them. But he manages to mix this in with his description of the sleazy café where the libérés from St. Laurent congregate, and the story of the homosexual bookmaker who was killed; it all shakes up into a final pre-war Maugham cocktail that still has quite a kick left in it today. Evelyn Waugh, reviewing *Christmas Holiday*,[17] admired its accuracy, economy and control, while Graham Greene found the story within a story so maladroitly handled that it seemed incredible to him that Maugham could have used this device so well in *Cakes and Ale*.[18]

[5.]

Maugham continued to travel, enlarging his 'pattern' all the time. A trip to the Caribbean at the suggestion of Kipling, who told him that he would find good material for stories there, proved strangely fruitless from this point of view. It was in a different corner of the globe altogether that his imagination was fired. In 1938 Maugham toured extensively in India, meeting a huge hierarchy of people there from the Viceroy and governors to mystics and yogis; he studied sufis, fakirs, occultists, making copious notes on means of self-discipline and mortification practised by the holy men. At Benares he observed that, 'Nothing can be more impressive than to saunter down the Ganges by boat in the evening just before the sun sets . . . A wonderful sense of peace descends upon you. There is a great silence'; and in the morning he found the ritual bathing in the river of hundreds of people 'a moving, a wonderfully thrilling spectacle'. The following year Maugham went on working excursions to Lens where, in emulation of Zola in *Germinal*, he lived among coal-miners and acquired material afterwards used for Larry's labours with Polish miners below ground in *The Razor's Edge*. When he was in England at the end of the year, he spent much time in Bermondsey, finding a rich crop of anecdotes among the working people for a projected novel about the Cockney in the modern world. Maugham's receptivity to anecdote, his flair for the vital germ was such that potential material came his way in his own backyard in the Riviera just as readily as on his travels. A murder at San Rafael, the death of a café-owner in Nice—they all went down into the *Notebook*, inchoate short stories about creatures of circumstance, along with others of Monaco in the eighteenth century during a visit from George III's brother, the Duke of York, none of them in fact ever to be written up further.

Maugham returned to the Riviera in July of 1939 from London. His daughter and her husband were to join him and he looked forward to a pleasant family party spent partly at the Mauresque and partly on Gerald Haxton's yacht *Sara* which was moored at Villefranche. For once he was not putting a work of fiction down on paper but planning one in his mind:

I intended to go back to London for a month before starting for India, where I meant to pass the winter. I had spent a winter there two years before and had found in that wonderful country much to excite my imagination, and I was eager to go back. I have never been able to write anything unless I had a solid and ample store of information for my wits to work upon. I expected this second visit to enable me to get some shape into the multitudinous impressions I had received and to complete the pattern that was vaguely outlined in my fancy.[19]

The possibility of war was talked about but not taken seriously, somehow, in a leisurely holiday pattern of life. 'We dined,' says Maugham, 'on the terrace among the orange trees, and when the moon was full over the sea, strewing her brilliance on the calm water in a great highway of white light, the scene was so lovely it took your breath away.'[20] Abruptly it all came to an end. 'I once,' he said, 'saw a waiter carrying an immense pile of plates suddenly trip and all the plates crashed noisily to the floor; things went wrong with just that unexpected and startling effect.'[21]

In *Strictly Personal* (1942), from which the above quotations come, Maugham told of his own adventures in the early part of the Second World War. It is a first-person narrative of a kind unique in his œuvre, written out of the direct pressure of events. His guests and family all went back to England; several of his Italian servants defected across the border; the Senghalese troops moved in along the Riviera. Maugham and Gerald went aboard the *Sara* with its crew of three (two Italians and a French cabin boy) and they sailed to Bandol. After a week Gerald returned on board one day with the news that the Germans had marched into Poland. Maugham, who had already offered his services to the Ministry of Information when he had been in England, sent a telegram reminding them of his offer.

Meanwhile, German residents in France, many of them refugees from the Nazis, were being interned, as later their counterparts in Britain would be on the Isle of Man, among them Lion Feuchtwanger, author of *Jew Süss*. Maugham intervened through his acquaintance Jean Giraudoux, who was a high-ranking official in the French Ministry of Information, to get him released, and eventually succeeded. It is piquant to contemplate the master of the plain style in English and the master of the *précieux* style in French, corresponding on this matter at a time of national crisis. After a few weeks of this Maugham and Gerald got fed up with life aboard the *Sara* and they took a taxi back to the Mauresque. Maugham toyed with an anthology he was preparing of his own views on literature. At length the Ministry of Information gave him an assignment. It was to write a series of articles about France and the French war effort and to sound out the French attitude to their British allies. In order to write the articles Maugham travelled around France visiting troops and civilians. He went to Nancy, to Strasbourg, to Toulon. He went to factories to talk to munitions workers and aboard ships to chat with matelots and admirals. He returned home just before Christmas and began to write up the material he had assembled. It was the only time in his life that he essayed reportage and it did not come easily to him: 'I find this sort of writing more difficult than fiction. I am hampered by the facts I have to deal with and I need time and reflection to set them in order.' However, they were soon written and Maugham went to London in their wake, travelling by air for the first time in his life.

Maugham's pieces about France were published first as articles and then in March 1940 as a sixpenny pamphlet under the title *France at War*. These informed eulogies of French morale and French determination to put an end to the German menace read strangely now; they are evidence of his deep affection for the country in which he had made his home for so long, but they show how dangerous it is for a writer to go in for propaganda even at a time of crisis. Yet inaccurate as they were in all their prophecies, they still are by Maugham, and even under the pressure of this uncongenial work his true touch has not completely deserted him. He is fascinating on the difference in modes of address of the French army and the French naval officer. Of the latter he says: 'They work so hard that I could not believe the French navy would ever produce another Loti . . . it will be hard in future for a naval officer, obliged to concentrate on his ceaseless duties, to attain high rank and to achieve as well the distinction as a novelist which was won by the author of *Pêcheurs d'Islande*.'[22] (This is a rare reference in Maugham's work to his fictional forebear in the Pacific.) The articles were such a success that someone in the Ministry of Information proposed that Maugham should write a similar series about England. 'We set about getting the various permissions that were necessary,' Maugham commented wryly, 'but they were not so easy to get as they had been in France. There I had been a distinguished English writer to whom all facilities should be granted; in England I was just another of those damned authors who came round interfering with people's business.'[23] It all came to nothing and he was sent back to France to report on the situation there. Shortly after his return the Germans invaded Belgium and Holland.

No one in France could quite believe that the end was so near. When Pétain broadcast to the nation that they must sue for peace, the wife of Maugham's gardener spoke for them all—'La pauvre France,' she murmured. Maugham went to the consul in Nice who told him to board a cargo-ship now at Cannes and make his way back to England via Gibraltar. Haxton, as an American citizen, stayed on at the Mauresque to do what he could to save its treasures. Maugham packed minimal baggage in which there was room for three books: Plato's *Trial and Death of Socrates, Esmond* and *Villette.* 'Both of these novels,' he commented of the two last, 'were long and would take a considerable time to read, and I had read neither for many years.' Ever since the episode of the Bore, Maugham had had a horror of death by drowning and he inquired of a doctor friend the quickest way to go if the ship was struck. The answer was not to struggle but to open his mouth and let the water pour into it. Fortunately it was not necessary, and during the long nightmare voyage back to England aboard the collier *Saltersgate,* in the company of 500 other refugees, Maugham had ample time in which to finish reading all three books. His account of the hazards of the journey, the straitened conditions of life, the various people he met, and the manner in which they stood up to the harsh necessities of that existence, is one of his finest pieces of writing. There was little means of distraction or amusement during the course of the interminable weeks but Maugham managed to provide some entertainment by telling stories to his fellow-passengers which proved enormously popular. Even amidst these extremities he remained a professional.

Maugham arrived in London in time to experience part of the Blitz, which he spent in the Dorchester Hotel, analysing the reasons for the French collapse. There was quite a gathering at night in the lounges and restaurant when the air-raid alert sounded. On one occasion an elderly woman-friend reproved Maugham for wearing his day clothes. 'I can see no reason,' she said, 'why just because there's a raid, a gentleman shouldn't dress like a gentleman.' Maugham took the point but his stay in this outpost of pre-war gentility was destined to be cut short. The Ministry of Information suggested that he should leave Britain for the United States and use all his formidable powers of persuasion to improve our relations with that country.

CHAPTER ELEVEN

At Work in the States

[1.]

SOMERSET MAUGHAM'S AMERICAN publisher, Nelson P. Doubleday and his wife Ellen, met their distinguished sexagenarian British author at La Guardia in October 1940. For his first reaction on landing here is Garson Kanin, ever ready with the appropriate anecdote:

> As soon as he had completed the formalities, he asked if he might have a bourbon old-fashioned. They took him to the airport bar, where he ordered his drink carefully, with complete instructions. In time it was served. He drank it with great relish and thanked the Doubledays. Whereupon he took an ampoule of poison out of his vest pocket, put it on the floor, and crushed it under his heel, saying 'I won't need this now Nelson.'[1]

In 1946 Maugham made handsome acknowledgement in a speech to the Library of Congress, of the hospitality both he and his family had enjoyed in America during the war, and as a token of his gratitude he presented the Library with the manuscript of *Of Human Bondage*, and later in 1950 with its ancestor *The Artistic Temperament of Stephen Carey*, insisting that this piece of apprentice work should never be published. In the dark uncertain days of 1940 the plan was that the Doubledays would build a house for him on their estate, Parker's Ferry, at Yemasee in South Carolina; in the meantime he stayed in New York, acclimatizing himself and giving interviews and lectures. His very first leading man in the theatre, Harley Granville Barker, was there also working for the British Information Service. Forty years later and they were colleagues again! H. G. Wells had been in New York looking, according to

Maugham, 'old, tired and shrivelled. He was as perky as he has always been but with something of an effort. His lectures were a failure. People couldn't hear what he said and didn't want to listen to what they could hear. They left in droves . . .'[2] One journalist announced that Maugham had come to the States as a British agent, Ashenden *redivivus*, but his efforts on behalf of the British Government were confined to literary work. He began by telling the true story of the Fall of France, his own escape and life aboard the cargo ship, publishing in magazine form material that afterwards appeared in *Strictly Personal*. It was during this period, while in some financial uncertainty, that Maugham discovered his personal vein of literary reminiscence could prove rewarding. The first of his *causerie* volumes *Books and You*, carefully chosen menus of reading in English and American literature with appropriate comments, had appeared in 1940,[3] and now he turned his hand to discussion of the detective story, reading under bombing, favourite paintings, in articles in *Redbook* magazine. In December he visited Chicago where he always enjoyed seeing the Seurats in the Art Institute. In January 1941 he went to Hollywood where he was not the only well-known British novelist to be found in film-land. Christopher Isherwood had arrived in the spring of 1939 to clarify his ideas about pacifism with Aldous Huxley and Gerald Heard, who had both settled in Los Angeles some years earlier. 'I found,' Isherwood writes, 'that Heard and Huxley were engaged in the study of Vedanta philosophy and the practice of meditation. They introduced me to their friend Swami Prabhavananda, a Hindu monk of the Ramakrishna Order who had founded a small Vedanta centre in Hollywood.'[4] Great minds were meditating alike: Maugham was mulling over his pre-war journeys in India, shaping them as an integral part of a long fictional narrative, but it would be some time before he would be able to get any of this down on paper. What came next from his pen, published in the spring, was *Up at the Villa*, a slight *nouvelle* elaborated from an unpublished story about the amorous prospects of an English widow in pre-war Florence. It has a somewhat *réchauffé* readability with echoes of both *The Letter* and *Caesar's Wife*: after an ugly shooting incident in which her bedfellow of the night is killed, the stuffy British diplomat, and the raffish bon viveur, both in love with her, behave like gentle-men and get her off the hook. Pamela Hansford Johnson, in *Books of the Month*, thought it 'fascinating and elegant'[5] and Anthony West in the early days of his career as a critic for the *New Statesman*, while admitting that the main episode was 'incredibly melodramatic', made a good point when he said that the story displayed 'three completely different types of male pride . . . exposed to a particularly deadly type of female sexual ethics'.[6] Otherwise it got pretty terrible reviews on both sides of the Atlantic. Still, this was not exactly being ignored by the intelligentsia. Isherwood worked on a screen play for a film of the book that was never made.

As soon as the house at Yemasee was ready Maugham moved to South Carolina. 'The moan of the wind in the pine trees was like the distant singing of the coloured people, singing their sad song to a heedless or helpless God,'[7] he wrote with a nostalgic splash of the old 'nineties purple. Three such coloured people were deputed to look after him, a cook, a maid and a gardener, and he had his own writing-shack separate from the house; sitting at his desk he reflected upon some American delusions:

(i)   That there is no class-consciousness in this country.
(ii)   That American coffee is good.
(iii)   That Americans are business-like.
(iv)   That Americans are highly sexed and that red-heads are more highly sexed than others.[8]

For his main professional work he was putting together some articles designed to show how one middle-class British family responded to the challenge of the war; these pieces were later elaborated into a novel that appeared in 1942 called *The Hour Before the Dawn*. The every-word-he-ever-wrote Maugham *aficionado* will want to hunt it down to look at, but it cannot seriously be recommended to anyone else. As a self-banished exile Maugham's knowledge of English life had for years been confined to the view from the penthouse suite of the Dorchester Hotel, a commanding but remote prospect, and he had not been back in England anything like long enough to des-cribe in convincing detail how the well-to-do country-bred Hendersons coped as their menfolk were called up and the evacuees descended upon their remaining women. Maugham put among them one conscientiously objecting son and one attractive female refugee who turns out to be a spy. The novel quite lacks that authentic sultry atmosphere of wartime treachery evoked by Elizabeth Bowen in *The Heat of the Day*, nor do its evacuees have the hilarious accuracy of Evelyn Waugh's in *Put Out More Flags*. Moreover, it contains things like the presentation of a white feather to the 'conchie' and expressions like 'women are queer cattle' that belong more to Maugham's Edwardian novels than anything recalling 1939. It has never been published in England.

In addition Maugham wrote numerous articles while he was in America with the aim of bringing the people of the two nations, allies after Pearl Harbor, into a greater measure of common understanding. These show him at his most professional, putting all his expertise and charm at the service of a wartime chore and making something thoroughly worthwhile out of it. One such article, 'Why d'you dislike us?' appeared in the *Saturday Evening Post* in April 1942; in it Maugham made no bones about the anti-British feeling he sensed throughout the States. It even extended, he felt, to the civilized area of literary criticism. 'Edmund Wilson,' he wrote, 'is, I believe, the most acute critic now writing in America, but when you read between the lines of his intelligent books you can hardly fail to notice his general attitude of exasperated contempt for the English.' Maugham proceeds to combat this hostility by pointing to some real differences between the two countries; what, for instance, they regard as funny: 'American humour depends on exaggeration, while English humour depends on irony.'[9] Finally he goes into his favourite question of class-consciousness and social snobbery, amplifying the point made in his *Notebook*. This particular article brought Maugham scores of letters.

Maugham also received requests to write for the Free French journal that had sprouted in England. He refused because he disliked the eulogistic Francophile Charles Morganic tone of these publications, believing now that one of the causes of the French defeat was their own complacency about their civilization. 'The war,' he said, 'has made manifest what only the very astute saw,' which was that for the past hundred years France had been a second-class power masquerading as a first-class one.[10] As we read these sour reflections on the French, published in the *Notebook*, we should remember Maugham's understanding of the ordinary French people. At the same time he wrote a story, *The Unconquered*, published first in *Colliers Magazine* in 1943, that has for its heroine a young French girl, raped by a German soldier, and driven eventually to infanticide rather than marry him. Her elderly parents gradually come to collaborate with him. Maugham assessed the situation astutely from afar. Gerald Haxton had eventually had to leave France and the Villa Mauresque to its fate. He was now working for the United States Government in Washington D.C., but he was not well and was taken to hospital in New York where Maugham was a constant visitor. Otherwise the Master lived in isolation at Yemasee with his black servants, instructing the cook how to make duck à l'orange, sometimes passing a whole day seeing no one else, and after the morning's writing was done, mooching about the woods which he loved. In the summer he would take a vacation and go East: to the Colonial Inn at Edgartown on Martha's Vineyard, continuing there his early rising, morning writing, and the rest of the day spent in relaxation, with a visit to the movies most evenings.[11]

[2.]

Now that he had cleared his desk of wartime chores, he had the time and space to work at the long novel that was to contain his most mature thoughts about life, and to be the last triumphant example of his technique of story-telling. He found a title for it in the Katha-Upanishad in a quotation that serves as an epigraph to the book: 'The sharp edge of a razor is difficult to pass over; thus the wise say the path to Salvation is hard.'

It appeared in the spring of 1944 and had two antecedents in previous works: one was a play called *The Road Uphill*, written in 1924 and never produced, and the other was a story *The Fall of Edward Barnard* that appeared in *The Trembling of a Leaf* in 1921. Both open by describing a small group of well-heeled, fashionable, 'socialite', successful people in the immediately post-First World War Chicago. For Maugham such ostensibly charming people embodied to perfection the drives motivating the majority of his fellow men and women in the modern world. One of them in the story reflects that,

> . . . he was glad that he had been born in the most important city in the United States. San Francisco was provincial, New York was effete; the future of America lay in the development of its economic possibilities, and Chicago, by its position and by the energy of its citizens, was destined to become the real capital of the country.

In the 1920s the antithesis of such energy for Maugham lay in the unconstrained, Loti-like, sun-drenched life of the South Seas and Edward Barnard, betrothed to Isabel Longstaffe, 'no city in the world could have produced her but Chicago', goes to Tahiti never to leave. He finds his salvation in the delectable company of a Polynesian girl and an ex-con man from his native city, both of whom seem much closer to truth, beauty and goodness than the respectable folk back home. In the play, discovered by the indefatigable Mander and Mitchenson among the Master's papers and acknowledged by him as an early work 'that came to nothing', salvation is sought in Paris where the hero goes—like his counterpart the would-be pianist in *The Alien Corn*—to try to escape from the Chicagoan values through art; on hearing that he will never be anything but a gifted amateur he tears up all his pictures and declares he must now seek 'unknown lands of the soul'. He does, however, undertake the intellectual effort of writing a book (shades of Ibsen's Eilert Lovborg) which, when it appears, is hailed as a revolutionary work by a professor at Chicago University. This is one of several strands in which this play's story-line anticipates the novel written thirty years later; another is the inclusion in it for comic purposes of the social snob.

Once these interesting antecedents have been noted one hastens to add that *The Razor's Edge* is a work much greater in depth and scope than either of them and needs to be viewed in isolation from them and in comparison with its peers. The simplistic antithesis of Edward Barnard's fall is replaced by Larry Darrell's conversion to one of the great religions of the

world, and the contrast between its values and those of the
modern world. No religious novel was ever penned with as
cunning a measure of scepticism. Here is 'Somerset Maugham',
the hard-working, man-of-the-world novelist in Chicago in 1919
when the book begins on his way to the Far East; thereafter he
shuttles back and forth to Paris and the South of France where
he lives, observing the while some American friends among
whom a new generation is coming to adulthood, and the
novelist invites his readers to share his prattle about them if we
will. In this confidential urbane manner his episodic narrative
breaks off from time to time to permit him some general reflections. 'I have never begun a novel with more misgiving,' he
announces to prepare us for those passages where the hero
makes an intensive study of religion and philosophy. 'If I call it
a novel it is only because I don't know what else to call it.' The
character of Larry was suggested to Maugham by a New York
taxi driver whom he spoke to for about twenty minutes.[12]
Because his hero is an obscure figure and not like Gauguin, an
historical one, he can pretend that this time in tracing the career
of a man who lived for the sake of an ideal he has 'invented
nothing'.

Yet if the novelist has invented nothing how odd that the
first Chicago section of the book should, in its structure, remind
one of that long-disowned early novel *The Hero* in that it concerns a young man who, having escaped death in war through
the gallantry of a comrade, comes home with his outlook on life
changed, to the dismay of the girl he left behind. Only this time
he is not an Englishman from a doting family in Kent but a
young, parentless American who has lied about his age to enlist
as an aviator in the First World War. To a Chicago seemingly
poised on the brink of a great period of economic expansion, he
has the eccentric attitude of wanting to do nothing, or as he puts
it, 'to loaf'. By loafing he means in fact an extended course of
reading in comparative religion, psychology and mysticism that
begins, as Maugham discovers to his surprise, with a ten-hour
stint at William James's *Principles of Psychology*. Larry Darrell
is a quiet, likeable American boy who exhibits from the start
two great Maugham characteristics: he is an orphan and he is
a self-educator whose studies are pursued with tremendous

application from a completely independent position. ('I felt I couldn't enter into a freshman's life. They wouldn't have liked me. I didn't want to act a part I didn't feel. And I didn't think the instructors would teach me the sort of things I wanted to know.')[13] Larry's studious non-conformity gradually becomes unacceptable to the world of fashionable Chicago in its Lake Shore Drive homes, and its eminently respectable and successful broking-house run by the father of his great rival, Gray Maturin, where he is offered a position in the firm which he refuses. He remains like Gerald Haxton immediately after the First World War: jobless in Chicago. Clearly he cannot stay for long in that city. The only place for him in his present frame of mind—maybe he is in 'a cloud of unknowing', says the novelist, deftly slipping his mystical pill into the jam, to puzzled Isabel—is that spiritual home of experimenting Americans, Paris, France. He becomes a Departer.

The Chicago-Paris axis along which this novel moves so smoothly is established through the formidable figure of Isabel's mother's brother, Elliot Templeton *'ce cher Elliot'*, as he has come to be known in the Proustian circles of the Faubourg St. Honoré, into which as an art connoisseur and dealer he has infiltrated himself over the years. Something of 'Chips' Channon may well, as Mr. Calder suggests, have gone into his making but his genealogy can, as I say, be traced right back to the Court Leys novels and pre-war comedies such as *Our Betters*. By the end of the book he has blossomed so richly that he seems quite *sui generis*. He is Maugham's most memorable comic creation who almost runs away with the show in the sense that Falstaff runs away with *Henry IV* and Lucifer with *Paradise Lost*. He has exactly the same function of epitomizing the values to which the protagonist is opposed, and which the writer has the difficult job of making seem less attractive than their opposite. But Elliot's sensitivity to social forms and social acceptance is carried to the point of absurdity; what humanizes him is great financial astuteness and generosity. If Elliot's Paris is centred on the Faubourg St. Honoré and Larry's around the Rue de Lappe, Maugham's lies somewhere between the two, not the Paris with the sword of Damocles hanging over it of *Christmas Holiday*, but the self-releasing Paris that most people from abroad who have spent any time in the city remember with such affection:

> It was very agreeable in the springtime, with the chestnuts in the Champs Elysées in bloom and the light in the streets so gay. There was pleasure in the air, a light transitory pleasure, sensual without grossness, that made your step more springy and your intelligence more alert. I was happy in the various company of my friends and, my heart filled with amiable memories of the past, I regained in spirit at least something of the glow of youth. I thought I should be a fool to allow work to interfere with a delight in the passing moment that I might never enjoy again so fully.

In spite of this euphoria Maugham's view of his leading lady Isabel is a pretty damning one; she is a charming and decorative creature to say the least, but—to mix my metaphors—when it comes to the crunch she knows on which side her bread is buttered; hence she marries the young stockbroker, Gray Maturin, rather than Larry whom she loves. She bears Gray two fine children, and sports her square-cut diamond and her sable coat as just rewards for fulfilling so gracefully her social and biological roles. Fair enough; many women have preferred to a hazardous love secure prospects and family approval (quite a few men have, too, if it comes to that). But at a later stage of the game Maugham shows us how, though Isabel has given Larry up, she refuses to let him go, and deliberately wrecks the chance of their childhood friend Sophie—who has come to a sticky alcoholic pass in Paris—of marrying him. Admitting that his offer to marry Sophie was prompted solely by a selfless wish to help her recover her self-respect, I am not convinced myself that he was really capable of marrying anyone. He seems to me to be a compassionate homosexual, always ready to help a lame duck, listen to the troubles and salve the wounds of his friends, but never seriously deflected from his own singleness of purpose. His occasional beddings with women, such as the Chaucerian episode in the hay loft of the farm near Zwingenberg, must be taken with a pinch of salt.

Larry is the first drop-out, the first Western hero to encase himself in an eastern mask. Unlike the On the Roaders and Dharma Bums whom he anticipated, he is a sexual abstainer, or rather, sexual aggression and conquest are not part of his pattern. He is 'aloof'. He lives that peculiar combination of omnivorous reading and worldly activity that Maugham suggested was his own salvation when he wrote *The Summing Up* though—and it is a very big though—he does have a comfortable private income on which to do it, until he gives this away. His life remains utterly baffling to all the other characters up to that black day in 1929—one of the very few historical events to be used by Maugham as a turning-point in a novel—when the stock-market crashes. The Maturins of this world are made bankrupt and inwardly shattered by the experience; Elliot escapes with his fortune intact through—a brilliant touch! —a tip-off from the Vatican. Larry's unworldliness seems now a source of strength to the worldly ones who rely on him for support in their crisis. Unfortunately he behaves like some quack faith-healer, and provides instant cures for migraine.

But these conjuring tricks are but the trappings of his newly acquired strength: where and how has Larry acquired it? Maugham goes to great trouble to show us the long ascesis through which Larry achieves his complete liberation from self; he makes it absorbing, humorous, dramatic, moving by turns. I cannot agree with Isherwood when he says in an interesting essay on *The Problem of the Religious Novel* that from this 'one gets the impression that becoming a saint is just no trouble at all'.[14] True, it is done Spanish-style as a series of picaresque adventures across France, Belgium, and Germany culminating in the moment of illumination on the mountain top in India, but as in *Don Fernando* you have the sense of an inner fatality guiding Larry's will from one point of enlightenment to the next. The process begins among the miners at Lens in northern France, utilizing Maugham's pre-war researches, where Larry falls in with the first of three exceptional people who are to enable him to change the course of his life; here, as so often in Maugham, the outstanding individual is the one whom the world has rejected: he is a cashiered Polish cavalry officer known as Kosti, a card-sharper and a Catholic now working as a coal-miner who, in the midst of all the racket of the bistro, would 'grow serious and start talking of all unlikely subjects— of mysticism. I knew nothing of it then but an essay of

Maeterlinck's on Ruysbroek that I'd read in Paris. But Kosti talked of Plotinus and Denis the Areopagite and Jacob Boehme the shoemaker and Meister Eckhart.'[15] Larry's next spiritual stopping-place is at a monastery in Alsace chez, the Benedictine Father Ensheim, where he learns about Roman Catholicism, makes extensive use of the monastic library and enjoys the company of the monks 'deeply impressed by their learning, their piety, and their unworldliness'. What he cannot accept, though, is their Christian God who allowed evil to exist and who built the world for his own glorification. He parts from these kindly fathers on very good terms, has his 'affair' with Suzanne Rouvier in Paris and then makes his way to Spain.

A seemingly chance encounter on a boat with a Swami of the Ramakrishna Order leads him to India where Larry becomes aware of an 'intense conviction that India had something to give me that I had to have'.[16] In Benares he is deeply moved, as Maugham was, by the sight of thousands of people taking their lustral baths and praying in the Ganges. He goes to Travancore where he has an audience with the saintly Shri Ganesha. He asks him to be his Guru. 'Brahman alone is the Guru,' the holy man replies. However, he allows Larry to become one of his disciples and under his instruction Larry learns the gospel of non-attachment: 'He taught that work done with no selfish interest purifies the mind and that duties are opportunities afforded to man to sink his separate self and become one with the universal self.' Larry stays in the Ashrama on and off for two years, completely absorbing this teaching in great happiness; then he goes off by himself to a bungalow up in the mountains to celebrate his birthday where he has his moment of truth: 'No words can tell the ecstasy of my bliss. When I came to myself I was exhausted and trembling.' After this he comes back into the world and eventually to Paris where he meets Maugham at a performance of *Bérénice* (a drama of sexual renunciation) by the *Comédie Française*.

My brisk little summary does violence to the patient, respectful and admiring manner in which Maugham mediates through the mouth of Larry some of the chief tenets of Vedanta with its wholly different view of evil from that of Christianity; nor does it show how realistically he punctuates the exposition, which is supposed to have taken place during a momentous nightlong conversation in the Brassèrie Graf on the Avenue de Clichy, with the comings and goings of the different specimens of unregenerate humanity, pimps, tarts, financiers, roisterers, white-collar workers who are the sad mute chorus to Larry's recital. The whole performance (which begins with an ironic piece of advice to the reader hungry only for the story that it may be skipped) is Maugham's most ambitious attempt to enhance the narrative structure of a fiction something more positive and lasting than the pleasure the working out of its pattern gives to the reader. It is not that Maugham himself has actually been wholly converted to the faith his hero describes, as Isherwood was; Maugham remained as he said at the end of his life 'a rationalist', but he felt that no picture of contemporary life such as he aimed to present in *The Razor's Edge* could be complete without including it among the possibilities. Maugham's position is as always that of an artist, not an apologist; and no saint can ever have made less effort to encourage disciples than Larry. He end his days, so we are told, as a New York taxi driver. But because he is a Maugham hero before he does this he leaves behind him a book of essays upon a number of famous persons, all of whom may be said to have made a success of their lives from Goethe to Akbar the Mogul conqueror. It is about the same length as Lytton Strachey's *Eminent Victorians* though presumably not so satirical. Maugham wishes to leave all the options open.

In this sense he works on a broader canvas than that of two other novels that have helped in the transmission of Hindu teaching to the Western world, Huxley's *Time Must Have a Stop* (1944) and Isherwood's *Meeting by the River* (1967). Each is remarkable for the skill with which the novelist uses all his art to convince us of the reality with which someone, whose background and education are roughly similar to our own, should have been converted to the non-attached life: each makes the conversion occur to the kind of character he has always admired. For Huxley in Bruno Rontini cleverly kept off-stage for most of the novel, he is a scholarly, self-effacing, antiquarian bookseller, ready to respond to the call of heroism when it eventually comes; for Isherwood (who writes from within the Hindu philosophy with the greatest knowledge) he is part of one of those middle-class mother-oriented English families where the sibling rivalry persists long into adult life and where the conversion has, fascinatingly, to come to terms with the family situation, as it did in a different context Maugham's Strickland. By contrast, the attractive, clean-limbed, quiet-voiced Larry is a loner; he emerges out of a situation of orphaned freedom that makes it more difficult for us to accept him as representative of the human condition however much we admire his integrity and capitulate to his charm.

Against this, Larry's experience of Hindu religion (which should be read in conjunction with both the Indian section of Maugham's *Notebook* and his essay on *The Saint* published in *Points of View*) does offer an alternative way of living not just to that of one English family group, whether in Florence or Bradford, but to that of people in various walks of life who we feel are the true embodiments of what drives our society forward on its course.

Cyril Connolly reviewing *The Razor's Edge* in the *New Statesman* was one of those who hailed it as Maugham's best novel since *Cakes and Ale* and as 'powerful propaganda for the new faith'.[17] *Time* magazine was prompt with its accolade 'the crowning triumph of that utterly dispassionate virtuosity to which he has always aspired—a persuasive as well as an enter-taining book, by a man of 70 who is still of the earth earthy—about a young man who has found a faith'.[18] The anonymous T.L.S. and Diana Trilling in the *Nation* were among the dissentient voices. 'Mysticism,' declared the latter, 'is bound to be inviting to the person who is afraid of the deep emotions; yet it can never fully win him, any more than humanity can fully win him. All the characters . . . inevitably inhabit the non-dimensional universe which is all that is left when deep emotions have been disavowed.'[19]

[3.]

Maugham did not disavow the deep emotions when, six months after the novel had been published in November, Gerald

Haxton died at the age of 52. On the contrary, he was heart-broken. 'His death,' he wrote later, 'was a bitter grief to me. We had gone through a great deal together.'[20] On reaching the allotted span of a man's life himself, Maugham prognosticated on his own future as an author.

He felt that he was unlikely 'at the age of seventy to write anything of great value. Incentive fails, energy fails, invention fails . . .' When he first came to America he had plans for four more novels floating about in his head. One was *The Razor's Edge* now written, and of the other three unwritten so far he explained in 1944 that,

> One was to be a miracle story set in sixteenth-century Spain; the second, a story of Machiavelli's stay with Cesare Borgia in the Romagna, which gave him the best material for *The Prince*, and I proposed to interweave with their conversations the material on which he founded his play *Mandragola*. Knowing how often the novelist makes up his fiction from incidents of his own experience, trifling perhaps and made interesting or dramatic only by his power of creation, I thought it would be amusing to reverse the process and from the play guess at the events that may have occasioned it. I meant to end up with a novel about a working-class family in the slums of Bermondsey. I thought it would form a pleasing termination to my career to finish with the same sort of story of the shiftless poor of London as I had begun with fifty years before. But I am content now to keep these three novels as an amusement for my idle reveries.[21]

In fact over the next four years two-thirds of this programme was completed. The novel about Machiavelli appeared in 1946 as *Then and Now*, and the Spanish miracle story in 1948 as *Catalina*; only the Bermondsey book remained unwritten. It is a common phenomena for the novelist who has excelled in the realistic depiction of contemporary life to seek a kind of creative sanctuary in a work of historical fiction at the end of his career: Gissing's *Veranilda* and Waugh's *Helena*, both favourite works of their authors and largely disregarded by their admirers, come to mind. These last novels of Maugham's are best seen as part of his vagrant mood, his wanderings in history and literature and resuscitation of real people who had played some exceptional part in their periods, with whom he found the same understanding to the point of identification as he had with the Stricklands and the Larrys of his fiction. In life Maugham had always been fascinated by ruthlessness and singleness of purpose, by a combination of charm, authority, cruelty, shrewdness and gambler's courage. He found a combination of all these qualities in the figures of Machiavelli and Cesare Borgia during the three months or so in 1502, the period of the Duke's most sensational and bloodthirsty coup, when the future author of *The Prince* was in close contact with him in the town of Imola from which he was conducting his military and diplomatic operations.

This is the setting of *Then and Now* in which Maugham applies his novelist's powers of invention to constructing an amorous intrigue for Machiavelli with a young wife at Imola, conducted in the interstices of political negotiation. The quick-change from matters of great political moment to the hazards of the bedchamber, from the world of *Mandragola* to that of *The Prince*, provides the alternating current for the book and takes some time to get switched on. Maugham has a complicated set of historical circumstances, involving the whole of the Romagna, the position of the King of France, the Pope and especially the city of Florence, to put before the reader in his first few chapters, and as Edmund Wilson pointed out in his devastating review *The Apotheosis of Somerset Maugham*, he makes rather heavy weather of it. However, even Wilson had to admit that once the narrative gets under way its hold is considerable. The domestic scene in which the object of Machiavelli's desire spreads out her fine long hair for it to be dyed by the sun has the quality of a late Renaissance painting, and the role-playing and mask-wearing of the scenes between the Secretary amd the Duke are masterly in their understanding of the formal double-talk of diplomatic negotiation and intrigue. Maugham has a great time showing how so skilled and wary an operator as Machiavelli, whose every word and gesture represents a cool calculation, is completely outwitted. Faced by the total rout of his amorous plans, humiliated by his young protégé who succeeds in bedding the wife, he decides, being a Maugham hero, that the only thing to do is to write a play about it. Thus the novel ends with, as it were, a historical reprise of two favourite Maugham themes, the sexual initiation of a young man and the discovery by an artist of a quickening of inspiration in a sexual defeat. Pattern-wise it brings to a full circle Maugham's fascination with Italian history that had begun almost fifty years before with *The Making of a Saint*. He had hoped to do the same with the London working people who were the subject of his first novel, but on returning to Bermondsey after the war, he found that the people he aimed to write about had all vanished and so had the ambience that had given him his inspiration. It was therefore his great historical passion for Spain that provided in *Catalina* his swan song as a novelist at the age of 72.

He calls *Catalina* a romance; and it is a less complicated operation than *Then and Now* but every inch as much the product of a mind so soaked in the period that it moves with ease among both political and domestic events. We saw in *Don Fernando* how Maugham relished the contrasts of Spanish life in its great age. He finds now what had hitherto eluded him, a single human being upon whom all the various pressures of the time, religious, military, literary, political and so on, can be seen to operate. She is a simple crippled girl, the Catalina of the title, to whom the Blessed Virgin appears in a vision, with instructions as to how her affliction may be cured, a behest that has an ambiguity worthy of the best tradition of *The Thousand And One Nights*. The healing touch, she is told, will be given her by the one of three brothers 'who has best served God'. One is an eminent bishop, another a famous general and the third a humble baker. I will leave anyone who has not yet read this novel to discover from it which of them performs the trick. It is in her approaches to these three men that Catalina becomes the centrepiece in a most beautiful wrangle involving Church and State, and even when she has been cured her troubles are by no means over. Indeed, they have only begun, for she has now become a valuable property, and Maugham shows us, mindful of such corrective institutions as the Inquisition, what this may mean to a person's freedom of manoeuvre. For a while Catalina is the subject of highly intriguing negotiations between the bishop and the nobly born Dona Beatriz de San Domingo, prioress of Castel Rodriguez and a fearless negotiator when it comes to advancing her convent's cause. This formidable lady

is the final apotheosis of Miss Ley, Maugham's last tribute to
feminine clarity of mind and power of decision. Her scenes are
the best things in the book; they have the sharp bite of a ripe
Spanish olive.

Eventually Catalina escapes into the theatre and ends her days
as part of a company of strolling players; in following her
latter-day fortunes Maugham takes a last fond look at the
theatre of Lope de Vega and somehow, in a rare piece of fantasy,
contrives the irruption of Don Quixote.

The reviews of the story were largely unsympathetic to what
was and remains the charming product of a still lively imagination. By the time the book was published Maugham was back
home again at the Mauresque with a devoted secretary and
companion to minister to his needs, and to enjoy the ready flow
of his wit, in his old friend Alan Searle.

CHAPTER TWELVE

Pantheon

[1.]

IN 1946 MAUGHAM and Searle returned to the Riviera to find the Mauresque had been occupied first by Italians and then by Germans; the entire contents had been looted and the eminence on which it stood shelled by the British. It was uninhabitable. They stayed at a hotel in Beaulieu. 'It took three months,' Maugham wrote in *Purely For My Pleasure*, the story of his art collection, 'for my architect, with a discreet use of the black market, to put the house in order.'[1] His pictures had been safely hidden for the duration by a French friend, and now there were new pictures acquired in Paris and America, including a Pissarro from Twentieth Century Fox as a reward for work done on a script (unused in the event) for the film of *The Razor's Edge*, made in Hollywood at the end of the war. 'We moved in,' continues Maugham. 'My pictures were returned to me and I placed them where they had been placed before. I resumed my interrupted life. A year or two later a friend brought me the two pictures I had left in the United States. I was obliged to hang them in my bedroom since, with the theatrical pictures and the Marie Laurencins, I had no place for them.'

Two things happened to Maugham after the war: he became a legend and he became an essayist. To those under the spell of the legend the Villa became a point of pilgrimage in the revived Riviera, or if not quite that an object of veneration from afar, a symbol of the rewards of success in literature as a career. Maugham abhorred sightseers or any kind of intrusion; like Pope in his days of glory at Twickenham, and Evelyn Waugh at Combe Florey in Somerset,[2] his whole concern was to be left alone to get on with his work. However, in 1948 the public were permitted a vicarious view of the Mauresque when Maugham 'the very old party' appeared in a film on the terrace, a tray of drinks at his elbow to introduce a movie made out of four of his short stories called *Quartet*; a success, it was followed by two more, *Trio* and *Encore*.

Maugham was not the only very old party at large on the Riviera after the war. Two others often to be found there, both friends of his and neighbours, were Winston Churchill and Lord Beaverbrook. A wag christened this particular trio 'the three wicked old men'. Each as he looked at this time may be studied in the portraits of them by Graham Sutherland. The often reproduced one of Maugham, that now hangs in the Tate Gallery, captures to perfection—as I said—the attribute that Maugham singled out in the heroes and heroines of his books, his aloofness, an invulnerable creative serenity attained only after a lifetime of dedicated effort; for all his charitableness Larry, you may recall, was aloof after his return to Paris from India; Julia Lambert was aloof before the footlights. But Maugham was not so aloof that he never wanted to see anyone. Life at the Mauresque was, after working hours, as full as ever, a succession of friends passing through its doors. 'In the last twenty-five years,' wrote Maugham at this time, 'I have had a lot of people staying with me, and sometimes I am tempted to write an essay on guests.'[3]

By all accounts he was an amusing and engrossing talker: a pity no one ever tape-recorded him speaking off-the-cuff. If at times he was malicious he was also searingly honest. His stammer only served to enhance the irony and polished acerbity of his discourse. So much is clear from the written records kept by Mr. Kanin and others. I never heard him but I have a notion, to use a Maugham phrase, that his table-talk was remarkable above all for three things: his power of hooking you on an anecdote, his dispassionate dissection of the personalities of his friends, and his unending absorption in the process of artistic creation. Happily it is this side of Maugham, applying his fine, shrewd, commonsensical mind to people and to books, that we are able to enjoy in the main work he did after the war, the essays that were collected in such volumes as *Ten Novelists and Their Novels* (1945), *The Writer's Point of View* (1951), *The Vagrant Mood* (1952), *Points of View* (1958) and in the single

volume of *A Writer's Notebook* (1949), which was all that he
allowed to survive of the fifteen volumes of the original, and
in the various lectures, prefaces and introductions.

Few novelists have written about the art of fiction, and those
who practise it, with such penetration. He examined his close
contemporaries and his illustrious predecessors in the same
spirit of judicial aloofness; they have their pretensions stripped
away, their virtues exposed with a surgical exactitude.
Maugham is an experienced citizen of the republic of letters
with as great an insight into the character of a suppressed Victorian homosexual like Emily Brontë as into an ebullient
twentieth-century Lothario like H. G. Wells. He often claimed
that the effect of success on people was to make them kindly and
mellow. Yet these are not quite the qualities that come through
his memorable essay (in emulation of Hazlitt's *My First
Acquaintance with Poets*), *Some Novelists I Have Known*. He is
wickedly, brilliantly funny about his friends, and generous with
his encomiums for those aspects of their work that he genuinely
admires. Obliquely through the essay we feel him empaling his
own piece of territory in the republic, and sealing it off. By
contrast, when Maugham is writing about Dashiell Hammett
and Raymond Chandler in *The Decline and Fall of the Detective
Story*, writers with whom he does not feel himself in any way
to be in competition, the warmth of his praise is unabated. His
greatest literary hostility was to Henry James whose vulnerable
flank, his plays (like both Shaw and Wells, Maugham was
present at the first night of *Guy Domville*) Maugham attacks,
and whose conversational manner he ridicules. Besides
Maugham's memory of James struggling to ask whether the
actress Ethel Irving was really a lady—'Is she, enfin, what
you'd call if you were asked point-blank, if so to speak you were
put with your back to the wall, is she a *femme du monde*?'—one
must put all these people culled together by Simon Nowell
Smith in *The Legend of the Master* for whom a conversation
with Henry James was among the greatest intellectual
experiences of their lives. And yet we owe to Maugham that
wonderful glimpse of James, whom he visited in America after
the death of his brother William, adrift in his own home town:
'I wander about these great empty streets of Boston,' he told

Maugham, 'and I never see a soul. I could not be more alone in the Sahara.'[4] James, or rather James's approach to the art of fiction, set out in the famous essay represented a threat to the illusion of realism. That is why he needed deflating. While Maugham was walking down those same Boston streets he would have taken in a dozen points of realistic detail for use later on, and one or two would have suggested a short story; on the other hand, Maugham was not interested in pursuing in fictional terms the nuancé distinction between a lady and a *femme du monde*. Maugham does, of course, realize perfectly well that though nothing is easier than, as we should say, to 'send up' Henry James, he cannot therefore as an artist be discounted. This is why in a final sentence of uncharacteristic tortuousness Maugham tried to pull back from the exposed position in which he had landed himself: 'The fact remains that those last novels of his, notwithstanding their unreality, make all other novels, except the very best, unreadable.'

Maugham is very conscious of the social situation out of which a novelist writes and its influence upon his work. James, he feels, was never really at home with English society, much as he loved it. 'He remained a friendly but critical alien'—now there, surely, Maugham does have a point. He observes that most of the English novelists have sprung from the middle class, two great exceptions to this rule being his contemporaries, Wells and Bennett: 'I think that H.G. and Arnold were drawn together because both were of modest origin and both had an arduous struggle to win recognition.' He is quite affectionate and highly entertaining about both of them. Bennett was 'cocksure and bumptious, and he was rather common' and Maugham tended to write him off as an artist until he picked up *The Old Wives' Tale*: 'I began reading it with misgiving, but this quickly changed to astonishment. I had never supposed that Arnold could write anything so good. I was deeply impressed. I thought it a great book.' The other aspect of Bennett that he admires is his poise and stability, his power of remaining neat and dapper and enthusiastic, of never lowering the mask, even under the most trying circumstances, and above all, his forbearance with the same disability as Maugham himself:

Few knew the distressing sense it gave rise to of a bar to complete contact with other men. It may be that except for the stammer which forced him to introspection Arnold would never have become a writer, but I think it is no small proof of his strong and sane character that notwithstanding this impediment he was able to retain his splendid balance and regard the normal life of man from a normal point of view.

Maugham was just as perceptive about the character of Wells, noting his 'strong sexual instincts', and his ruthlessness in terminating a relationship as soon as it became a bore. He praises his skill as a short-story writer and, as one would expect, does not see eye to eye with Wells's socially-oriented, rag-bag attitude to the novel, though he has a good word for *Tono Bungay* and points to the character of Trafford in *Marriage* as 'the portraits of the man H.G. thought he was, added to the man he would have liked to be'.

[2.]

Maugham, therefore, enjoyed cutting his contemporaries down to size. He does what one can only call a mini-cakes-and-ale on Edith Wharton, and he has some very disagreeable stories to tell about Elizabeth Russell who wrote *Elizabeth and her German Garden*. The one significant exception to this deflating critico-anecdotal approach is Kipling, who does not come into 'Some Novelists I Have Known', although he did sometimes stay at the Mauresque. He was, as we have seen, much more central to Maugham's own inspiration than the others, and deserving of separate and rather special treatment. Maugham was in the position of the second generation pioneer wishing to honour the founding father who opened up the territory. Consequently his introduction to *A Choice of Kipling's Prose* (1952) is by far the most positive and laudatory essay he ever wrote about a fellow writer. In championing Kipling with such exceptional fervour Maugham is not only focusing attention upon the merits of a great master in English of the short story but also tilting at his old enemy the intelligentsia who underrate Kipling too. Since Maugham wrote his introduction the pendulum of fashion has swung to the opposite extreme: it is the intelligentsia who now overrate Kipling and the common reader who neglects him.

But when Maugham went on his travels in those territories where the white man still shouldered his burden, he saw all around him, everywhere he went, living proof of Kipling's genius in the form of people whose personalities and whose attitudes had been moulded by Kipling's work. 'He not only created characters, he created men.' Maugham is at some pains to defend Kipling from 'one of the most absurd charges brought against him . . . that his stories were anecdotes'. Maugham quotes his favourite authority, the *Oxford Dictionary*, on anecdote: 'The narration of a detached incident, or of a single event, told as being in itself interesting or striking.' That, says Maugham, rubbing his hands,

> is a perfect definition of a short story. The story of Ruth, the story of the Matron of Ephesus, Boccaccio's story of Frederigo degli Alberighi and his falcon are all anecdotes. So are *Boule de Suif*, *La Parure* and *L'Heritage*. An anecdote is the bony structure of a story which gives it form and coherence and which the author clothes with flesh, blood and nerves.

Yet if we turn to some of Maugham's own stories for a moment, *Rain*, *The Book-Bag*, *The Round Dozen*, *Alien Corn*, they do seem to be rather more than just anecdotes: they seem to me to be dramatic structures moving to a definitive climax but including more than one event or detached incident.

But he would be a bold man who attempted to cross swords with Somerset Maugham on the nature of the short story. It was a subject to which, from the critical as well as the practical point of view, he devoted a great deal of thought. He first set his ideas about it down when he wrote a long introduction in 1939 to an anthology he made for Doubleday of '100 Short Stories from the United States, England, France, Russia and Germany';[5] he returned to it in a lecture he gave to the Royal Society of Literature, and finally went into it again in a long essay on *The Short Story* published in *Points of View*.

With his usual thoroughness Maugham traces the history of the form from its origins in the Annual through the rise of the

magazine and the newspaper story. This time he quotes
another master, Edgar Allen Poe, as having come up with the
canonical definition, '—having conceived with deliberate care,
a certain unique or single effect to be brought out, he then
invents such incidents—he then contrives such effects as may
best aid him in establishing this proconceived effect.' That
amplifies the *Oxford Dictionary*, but does it really cover
Chekhov? Maugham makes the inevitable comparison between
the Russian and Maupassant, pays his respects to Kipling and
ends with some qualified praise for Katherine Mansfield. He
takes his usual swipe at James, and he does not mention such
more modern exponents of the form as Joyce and Hemingway
though both are included in the 100 greats; it is a wonderfully
catholic choice including everyone under the sun from Stephen
Crane to Franz Werfel.

It is to American magazine editors and publishers, wishing
to provide their readers with lists of the hundred best of this
and the ten best of that, that we owe some of Maugham's most
enjoyable essays. His choice of the ten best novels in the world
began as a series of introductions to the novels abridged by
Maugham for an American public. It was a project close to
Maugham's heart, and after the abridgements were published
he began revising and expanding the essays to give us finally
Ten Novels and Their Authors which, thanks to Ian Fleming,
were serialized in the *Sunday Times*, and appeared in book
form, in 1954. These essays are all informed by Maugham's
opinion, stated most fully perhaps in a lecture he gave to the
National Book League in 1951, that 'when you come down to
brass tacks, the value of a work of art depends on the artist's
personality'.[6] In the essays he leads us in easy stages from the
novelist's character to those in the novel. He is scrupulous in
recognizing an immense debt throughout the whole operation
to the biographies written by other people, but Maugham's
focus on the subject is so sharp and idiosyncratic, that his work
has the semblance of originality; what he provides are pen-
portraits of engrossing vividness, the careers of Fielding,
Dickens and the rest are unfolded with a subtle sense of dramatic effect; nor is Maugham any more in awe of the great ones
of the past than of his eminent and distinguished contemporaries.

Lecherous, raffish Fielding he nonetheless approves of: 'he was a very proper man'; and he enjoys Jane Austen's caustic wit and sharp tongue in her letters, even though she was 'a provincial'. Stendhal was 'a vulgar buffoon' who happened to have 'a wonderful gift of accurate observation, and with a piercing insight into the intricacies, vagaries and bizarreries of the human heart'. Balzac, that giant among novelists, was 'a show-off; he adored luxury and he could not help spending money'. Dostoievsky 'was a singularly unamiable character . . . It never seems to have occurred to him that anyone could have enough of hearing him talk about himself and his works.' Herman Melville was 'a moody, unhappy man tormented by instincts he shrank from with horror . . . a man whom one can only regard with deep compassion'.

As a fellow-craftsman in the realistic tradition, Maugham pauses from time to time to animadvert upon the technical faults perpetrated by these great masters. *Wüthering Heights* is 'very clumsily constructed'; clumsiness even afflicted Miss Austen in *Persuasion* in the famous episode where Ann Wentworth jumps off the Cobb at Lyme Regis,

> even if the Cobb then were twice as high as it is now, she could not have been more than six feet from the ground and, as she was jumping down, it is impossible that she should have fallen on her head. In any case, she would have fallen against the stalwart sailor and, though, perhaps shaken and frightened, could hardly have hurt herself. Anyhow, she was unconscious and the fuss that ensued is unbelievable.[7]

Though Maugham regards *War and Peace* as the only work of fiction that can justly be called an epic, he wonders if it was necessary to make Pierre 'quite so silly'. Dickens, who was over-sensitive about his few months in the blacking factory, was ill at ease when dealing with characters in 'the higher walks of life', he is at his best 'when dealing with the rag tag and bobtail among whom his boyhood was spent'. Rosa Dartle is a somewhat baffling loose end of a character. 'I suspect that Dickens meant to make greater use of her in his story than he did.'

Maugham probes the strange relations between Dickens and his wife's sisters, and he goes discreetly into the affair with Ellen Ternan. Indeed, he peers into the novelists' secret lives

with a firmness and exhaustiveness which he went to astonishing lengths to prevent future commentators from applying to
his own. He notes such things as Melville's delight in 'male
beauty' and the tyranny exerted over Charlotte and Emily
Brontë by their parson father. He dwells on Flaubert's passion
for Eliza Schlesinger and traces the steps by which Tolstoy was
taken over by Chertkov to the impoverishment of the Countess.
He points out how shabbily Balzac treated his mother, but he is
the only one of the ten to whom Maugham would apply that
much over-used word 'genius'. He is the greatest of the greats
because his aim was 'to depict a civilization', and became the
first novelist to dwell on the importance of economics in
everybody's life.

The only thing that all ten greats have in common is that
'they tell good stories . . . in a very straightforward way. They
have narrated events and delved into motives without any of the
tiresome literary tricks, such as the stream of thought, the
throw-back, which makes so many modern novels tedious.
They have told the reader what they wished him to know, and
not, as is the present fashion, left him to guess who their
characters were, what their calling was and what their circumstances: in fact they have done all they could to make things
easy for him.'

Now this last point is not really true. Tolstoy, Dostoievsky
and Melville do not make things particularly easy for us even
if you could argue that the other seven do; but even to a
Frenchman is Flaubert an easy read? Maugham's concern here
is to seek confirmation in the work of the masters, that the sole
purpose of the novel is to give pleasure, and that the reader is
under no obligation to read any book or part of a book that
fails to please. He was a great advocate of skipping though he
rarely seems to have skipped anything himself. 'I have read all
the great novels three or four times already and they have
nothing more to tell me,' he explains. But Maugham is unwilling to recognize that he has lived through a period when the
art of the novel changed radically to include some highly
elusive areas of consciousness. He refused to recognize what
had happened on what Edmund Wilson called 'the higher
ground', and hence earned the strictures of that critic who, out

of fury at Maugham's patronizing attitude to Proust in his Library of Congress lecture,[8] went far too far in the opposite direction. Yes, even Proust has a story to tell, but he does not *only* have a story to tell, and therefore to advise the reader to skip the boring bits where he is being influenced by Bergson is not going to help him to understand the greatness of Proust. It is barbarous of Maugham, surely, to say, 'It may be that some day an abridged version of his immense novel will be issued from which will be omitted those passages that time has stripped of their value and only those retained which, because they are of the essence of a novel, remain of enduring interest.'

Sometimes even a novel-reader does have to make an intellectual effort. Maugham is inconsistent about this. He quite sees that if you are really going to get anywhere with *War and Peace* you have got to come to terms with Tolstoy's view of history. Under the influence of Isaiah Berlin Maugham read the work of Joseph de Maistre. 'I felt constrained to read *Les Soirées de Saint Petersbourg ...*' and finding how much Tolstoy owed to de Maistre he felt constrained also to defend him from the charge of borrowing his ideas from someone else. 'It is no more the novelist's business to originate ideas than it is to invent the persons who serve as his models.' Ah, now we are off on a different argument! We would all agree at least with the first part of that statement.

Novelists integrate highly abstruse ideas into the structure of their novels, often when they are at their most interesting. Maugham does it himself in *The Razor's Edge*. True, he feels constrained to say at one point that he wants 'to warn the reader that he can very well skip this chapter without losing the thread of such story as I have to tell ...' but then he immediately qualifies this by saying that should he in fact skip this chapter he will miss the whole point of the book. Maugham cannot be skipped with impunity any more than Proust.

These inconsistencies of Maugham's stem from his standpoint in all his essays of the plain self-educated man of goodwill who approaches the subject purely for his own pleasure and enlightenment;[9] it is an ironic position that makes them so unpedantically readable and delightful. Yet he has a hard time to preserve this purity of approach in a lengthy discussion of

Kant's aesthetic ideas in *Reflections on a Certain Book*, where he eventually lands in that ancient bunker, the concept of beauty, and then tries to find some correlation between the pleasure we take in the appreciation of works of art and the ennoblement of character that leads to behaving well. 'If the delight in aesthetic appreciation is no more than the opium of an intelligentsia it is no more than, as Kant says, a mischievous distraction. If it is more it should enable its possessor to acquire virtue.' After its strong biographical opening the Kant essay seems to me to be one of Maugham's rare failures. It is not often that we watch Maugham tying himself up into knots and failing to extricate himself, but the latter part of this essay is one of those strange occasions. For the most part the essays in *The Vagrant Mood* and *Points of View* successfully extend Maugham's range as an essayist from fiction into other major areas of his interests, such as art, history, mysticism, prose-style, diary-keeping, travel-writing, orphanhood, English social life, the Established Church.

They open the doors of a pantheon in which we find him paying conscientious homage to a number of singular human types. They are all people of great tallent or ability in some creative field, most of whom sprang from modest origins. Kant, the harness-maker's son, who changed the nature of philosophy; Venkataraman, who lost his father, a village lawyer, at the age of 12 and went on to become the Maharishi, the most celebrated and revered Swami in the whole of pre-war India; Tillotson, the Yorkshire clothier's boy, who became Archbishop of Canterbury in the dangerous seventeenth century and, more important to Maugham, one of the first masters of the plain style of writing English; Francisco de Zurbaran, brought up in Fuente de Cantos near Guadalupe, among his father's livestock, who became the master of the plain style of portraiture and still life, and who painted that picture of the Blessed John Houghton that Maugham had found so haunting. 'Talent,' comments Maugham, 'is a mysterious gift of nature for which there is no accounting.'

Through the lives and careers of such people Maugham returns to those themes and interests that he first took up as a young writer before the First World War, and through a series of biographical distillations, as it were, completes the various figures of his own pattern. The essay on Kant, and a lengthy companion one on Goethe, in which he sorts out the autobiographical strands in the three novels, takes him back to the Germany of his youth, to which he returned on a trip after the war; Zurbaran represented a last look at seventeenth-century Spain; *Three Journalists* (that is, people who kept journals, the Goncourts, Jules Rénard and Paul Léautaud) between them cover a hundred years of French literature and intellectual life in Paris; while finally *Augustus*, a memoir and account of the writings and travels of his friend Augustus Hare, recalls the self-contained world of the Edwardian country house ruled by a figurehead who was both an eccentric and a gentleman.

All these people possess some gift that sets them apart from their fellow mortals: they are aloof and their behaviour to their own families must seem strange when judged by ordinary standards. They have qualities without which the sum total of human happiness might have been, indeed would have been, very much poorer but niceness and considerateness to those whom the common run of mortals would regard as their nearest and dearest are not among them. Kant, for example, had two married sisters who lived in Köningsberg. He never spoke to them for twenty-five years. 'The reason he gave for this,' Maugham tells us, 'was that he had nothing to say to them. This seems sensible enough, and though we may deplore his lack of heart, when we remember how often our pusillanimity has led us to rack our brains in the effort to make conversation with persons with whom we have nothing in common but tie of blood, we cannot but admire his strength of mind.' By the same token, Goethe 'was curiously insensitive to the pain he caused'. Rénard was 'grossly selfish, ill-mannered, envious, hard and sometimes even cruel' and in common with him the other journal-writers 'were monstrously touchy . . . callous to the feelings of others . . . malicious and unkind'. Even the saintly Maharisi wished to have no truck with his mother once he had seen the light, and took a lot of persuading to accept her as one of his flock.

In mitigation of this unnatural behaviour to kith and kin, a high proportion of the Maugham pantheon suffered from some kind of childhood dislocation of environment and experienced full or partial orphanhood. Augustus was given away at a tender age by his mother for adoption by her husband's child-less widowed sister. ('Yes, certainly the baby shall be sent as soon as it is weaned; if anyone else would like one, would you kindly remember that we have others.') Léautaud, the product of a broken theatrical marriage, was separated from his mother when he was two, brought up by a nurse, and when after twenty years he saw his mother again, he fell in love with her physically. Rénard's mother hated him; as a punishment for wetting his bed she made him drink his urine and treated him as a menial. He said in his autobiographical novel *Poil de Carotte*: 'Tout le monde ne peut pas être orphelin.' The Goncourts' father died when they were boys; the brothers were very close; after Jules's death Edmund manifested a strikingly unfeeling aspect to his character when it came to publishing intimate facts about his friends that they wished to keep hidden from the public, such as the locomotor ataxy, a distressing after-effect of syphilis, from which Daudet suffered. Maugham seems throughout these essays to be making the point that unnatural behaviour, even to the extent of betraying the confidence of those closest to them, is not uncommon in people of exceptional gifts.

[3.]

When *Points of View* came out in 1958 it contained a prefatory note that read:

> Mr Maugham has announced that this is the last book he will ever publish and since he seems to have a way of doing what he says he is going to do, we may safely assume that with this volume of essays he will take his leave of the reading public and so put an end to a relationship that with *Liza of Lambeth* began just over sixty years ago.[10]

Positively his last farewell appearance? The great pattern at long last complete? For some years it seemed as if this was indeed so. Gradually the very old party was turning into a

grand old man. He had been made a Companion of Honour in
1954 and in that year, on his eightieth birthday, he was wined
and dined by the Garrick Club. He made a genial speech, containing one long hiatus I gather, and he spoke to the nation
as a whole on radio: *Looking Back on Eighty Years*. Like his
fellow octogenarians on the Riviera he was now an elder statesman (of literature) whose occasional public utterances had a
quavering *gravitas* and who succeeded amazingly in keeping
abreast of the times. When *Lucky Jim* by Kingsley Amis
appeared in 1956 Maugham read it and pronounced the new
state-educated provincial hero to be 'ss . . . scum', and when in
London Maugham continued to go to the theatre; on seeing
Look Back in Anger he immediately recognized a major new
talent and pronounced Osborne to possess that mysterious
knack 'without which you will never write plays'. But even in
his eighties Maugham continued to write; the habit was too
strong for him to give it up completely. It was rumoured that he
was working on an autobiographical book of a more intimate
kind than *The Summing Up*, which recalled his early years in
London and filled in many of the gaps in his own story, but not
perhaps with any notion of publication. He continued to travel
and revisit most of the places in which his work had been set,
thus rounding off the pattern on foot as well as on paper.
Wherever he went he was fêted and besieged by admirers who
wanted him to sign copies of his book. But people who met
Maugham in these last years reported that he seemed very tired
and old, that though still capable of the former flashes of penetration, his concentration was going; like General de Gaulle he
had Niehans injections that appeared to have given him a new
lease of life, but he had begun to live more and more in a world
of his own.

It seemed as if he must be dwindling away but then, in the
autumn of 1962, readers of Lord Beaverbrook's *Sunday Express*
were told that,

> Once in a decade the world of publishing is galvanised by some
> truly stupendous event. There comes a book which, by reason of
> the stature of its author, its public appeal, and its importance,
> dominates the whole scene . . . The event is this: the greatest story-
> teller in the English language has written his greatest story of

all—the story of his own strange, fascinating life. Don't miss
Maugham LOOKING BACK on his long life . . .[11]

For the next eight weeks readers were given a two-page instal-
ment of Maugham's rememberings. At first, when he had completed this autobiographical work, he wished for it to have a
wide circulation but as the moment of publication approached
he began to have second thoughts. By then, however, he had
closed with Beaverbrook, and with the proprietor of *Show*
magazine in the United States, to let them both serialize parts
of it for a large sum, and it was too late to withdraw. The manuscript of *Looking Back* has not so far been published in book
form; nor I gather is it ever likely to be during the lifetime of
the present executors.

The extracts from it that were published began innocuously
enough with an amusing apologia on the part of the author for
writing another book, followed by a touching childhood portrait
of Maugham in the late 1870s, with his mother and brothers
when they were spending a summer holiday at Trouville. On
the beach a shabby little painter in a beret is offering to paint
portraits of the holiday-makers at five francs a time. As
Maugham walks along the promenade with his mother another
elegant woman passes them: she and Mrs. Maugham look each
other up and down. Then it is little Willie's seventh birthday
and his mother's best friend, Lady Anglesey, gives him twenty
francs (a staggeringly generous present in those days, surely
even from an American). Willie is asked how he wishes to
spend it, and he says to see Sarah Bernhardt,

> How I could ever have had the idea I cannot imagine. Anyhow,
> on that night I was taken by my eldest brother to the theatre for
> the first time in my life. The play was called *Nana Sahib* and it was
> an atrocious melodrama by Sardou. To me it was wonderfully
> thrilling.[12]

The moral of all this is that if you are going to be a highly
successful English writer you should have stored away
memories of Boudin, Lily Langtry and Bernhardt by the age of
seven. If it had all been on this nostalgic level (with a somewhat
fuller account than hitherto of his intelligence work in Russia
naming William Wiseman as his boss) the personal story would

have taken its place as being among the most agreeable of the Master's pieces of self-revelation; unfortunately some vengeful senile pressure compelled Maugham to unfold in a series of anecdotes, bathed in acid, the steps leading to his marriage, his long love-affair with Rosie (identified by Mr. Calder in conversation with Gerald Kelly as Ethelwyn Sylvia Jones, the second daughter of Henry Arthur Jones) and when she had chucked him for an earl, his involvement with the estranged wife of Henry Wellcome.

Every reader of *The Razor's Edge* remembers the moment when the author, who is telling the story, probes Isabel's motives in marrying Gray and not Larry with cruel accuracy. She flings a plate of bread and butter at him. He catches the plate but the contents scatter all over the floor.

> 'And you call yourself an English gentleman,' she exclaimed savagely.
> 'No, that's a thing I have never done in all my life.'[13]

It was perfectly true; he had, as we have seen in his books and plays, ripped that mask aside many times from his fictional characters, but there were many of Maugham's warmest admirers who wished that he could have left it in front of his own countenance until the end. Even then what he wrote might have been understandable if the mask had been dropped in the interests of telling the whole truth. But the private face that stared out of *Looking Back* was yet another mask, a half-mask: there was no frank admission of his kinship in temperament to a writer like André Gide who married his cousin Emanuele but spent his happiest erotic moments with Arab boys in Tunisia. Gide made this dilemma the subject of books that shock the reader into facing a problem that has faced so many writers in our society. He came clean with his public. But Maugham had judged, like Dickens before him, in a somewhat different but just as awkward situation, that had he come clean his public would have forsaken him. In the end Maugham was too much of a gentleman to be wholly frank and too much of an artist to be wholly reticent. The compromise was not a happy one.

The equivocal references to Haxton, or rather the all too few references to him, and the picture painted of Syrie, outraged many of Maugham's closest friends. Beverley Nichols rushed to her defence with precipitate haste after Maugham's death in a book that seemed even more distorted and one-sided than the work it claimed to expose. Noël Coward, who knew Maugham as well as any other writer could know him, even though he said that 'I cannot truthfully say that I really knew him intimately', and who also knew about this particular problem, imagined a situation in which the Master was called to account for his concealment and had to face the possibility of the mask being torn down by a former mistress while he was still alive. Coward made it the plot of one of his last plays, *A Song at Twilight*. He gives a prickly aloofness to the distinguished writer, Sir Hugo Latymer, whom he played himself. The sage lives in Switzerland with his devoted German secretary-wife, and he is awaiting a visit from an actress with whom, many years ago, he had a love-affair. The lady has a time-bomb in her handbag in the form of a bundle of love-letters from Sir Hugo to his deceased secretary, Perry Sheldon, which she threatens to make use of in a forthcoming book. Coward raises all the delicate and indelicate moral questions about public and private faces, betrayal and concealment, in a lengthy duologue of wounding emotional in-fighting that has the intensity of a bout between Fischer and Spassky plus a great deal more humour. It is as if Ben Jonson had written a play in which the chief characters were based on Shakespeare, the Earl of Southampton and the Dark Lady. Present wife and former mistress discuss the Master's imperturbable mask:

Carlotta: It was as though he had made a private vow to remain Captain of his Soul no matter what emotional hurricanes he might encounter. But it was all so long long ago. He had ample time to change as indeed we all have.

Hilde (with a faint smile): I agree that Hugo has not the sort of temperament to be easily battered by 'emotional hurricanes' as you put it, but that is not quite what I meant.

Carlotta: He has certainly had a wonderful career. It wouldn't be surprising if he sometimes found the burden of his eminence a trifle nerve-racking.

Hilde: (not quite pleased with this either): Nerve-racking?

Carlotta: The continual demands made upon his time, the constant strain of having to live up to the self-created image he had implanted in the public mind . . .[14]

Let us leave it there.

[4.]

Somerset Maugham died at the Mauresque on December 16, 1965. He had been brought home from the British American hospital in Nice where he had been taken earlier, and moved only when there was no longer any hope of prolonging much more that very long and very full life. He was two months short of his ninety-second birthday. According to his wishes he was cremated and his ashes taken to England. It may come as a surprise to readers of *Of Human Bondage* to learn that he asked that his ashes should be buried in the grounds of The King's School, Canterbury. But the fact is that ever since the 1930s Maugham had been atavistically and systematically reforging the links that his premature departure as a pupil had severed. He sat on the governing body and would time his visits to London to coincide with its meetings. One of Maugham's fellow alumni was, by a curious chance, Hugh Walpole, who had been generous with gifts to the school of money and of manuscripts, and so indeed in competitive spirit, perhaps, was Maugham. Running through my portrait of him, the most eye-catching figure in the pattern, has been his insistence on the limitations of the code of conduct instilled in youth into the character of the English gentleman, and it is interesting to find Maugham using his money to try to give some young gentlemen in Canterbury a wider perspective on life. In 1948 he wrote to the headmaster, Canon F. J. Shirley, with the aim of setting up a fund,

to provide [as Maugham put it] education in a public school for the sons of working men, and the motive for its institution was to diminish the class-consciousness of the ordinary schoolboy by throwing him into contact at a formative period of his life with boys of another class, and thus to some extent to diminish the exclusiveness and snobbery which have resulted in the universal dislike for the English which no traveller abroad can fail to notice.

The Duke of Wellington is supposed to have said that the Battle of Waterloo was won on the playing fields of Eton. I think that a future historian may with more truth say that India was lost in the public schools of England.[15]

Maugham's idea was about a decade ahead of its time and it foundered. He began to suspect that Shirley would use the money to 'provide education for the sons of needy colonels and distressed gentlewomen'. Eventually, instead of poor boy scholarships, Maugham's munificence provided a new science block, new boathouses and the Maugham library. It was beside the wall of this library and the adjoining laboratory that his ashes were buried on the morning of December 22 at a short private service conducted by the dean and headmaster in the presence of Lady Glendevon, Maugham's daughter, and some thirty boys who interrupted their Christmas holidays to attend the ceremony. There was no public memorial service such as is customary when a writer of such eminence dies. This again was in accordance with Maugham's wish:

> The memorial service is an ugly feature of contemporary manners. It was all very well when the deceased was a person of eminence or one who had been outstanding benefit to the country. It was then a decent mark of respect for one who deserved it. But now memorial services are held for persons whose lives have been obscure, whose activities have been so unimportant, that they have been of account only in the small circle in which they moved.[16]

Of no one was this less true than the writer of those words. Every newspaper in the world carried an obituary and the *New York Times* gave him an entire page, an honour it tends to reserve for former presidents, and other men of destiny. In Canterbury, in a sunken garden at The King's School, a memorial plaque reads: 'WILLIAM SOMERSET MAUGHAM, K.S.C. 1885–1889. Born 1874. Died 1965.'

Maugham often said that an author has the right to be judged by his best work. It amused him when he was writing his own obituary, which in a sense he did several times, to speculate on what that best work was. He believed that he had written a few short stories and one or two plays that would live as long as the language, his 'baggage for eternity', he called it whimsically.

I suppose that at the end of a critical portrait in which I have
tried to present to the reader Maugham's work as a unity, and
to show its relation to the different periods through which he
lived, I should open his baggage, and like some critical *douanier*
see what he has to declare, before he catches the celestial airport
omnibus to that *grande corniche* from which no tourist returns.
The list would not contain any shock inclusions or omissions.
Among the novels I should put *Of Human Bondage* firmly and
obviously at the head as his major achievement, a novel that is
both highly individual and yet part of a continuing tradition,
then would come *The Moon and Sixpence* in which he worked
out so memorably that artist-gentleman dilemma which in his
own life he never succeeded in resolving; then *Cakes and Ale* for
its withering view of the literary reputation-makers at work,
blended with its nostalgic evocation of Edwardian Whitstable
like sweet and sour pork; and *The Razor's Edge* for Elliot and
for Larry and for Paris. The plays? I accept the majority opinion
that *The Circle* is his most perfect comedy but there are at least
half a dozen other pieces that I want to see as part of a national
repertory; some are middle period like *Our Betters* and *Caesar's
Wife* and others are late like *For Services Rendered* and *Sheppey*.
And if I were to make a list of all the stories I want to re-read,
starting with *The Book-Bag* and *The Round Dozen*, I should be
compiling another bibliography; in fact I should want to include
volumes of short stories: *The Trembling of a Leaf*, *Ah King*,
Ashenden, *First Person Singular*. And I most certainly would not
want to let him get away without the essays: *Don Fernando*, the
Notebook, *The Summing Up* . . . No, it's no good. The essential
Maugham is Maugham.

In his beautiful essay on Zurbaran he describes how the
painter went to *imaginero* to learn his trade. The word means
here a carver of religious images, but we need some such term
in English to describe the kind of writer Maugham was. Certainly other writers will go to him to learn their trade, however
far they may aspire beyond realism to the higher ground. He
made images of a palpable kind; solid, strongly-carved, striking
images, around which crowds clustered and stared, in which the
people saw some illumination of life as they had experienced it.
His plain, lucid, honest prose, even at its most bare, never fails

to serve his purpose: to lead one into a situation of perennial human interest. Maugham self-consciously avoided the higher ground but it is a region which no lover of literature wishes to inhabit all the time. The air is too thin on those heights, breathing is difficult, the cold is intense, the whole expedition not to be undertaken lightly. I have ascended the North Face of Henry James, and the Annapurna of Proust, and I have been greatly exhilarated by the conquest of these great mountains, planting here and there my puny flags of understanding. The views from the summit are among my most cherished memories. But I cannot live there permanently. I come back to the open, green, cultivated lowlands of Maugham. I wander there happily until it is time to set out on the next hazardous ascent of Mount Tolstoy or Mount Dostoievsky. Maugham is where I live. He continually delights me by his insights into the literary life and he frequently astounds me by a skill so fine that it seems to me to be the most perfect expression of the art of narrative in our literature.

Bibliography and Notes

Maugham's works are published in the U.K. and British Commonwealth by Heinemann and in paperback by Penguin books; in the United States in hardback by Doubleday. For the general reader a convenient checklist of his main works will be found on the wrapper and in the fly-leaf of the Collected Edition which is currently available from bookshops. For the collector and student the most complete and up-to-date bibliography, which gives in addition to the published works descriptions and whereabouts of manuscripts, collections of letters, articles and so on, is *A Bibliography of the Works of W. Somerset Maugham* by Raymond Toole Stott (Kaye and Ward, 1973). This volume to a great extent supersedes the same author's *The Writings of William Somerset Maugham: a bibliography* (Bertram Rota, 1956) and his *Maughamiana* (Heinemann, 1950.)

For detailed information about Maugham's career as a playwright the *Theatrical Companion to Maugham* by Raymond Mander and Joe Mitchenson (Rockliff, 1955) gives not only cast-lists, plots, photographs and reviews of the original productions, but also particulars of subsequent revivals, films and dramatic adaptations by other hands, and a synopsis of the unperformed, *The Road Uphill*. A comprehensive, chronological view of the critical reaction to Maugham's work, from 1897 to 1968 in Britain, the United States and France, may be gained from *W. Somerset Maugham* compiled and edited by Charles Sanders (Northern Illinois University Press, De Kalb, Illinois, 1970) in the Annotated Bibliography Series on English Literature in Transition, 1880–1920, general editor Helmut E. Gerber.

From the previously published volumes about Maugham here is a highly selective list of suggestions for further reading about the man and his work:

W. Somerset Maugham and the Quest for Freedom by Robert Lorin Calder (Heinemann, 1972).

W. Somerset Maugham by Ivor Brown (International Profiles, 1970)

Remembering Mr Maugham by Garson Kanin (Hamish Hamilton, 1966)

Somerset and all the Maughams by Robin Maugham (Longman and Heinemann, 1966)

The Two Worlds of Somerset Maugham by Wilmon Menard (Sherbourne Press, Los Angeles, 1965)

Somerset Maugham: A Guide by L. Brander (Oliver and Boyd, 1963)

Somerset Maugham: a biographical and critical study by Richard Cordell (Heinemann, 1961)

The World of Somerset Maugham: an anthology edited by Klaus W. Jones (Peter Owen, 1959)

Most readers possess Maugham's works in a medley of different editions, hard and soft cover, book clubs, anthologies, reprints. In the Notes that follow I have, therefore, identified quotations where necessary not by page numbers but by chapters or acts, and in the case of stories by the volume in which they originally appeared. References to the Mander and Mitchenson volume are abbreviated to M. and M., quotes from reviews noted in the Sanders volume are identified by S.

Chapter 1: *Œuvre and Environs*

1. Edmund Wilson's review of *Then and Now* appeared as 'Somerset Maugham and an Antidote' in *The New Yorker* of June 8, 1946 and was reprinted as 'The Apotheosis of Somerset Maugham' in *Classics and Commercials*, 1950.

2. Desmond MacCarthy's 'William Somerset Maugham "The English Maupassant" An Appreciation' appeared in Nash's *Pall Mall Magazine*, May 1933 and was reprinted the following year by Heinemann as a pamphlet.

3. See Harold Nicolson *Diaries and Letters, 1930–1939*, edited by Nigel Nicolson (Collins, 1966), p. 350.

4. See *The Summing Up* VII for the origin of this Maugham-mark. 'My father took it into his head to build a house to live in during the summer. He bought a piece of land on the top of a hill at Suresnes . . . He ordered a great quantity of glass on which he had engraved a sign against the Evil Eye which he had found in Morocco and which the reader may see on the cover of this book.' (But not, alas, on that of the most recent edition by Penguin Books.)

5. The Bertram Alanson Maugham collection is now in the University of Stanford, California, and Jerome R. Zipkin's collection in the University of Texas.
6. 'After Reading Burke', *The Vagrant Mood*, 1952.
7. George Rylands in a letter to the author, March 21, 1972.
8. James Thomson, *The City of Dreadful Night* (Dobell, 1910), p. 47ff.

Chapter 2: *Orientations*

1. Maugham left a sizeable part of his library to his old school and the manuscripts of his first and last novels, *Liza of Lambeth* and *Catalina*.
2. The Pseudonym Library. See *The Publishing Unwins* (Heinemann, 1972) by Philip Unwin, p. 42.
3. Some of Booth's findings may be conveniently sampled in *Charles Booth's London* (Hutchinson, 1969) selected and edited by Albert Fried and Richard M. Elman.
4. Sir Arthur Quiller-Couch: *Memories and Opinions*, (Cambridge, 1944) p. 73.
5. Biographical material about Arthur Morrison is contained in P. J. Keating's introduction to his edition of *A Child of the Jago*, (MacGibbon and Kee, 1969.)
6. P. J. Keating: *The Working Classes in Victorian Fiction* (Routledge, 1971).
7. *Liza of Lambeth*, Chapter 1.
8. Ibid., Chapter 12.
9. Maugham did not reprint 'The Record of Badalia Herodsfoot' in his *A Choice of Kipling's Prose* (Macmillan, 1952). It is in *Many Inventions* or may be read in the context of other examples of Cockney dialect in fiction in *Working-class Stories of the 1890s*, edited by P. J. Keating (Routledge, 1971).
10. The fullest account of Maugham's background is given in *Somerset and all the Maughams* (Longman and Heinemann, 1966) by Robin Maugham.
11. *The Summing Up*, XLIII.
12. *Liza of Lambeth*, Chapter 8.
13. For the demise of the three-decker see *Mudies Circulating Library and the Victorian Novel* (David and Charles, 1970) by Guinevere L. Griest.
14. Reprinted in *Essays and Historiettes* (Chatto & Windus, 1903) by Walter Besant.
15. Henry James's essay on 'The Art of Fiction' first appeared in *Longman's Magazine* in September, 1884. For a discussion of the

different approaches of Besant and James see John Goode's essay in *Tradition and Tolerance in Nineteenth-Century Fiction* (Routledge, 1966).

16. *A Writer's Notebook*, 1896.
17. Ibid., 1894.
18. Ibid., 1896.
19. Machiavelli, *History of Florence*, (1532), Book VIII.
20. *The Making of A Saint*, Chapter 15.
21. *Literature as a Career*.
22. Many of Maugham's early uncollected stories are listed by Toole Stott in *Maughamiana* (Heinemann, 1950).
23. *Maughamiana*, p. 53.
24. 'Augustus' in *The Vagrant Mood*.
25. *The Hero*, Chapter 6.
26. *Born in Exile*, Part the First, Chapter 11.
27. *The Hero*, Chapter 6.
28. *Mrs. Craddock*, Chapter 1.
29. Preface to *Mrs. Craddock*, 1955.
30. *The Summing Up*, XLIV.
31 *The Merry-Go-Round*, Chapter 12.
32. Ibid., Chapter 15.
33. Ibid., Chapter 15.
34. Ibid., Chapter 15.
35. *The Speaker*, November 19, 1904.
36. *The Explorer*, Chapter 2.

Chapter 3: *Going Lightly*

1. *Schiffbrüchig*. See M. and M. p. 17ff.
2. Alexander and Wyndham. See *The Victorian Theatre* (Oxford, 1956) by George Rowell, and 'The Role of the Reasoner' by Rowell in *The Rise and Fall of the Matinée Idol* edited by Anthony Curtis (Weidenfeld, 1974); and *The Actor Managers*, (Weidenfeld, 1970) by Frances Donaldson.
3. A list of the first ten years' productions is given in *The Incorporated Stage Society*, 1909.
4. From the version published by Heinemann, 1912.
5. In the *Sunday Special*, March 1, 1903. Quoted by M. and M. p. 24.
6. *The Times*, February 24, 1903.
7. *The Saturday Review*, March 5, 1904, Reprinted in Max Beerbohm, *Last Theatres* edited by Rupert Hart-Davis (Hart-Davis, 1970).

8. Ibid., p. 358ff.
9. Preface to Volume 1 of *The Plays of W. Somerset Maugham*.
10. Ibid., for Maugham's version and *Whatever Goes Up*, 1934, by George C. Tyler and J. C. Furnas for Tyler's.
11. *Seven Friends* (Richards Press, 1953) by Louis Marlow.
12. *The Journals of Arnold Bennett*, edited by Newman Flower (Cassell, 1932).
13. 'A Fragment of Autobiography' printed as a preface to the Collected Edition of *The Magician*, 1956.
14. Ibid.
15. *The Great Beast: The Life and Magick of Aleister Crowley* by John Symonds (Macdonald, new edition 1971), Chapter 12.
16. *Mrs. Dot*, Act one.
17. *Jack Straw, The Saturday Review*, 1908, reprinted in *Last Theatres*, p. 359.
18. 'How "Dare" He', *The Saturday Review*, June 20, 1908, reprinted *Last Theatres*, p. 378.
19. *A Writer's Notebook*, 1908.
20. Candidates Book, 1909, The Garrick Club.
21. 'Reggie Turner', *Seven Friends* (Richards Press, 1953) by Louis Marlow.
22. *The Summing Up*, Chapter III. XXXIII.
23. Ibid.
24. *Smith*, Act one (description of set).
25. *Penelope*, Act one.
26. Introduction to *Complete Works of Oscar Wilde* (Collins, 1948.)
27. *Charles Frohman: Manager and Man* by Isaac F. Marcosson and Daniel Frohman (John Lane, 1916).
28. No mention of this Maugham work has, so far as I know, appeared before and I am indebted to the kindness of Mander and Mitchenson for this information.
29. The returning colonial acting as a catalyst was anticipated in Alfred Sutro's *The Walls of Jericho*, 1904. For a discussion of the relation between this play and Maugham's see *English Drama 1900–1930* by Allardyce Nicoll (Cambridge U.P., 1973), Chapter six.
30. *The Times*, October 1, 1909.
31. *The Summing Up*, XXXIII.
32. See above, Marcosson and Frohman.

Chapter 4: *Limping Earnestly*

1. *The Limit* (Grant Richards, 1911).

2. *Of Human Bondage*, Chapter XVIII.
3. Maugham saw plays by Ibsen, Sudermann and Henry Becque at Heidelberg. See Richard Cordell, *Somerset Maugham* (Heinemann, 1961), pages 15 and 174.
4. *Modern French Painters* by R. H. Wilenski (Faber, 1940, reprinted 1963).
5. *Avowals* by George Moore (Society for Irish Folklore, 1919).
6. *O.H.B.*, Chapter XLIV.
7. Ibid., Chapter XLV. Fol. O'Conor's career see "An Irish Painter in Paris" by Denys Sutton *Studio*, 1960, CLX, pages 173 ff.
8. Ibid., Chapter LV.
9. *A Case of Human Bondage*, 1900, p. 143.
10. *O.H.B.*, Chapter LXV.
11. Ibid., Chapter LXIV.
12. Ibid., Chapter LXXXVIII.

Chapter 5: *A Double Life*

1. *William Somerset Maugham:* 'The English Maupassant'—An Appreciation by Desmond MacCarthy (Nash's Pall Mall Magazine, May 1933).
2. *Looking Back*, part three. *Sunday Express*, September 23, 1962
3. *A Writer's Notebook*, 1914.
4. Ibid.
5. *Escape from the Shadows* (Hodder & Stoughton, 1972) by Robin Maugham.
6. *Looking Back*, part eight, *Sunday Express*, October 28, 1962.
7. 'Miss King.'
8. *The Two Worlds of Somerset Maugham* (Los Angeles: Sherbourne Press, 1965) by Wilmon Menard.
9. *A Writer's Notebook*, 1916.
10. *Looking Back*, Ibid.
11. *The Moon and Sixpence*, Chapter XLV.
12. *A Writer's Notebook*, 1916.
13. *A Portrait of the Artist as a Young Man.*
14. Quoted by Emile Delavaney in *D. H. Lawrence: The Man and His Work* (Heinemann, 1972) Chapter 7.
15. 1895 see *The Complete Tales of Henry James* edited by Leon Edel (Hart-Davis, 1964) Vol. 9.
16. *The Moon and Sixpence*, Chapter XXL.
17. Quoted by Wayne Andersen in *Gauguin's Paradise Lost* (Secker & Warburg, 1972).
18. *The Moon and Sixpence*, Chapter XLI.

19. *The Saturday Review*, 17 May 1919.
20. *Athenaeum*, 9 May, 1919, for this and following quotes from Katherine Mansfield.
21. *Looking Back*, part five, *Sunday Express*, Sept. 30, 1962.
22. *Vogue*, July 1928. Reprinted in *D. H. Lawrence: Selected Literary Criticism* edited by Anthony Beal (Heinemann, 1955).
23. Preface to *Collected Plays*, Vol. III, 1932.

Chapter 6: *Mainly Heroines*

1. St. John Ervine, *The Theatre in My Time* (Rich & Cowan, 1933) Chapter XXX.
2. *The Sunday Telegraph*, 13 October, 1968.
3. *The Circle*, Act II.
4. *The Summing Up*, I.
5. *Caroline*, Act II. The play was originally called, and published under the title of, *The Unattainable*.
6. *New Statesmen*, October 6, 1923. Quoted in full in M. and M., p. 118ff with the subsequent correspondence revealing the Lord Chamberlain's objections.
7. *Our Betters*, Act three.
8. Preface to *The Plays of Somerset Maugham*, Vol. III, 1932.
9. *Caesar's Wife*, Act I.
10. James Agate, *The Saturday Review*, September 17, 1922. (M. and M. p. 171ff.)
11. See Basil Dean, *Seven Ages* (Hutchinson, 1970), p. 304 ff.
12. *The Constant Wife*, Act I.
13. Ibid.
14. Ibid.
15. Ibid.
16. Herbert Farjeon, *Graphic*, April 16, 1527. S.665.
17. *The Unknown*, Act I.
18. *The Sacred Flame*, Act III.
19. *Introduction to the Tale of the Dark Ladie*.
20. *The Breadwinner*, Act III.
21. Preface to *The Plays of Somerset Maugham*, Vol. VI, 1934.
22. 'Off with the Motley', *Theatre World*, July 1933.
23. *The Times*, September 15, 1933.
24. Preface to *The Plays of Somerset Maugham*, Vol. VI, 1935.

Chapter 7: *Bicycling Down Joy Lane*

1. Author's Preface to *Cakes and Ale*. (Penguin edition, 1948.)

2. Robert Lorin Calder, *W. Somerset Maugham and the Quest for Freedom*, 1972. See Appendix A. 'Rosie'.
3. *Cakes and Ale*, XXIV.
4. This was first pointed out by Q. D. Leavis in her essay, 'Gissing and the English Novel', *Scrutiny*, Vol. VII, 1938. 'Jasper Milvain,' says Mrs. Leavis, 'differs from Alroy Kear only in being a simpler psychological study.'
5. According to Beverley Nichols in *A Case of Human Bondage* (Secker and Warburg, 1966), I, Haxton had been declared an undesirable alien by an English police court in 1916 and was never allowed to set foot in England again.
6. *Cakes and Ale*, V.
7. Ibid., VIII.
8. See *Sweet Saturday Night* by Colin MacInnes (MacGibbon and Kee, 1967), p. 57.
9. *Cakes and Ale*, X.
10. Ibid., XI.
11. *Ten Novels and Their Authors*, Chapter Eleven.
12. *Cakes and Ale*, XXIV.
13. *The Tragic Muse* (Macmillan, 1890), XLI.
14. *Theatre*, XIV.
15. Ibid., XXIII.
16. *The Summing Up*, LVI.

Chapter 8: *Streaks of Yellow*

1. A copy of the *Illustrated Guide to the Federated Malay States* will be found in the London Library. It was first published in 1910.
2. Published in 1952. T. S. Eliot's *A Choice of Kipling's Verse* (Faber & Faber) had appeared in 1941.
3. In *A Writer's Notebook*, Maugham described the Bore episode of 1922 and ever afterwards suffered from a fear of death by drowning (*see* Chapter ten, p. 155).
4. *The White Rajahs*: A History of Sarawak from 1841 to 1946 (Cambridge U.P., 1960), p. 236.
5. Published in *Life's Handicap*, 1891.
6. *The Modern Movement*: 100 Key Books from England, France and America (André Deutsch and Hamish Hamilton, 1965).
7. S.568.
8. P. C. Kennedy in *New Statesman*, S.561.
9. S.570.
10. Preface to *Cosmopolitans*: Very Short Stories, (1936.)

11. Ibid., 'The Four Dutchmen'; it was the final story in the book.
12. *On A Chinese Screen*, (1922), 'The Stranger', XXXV.
13. *The Narrow Corner*, V.
14. Ibid., XXII.
15. Ibid., XXV.

Chapter 9:   *On the Judgment Seat*

1. *Spectator*, April 17, 1936. S.1197.
2. The two 'Ned Preston' stories 'Episode' and 'The Kite' are the last two stories in *Creatures of Circumstance* (1947).
3. Included in *The Mixture as Before* (1940). Made into a film as part of *Encore* (1951) with screenplay by Eric Ambler.
4. 'Some Novelists I Have Known', the last essay in *The Vagrant Mood* (1952). Henry James's *The Author of 'Beltraffio'* appeared in 1884. Leon Edel says that this cannot truly be considered one of James's stories of writers. 'It is in reality a Medea-like tale, of a female figure who sacrifices innocence to her own cruel destructive vision; in this and in certain of James's tales to come, the piping voice of childhood is smothered by a righteousness more evil than the evil it imagines and seeks to defy. "The Author of 'Beltraffio'" is a harbinger of "The Pupil" and "The Turn of the Screw", those stories in which an adult world makes its cruel offerings on the altars of its own egotism.' (Introduction to *The Complete Tales of Henry James*, Volume Five, 1963). Maybe, but this does not invalidate Maugham's animadversion. The story of Henry James that Maugham chose for inclusion in his anthology *Tellers of Tales* (1939)—'100 short stories from the United States, England, France, Russia and Germany'—was 'The Jolly Corner.'
5. The opening story in *Creatures of Circumstance*. Filmed in *Quartet* (1948) with screenplay by R. C. Sherriff.
6. The final story in *Six Stories Written in the First Person Singular* (1931).
7. Included in *The Mixture as Before* (1940).
8. As above.
9. See 'Somerset Maugham and Posterity' in *Images of Truth* (Hamish Hamilton, 1963).
10. *The Mixture as Before* (1940).
11. Made into a film in *Trio* (1950).
12. *Cosmopolitans*.
13. *Six Stories Written in the First Person Singular*.

14. *Cosmopolitans.*
15. Published as 'The Princess and the Nightingale' in *The Book of the Queen's Doll's House Library*, edited by E. V. Lucas (1924). It was included in *The Gentleman in the Parlour* (1930) and published on its own for children in America as *Princess September and the Nightingale* (1939) and is included in the *Collected Short Stories* as 'Princess September.'
16. *Remembering Mr. Maugham* (Hamish Hamilton, 1966), p. 210ff.
17. Published on its own in a limited edition in America in 1944 and then in *Creatures of Circumstance.*
18. 'The Mother' is an interesting case, as Toole Stott points out, of a story published originally in a magazine in 1909, just at the time of Maugham's great theatrical bonanza, and later reprinted thirty-eight years later with some but not vast revision in book form in *Creatures of Circumstance.* (See *Somerset Maugham: a bibliography.* Bertram Rota, 1956, p. 109.)
19. *Creatures of Circumstance.* Compare *The Punctiliousness of Don Sebastian* in *Orientations.*
20. *Creatures of Circumstance.*
21. *Cosmopolitans.*
22. Maugham made a recording of this story in the U.S. in 1950 for Columbia records.
23. 'Chagrin in Three Parts' in *May We Borrow Your Husband?* (Bodley Head, 1967).

24. *First Person Singular.*
25. *Creatures of Circumstance.*
26. *First Person Singular.*
27. Published in a limited edition in 1934 by the Centaur Press and then in *Cosmopolitans.*
28. *A Certain World*, 1970, p. 248.
29. The first story in *First Person Singular.*
30. *Le Bonheur.* The English translation is by Jonathan Sturges, 1891.

Chapter 10: *Don Guillermo and other Portraits of the Artist*

1. Preface to W. Somerset Maugham, *The Travel Books*, 1955.
2. *The Gentleman in the Parlour*, II.
3. *Table Talk*, XIX. First published in *The New Monthly Magazine*, 1822.
4. *Don Fernando*, III.
5. Ibid., IX.

6. *Spectator*, June 21, 1935. This review is included in 'Some Notes on Somerset Maugham' in the *Collected Essays*, 1969.

7. *London Mercury*, September 1935.

8. *Remembering Mr. Maugham*, p. 141. The picture was Le Polisseur. Kanin explains that the polishing was such a dirty job that the polisher stripped naked to do it.

9. *The Razor's Edge*, V.8.

10. *The Summing Up*, LVII.

11. *Virginia Woolf* (The Hogarth Press, 1972), a biography by Quentin Bell. Vol. 1, *Virginia Stephen*, p. 80.

12. *Marcel Proust*, a biography. Vol. 2 (Chatto & Windus, 1965).

13. *W. Somerset Maugham and the Quest for Freedom* (Heinemann, 1972), Chapter IX.

14. Evelyn Waugh to the author, October 7, 1961. The fellow-novelist was Richard Hughes interviewed in *The Sunday Telegraph* about the forthcoming *The Fox in the Attic*.

15. *The Summing Up*, XXV.

16. *The Private Papers of Henry Ryecroft* (Constable, 1903), XVII.

17. *Spectator*, February 17, 1939. Reprinted in *The Maugham Enigma* edited by Klaus Jonas (Peter Owen, 1954), S.1380.

18. *London Mercury*, March 1939.

19. *Strictly Personal*, p. 8.

20. Ibid.

21. Ibid.

22. *France at War*, p. 65.

23. Ibid.

Chapter 11:   *At Work in the States*

1. *Remembering Mr. Maugham*, p. 182.

2. *A Writer's Notebook*, 1941.

3. Originally commissioned as articles by *The Saturday Evening Post* in which they appeared in 1939.

4. *Exhumations* (Methuen, 1966), 'Vedanta and the West,' p. 97.

5. *Books of the Month*, June 1941. S.1443.

6. *New Statesman and Nation*, May 31, 1941. S.1467.

7. *A Writer's Notebook*, 1941.

8. Ibid.

9. Several of Maugham's articles from this period, like this one, remain uncollected in book form.

10. *Strictly Personal*.

11. *Remembering Mr. Maugham* where a notable dinner party featuring duck à l'orange is recalled on p. 184.

12. Alan Searle to the author, July 6, 1973.
13. *The Razor's Edge*, I 6. 'Maugham's' reply to Larry is interesting: 'I never went to Cambridge as my brothers did. I had the chance, but I refused it. I wanted to get out into the world. I've always regretted it. I think it would have saved me a lot of mistakes.'
14. *Exhumations*, p. 120.
15. Ibid., III, 1.
16. Ibid., VIff for Larry's account of his Indian experiences.
17. *New Statesman and Nation*, August 26, 1944. Reprinted in *The Condemned Playground* (Routledge, 1945), S.1517.
18. *Time*, April 24, 1944. S.1515.
19. *Nation* (N.Y.), May 6, 1944. S.1553.
20. *Looking Back*, part 8. *Sunday Express*, October 28, 1962.
21. *A Writer's Notebook*, see 1944.

Chapter 12: *Pantheon*

1. *Purely For My Pleasure*, 1962. This handsome volume contains colour reproductions of many of Maugham's pictures including those by Roderic O'Conor, and interesting portraits of Maugham by Marie Laurencin and Edouard MacAvoy. (See the dust jacket of this book.)
2. A notice outside the gate of Waugh's house read: 'No admittance on business.'
3. 'Some Novelists I Have Known' in *The Vagrant Mood* (1952).
4. It was the winter of 1910 while James was staying with his brother's widow. See also *Henry James: The Master* by Leon Edel (Hart-Davis, 1972), p. 452ff.
5. *Tellers of Tales:* 100 Short Stories from the United States, England, France, Russia and Germany. Selected and with an introduction by W. Somerset Maugham. Doubleday, Doran, 1939. It was never published in England.
6. *The Writer's Point of View*. Published as a booklet by the Cambridge University Press for the National Book League.
7. 'Jane Austen and *Pride and Prejudice*' in *Ten Novels and Their Authors*. Other quotations in this section are from the essays in this book on the novelists mentioned. The ten novels Maugham chose are: *Tom Jones, Pride and Prejudice, Le Rouge et le Noir, Le Père Goriot, David Copperfield, Madame Bovary, Moby Dick, Wuthering Heights, The Brothers Karamazov* and *War and Peace*.
8. Of Human Bondage: An Address by W. Somerset Maugham,

1946. It was delivered in the Coolidge Auditorium of the Library of Congress when he presented the manuscript of the novel to the library.

9. 'The plain man with a proper interest in humanity' is how he described himself in *Books and You.*

10. Printed as the entire blurb on the jacket and as a Note at the beginning and, presumably, written by Maugham himself?

11. *The Sunday Express,* September 2, 1962.

12. Ibid. *Looking Back,* Part one, September 9, 1962.

13. *The Razor's Edge,* V 4.

14. *A Song at Twilight,* Act One. It was one of three plays with the same setting published in *Suite in Three Keys* (Heinemann, 1966), Coward's final work for the theatre.

15. Quoted by David L. Edwards in *F. J. Shirley: An Extraordinary Headmaster,* 1965. For information about Maugham's association with his old school in later life I am indebted to P. Pollak, the present archivist.

16. *The Sunday Express, Looking Back,* part one, September 9, 1962.

Index